ALSO BY DAVID MATTHEWS

ACE OF SPADES

THE PENGUIN PRESS   NEW YORK   2011

KICKING ASS
AND
SAVING SOULS

A TRUE STORY OF
A LIFE OVER THE LINE

DAVID MATTHEWS

THE PENGUIN PRESS
Published by the Penguin Group
Penguin Group (USA) Inc., 375 Hudson Street, New York, New York 10014, U.S.A. • Penguin Group
(Canada), 90 Eglinton Avenue East, Suite 700, Toronto, Ontario, Canada M4P 2Y3 (a division of Pearson
Penguin Canada Inc.) • Penguin Books Ltd, 80 Strand, London WC2R 0RL, England • Penguin Ireland,
25 St. Stephen's Green, Dublin 2, Ireland (a division of Penguin Books Ltd) • Penguin Books
Australia Ltd, 250 Camberwell Road, Camberwell, Victoria 3124, Australia (a division of Pearson Australia
Group Pty Ltd) • Penguin Books India Pvt Ltd, 11 Community Centre, Panchsheel Park, New Delhi–
110 017, India • Penguin Group (NZ), 67 Apollo Drive, Rosedale, Auckland 0632, New Zealand (a division
of Pearson New Zealand Ltd) • Penguin Books (South Africa) (Pty) Ltd, 24 Sturdee Avenue, Rosebank,
Johannesburg 2196, South Africa

Penguin Books Ltd, Registered Offices: 80 Strand, London WC2R 0RL, England

First published in 2011 by The Penguin Press,
a member of Penguin Group (USA) Inc.

Photograph credits
Insert page 1 (middle and bottom), 2 (top and middle left): Courtesy of Roye Templeton; 3 (upper left):
Courtesy of David Matthews. Other photographs courtesy of Stefan Templeton.

Library of Congress Cataloging-in-Publication Data

Matthews, David, 1967–
Kicking ass and saving souls : a true story of a life over the line / David Matthews.
p. cm.
ISBN 978-1-59420-296-4
1. Templeton, Stefan, 1967– 2. Templeton, Stefan, 1967– —Travel. 3. Templeton, Stefan, 1967– —
Homes and haunts. 4. Human rights workers—Biography. 5. Humanitarian assistance. 6. Disaster
relief. 7. Scuba divers—Biography. 8. Thieves—Biography. I. Title.
HV28.T43M37 2011
363.34092—dc22
[B]   2010053091

Printed in the United States of America
10 9 8 7 6 5 4 3 2 1

DESIGNED BY MEIGHAN CAVANAUGH

FOR MY FATHER

This is a work of nonfiction. In instances where no documentation was possible or extant, the events depicted herein have been faithfully rendered as the author, his subject, and corroborating witnesses remember them. Some names, identities, and locales where any laws may have been transgressed have been altered to protect the innocent and the not so.

PROLOGUE

Stefan Templeton pulled the eviction notice from the door and crumpled it in his fist. Beneath it, the construction paper, crayon, and glitter castle his four-year-old son, Stormy, had drawn lay ripped in half from where the landlord had taped over it.

You ripped it, Stormy said, jerking his hand from his father's.

No, Stormy-bear, someone left us a note saying how nice your picture was, but they made a mistake and put too much tape on.

Stormy looked up at me. Auburn eyes set wide on his face, he was teetering on the brink between tears and hopeful optimism and looked like he needed a swing vote. I nodded like a madman. Patted his sandy head in what I hoped came off as carefree affirmation.

See? his father said. *I think this means you should draw a bigger one.*

Once inside, Stormy bounded into his room—a small alcove just off the living room—and fished through the sprawl of toys for his box of crayons. Stefan sighed, deep and long, and smoothed the notice just enough to read the deadline: *ten days*.

His wife, Elena—Russian, and at twenty-five, fourteen years his junior—looked over from her pot of borscht on the stove. Saw the piece of paper in his hand. Stefan waved it off.

No sweat, baby. I'll take care of it. A pivot off her look: *Dinner smells good.*

You're still going, aren't you? she asked.

I have to, he said. *There are problems,* waving the eviction notice, *and then there are* problems.

Elena nodded and turned her hazel eyes back to the pot. Beets and onion and beef murmured low bubbles.

Come hang while I pack, he said to me. There was a large duffel bag spread out on the living room floor of his one-bedroom apartment. A beige pair of dusty combat boots lay atop an orange jumpsuit. The letters *NKAB+* were Sharpie'd on the backs of the boots and onto the collar of the jumpsuit.

What's that mean? I asked him. *Those letters?*

Means "No Known Allergies," and my blood type—"B positive." In case I can't speak for myself.

In two days' time he would be in Sudan, only a few hours away from Darfur, on a well-building humanitarian mission. This would be his second trip in a year to the area. Renewed fighting between north and south Sudan was a real possibility, despite a treaty that had maintained a fragile peace since 2005. He was going there—funded in part by the NGO KUSH—to map underground water sources, so that if war returned, the villagers would have access to water along a proposed evacuation route.

Stefan had become something of a recurring presence in the aftermath of some of the last decade's worst man-made and natural disasters. He'd helped distribute water, food, and medicine during Honduras's Hurricane Mitch, in 1998. Provided logistical support in the form of inoculating and hydrating displaced villagers during the late 2004 South Asia tsunami. And now, in January 2007, the genocide-ravaged Horn of Africa.

His family struggled by, month to month, on the income from translating work he'd done. His absences were a hardship to his wife and son, both emotionally and financially. Elena was in law school at the University of the District of Columbia, her time stretched thin to breaking between her studies and frequent solo care for their son. Stefan was the sole provider. Money would only get tighter when he left for Sudan. The trip would last weeks.

On this mission, as on all the others, he would receive no payment.

He dove into the closet and yanked out a pair of plastic Pelican briefcases, buried beneath an old acoustic guitar case, snowshoes, and a few years' worth of Stormy's loot from Christmases past. He mumbled something about not knowing where his sat-phone was and lumbered into the bedroom. He was big. Maybe 220 pounds on five-eleven of him. Bigger than I'd ever seen him. But it had been a long time. With the exception of a weekend in the summer of 1995, and a few months in late 1999, about twenty years had gone by since we'd spent any real time together. Geography was to blame for some of it. He'd lived all over the world—mostly in Scandinavia, continental Europe, and Asia—since high school, and I'd remained on the East Coast.

Time, distance, whatever. We were boys. That would never change. He'd looked out for me growing up in Baltimore City. In the 1980s, Baltimore's West Side wasn't a place you came from, it was a place you lived through. Stefan was bigger, badder, more worldly. And I think I may have amused him. Despite the years apart, I always knew that if I was in a jam—if a body needed disappearing, or I needed a safe house in Gdansk to wait out some unforeseen troubles—he'd come through for me.

I sat on the overstuffed couch and fidgeted with my canvas satchel. Inside was the advance galley copy of my first book, a memoir about growing up in Baltimore. I had called to tell him about the book and suggested we meet. He said he was pressed for time but excited to catch up.

Memoir? Have you done anything memoir-worthy? He'd laughed. Truth was, I wasn't sure I had. But it was important to me that he like the book: he was in it.

I first met Stefan Templeton in the fall of 1977. The only two mixed-race kids at our Baltimore City elementary/middle school—Mount Royal, PS 66—we were drawn together by our outsider status. *My* outsider status, to be precise. When I transferred to the school in the fourth grade, I was a pasty, spindly suburban transplant. At ten, Stefan was brown and stocky and fearsome—already a playground legend. He noticed me in the hallway my first day and asked me two questions:

Are you mixed?

and

Can you fight?

I answered yes to the former and no to the latter, and he looked at me and said, *Then you've got a friend.*

I didn't know whether to laugh in his face or pump his hand in gratitude. I split the difference and just stared at him. As long as he didn't kick my ass, we were blood brothers, bosom buddies, life-long pals.

We were an unlikely pair. By the time I'd met him, Stefan had traveled the world several times over, was a finely tuned martial artist, and spoke a couple of languages fluently. Washington, D.C., and Baltimore, Maryland, had been the extent of my travels. I weighed about sixty pounds soaking wet and could have been beaten up by the Teen Miss Muscular Dystrophy.

We were inseparable from the ages of ten until seventeen. Inseparable when he was home, at least. He'd often move to Europe to be with his mother, for months or years at a time. He'd return with matter-of-fact accounts of his time abroad. He'd say he'd lived in castles, ridden motorcycles, gone hunting in the French country-side, slept under starry desert skies with Bedouins, gone snorkeling off the coast of Spain.

I found his stories boring. I tuned him out. I lived in a world of books and TV shows, bordered by the two blocks of my neighbor-hood in that small, segregated, provincial city. He may just as well have been talking about a trip to the moon. And the *way* he'd relay his experiences: the guy had zero sense of humor. He was cheerful enough, but he had no feel for irony or self-deprecation. He'd think nothing of coming back home after a long absence and answering my *Didja do anything fun?* with *I've seen some things, man.*

Ten-year-olds should not speak that way. No one outside of a Michener novel should. So I'd only half listened to his adventures— probably pissed that I'd never gone anywhere or done anything.

He left Baltimore immediately after high school and moved to

Europe. That was 1985. I was in contact with him only sporadically over the next twenty years. A cryptic postcard here, a garbled international phone call there.

My childhood best friend and I had been virtual strangers for our adult lives. I had no idea what the hell *he'd* done during his years abroad. Now he was some kind of humanitarian, risking his family's well-being to go to one of the most dangerous places on earth without any possibility of financial reward. How he'd gotten here was a mystery.

You taking all this stuff? I yelled to him in the bedroom.

Nah, just some of it.

I walked over to one of the Pelican cases and flipped the lid. Inside a series of foam cutouts was a black electronic square device, a coiled length of what looked to be electric wires, and a pair of walkie-talkies.

What are you doing? He was standing above me, squinting hard. Some edge in his voice.

Thought maybe your phone was in here, I lied. I was snooping. *What's this?* I pointed at the black square.

Take it out, he said.

I removed the device. A block of plastic the size of a primordial cell phone.

He shook his head. *It's a Taser, knucklehead.*

Jesus, I said. *Get pretty rough out there saving babies?*

Stormy clambered into the room, midway through his drawing. *What's a Taser, Poppa?*

A Taser makes bad people jump, Stormy-bear. Stormy held up his drawing. I could make out some red and black stick people with what looked like blue arrows raining down on them.

That's amaaazing, Stefan said.

It's the African children when you put water on them, Poppa.

And what's this? I asked, pointing to the wound cable in the case, still trying to wrap my head around the Taser.

He swatted Stormy along with more praise and a couple of editorial suggestions and knelt next to me, closing the case with thick brown fingers.

A fiber optic video cable, he said. It was one of those cables you see in spy movies—a flexible piece of wire with a tiny camera lens on one end that snakes under doors and through air-conditioning vents.

What's with this stuff? I asked.

He was silent.

Hey, I said. *You remember that time I ate your grandmother's leftovers?*—

He started cracking up. *Oh shit! And I had to walk you all the way*—

And I started doing a Frankenstein walk across his living room floor, knees locked, as he collapsed onto his back in hysterics. The walk, my grimacing mug, brought it all back.

Just after we'd first met, back in 1977, I'd shit myself.

It was the Baltimore City Fair. Summer. We'd gone to his grandmother's apartment to beg some money from her so we could go on rides, eat fried carbohydrates, and guzzle sugary, incandescent beverages. On the way there, he'd warned me—*No matter how much she offers, do not eat anything she gives you, man. She never throws anything away.*

I was a fawning little suck-up, and, sure enough, when she offered me some pickles from her fridge, I smiled like a lobotomized Eddie Haskell and ate them.

Forty minutes later, while we waited to get on the Tilt-A-Whirl, my legs, socks, shoes, were covered in a diarrheic sheen.

He'd walked me back the—thirty? forty?—blocks home, while I sloshed across the city in the same Frankenstein lumber I was presently reenacting in his living room. He had seen me and loved me at my worst.

Stop it! Stop it, he pleaded.

Okay then, motherfucker—I nodded at the case—*tell me what's going on.*

He caught his breath. Sat up. Took inventory. Of the case. Maybe of his life. Or our friendship. Finally:

I've uh . . . I've done some—

Elena called out. Dinner was ready.

We rose and went into the dining nook just off the kitchen. The windows were steamed on the inside and frosted on the outside. Beyond them, the dim lights and dull whine of car engines swirled, as young professionals made their way back into the neighborhood from their nine-to-fives. Seven o'clock and everybody was settling in to dinner. Back in New York, I would have just finished lunch. I went to sit in an empty chair, leaving the head-of-the-table seat for him. But he just stood there.

Hey man, let's switch seats, he said. *I don't sit with my back to the door.*

I looked at Elena to see if her husband was kidding. She was spooning crimson borscht into Stormy's bowl. I guessed this passed for normal in the Templeton household. I squeaked my chair back on the hardwood and switched seats with him. Everyone tucked into their borscht. Small talk was made. He reached over and touched my arm as Elena escorted Stormy from the table into the bathroom to brush his teeth before bedtime: *Let them go to bed, and we'll talk. For real.*

An hour later, we sat in the living room as he piled more gear—

dehydrated meal packets, a tent, mosquito netting—into his ruck-sack. I'd forgotten about my book and his reaction to it. I wanted to know what the hell was going on.

You have to understand, man . . . everything I do now, the disaster-management stuff, that's who I am. . . .

He'd landed hard on the word *that's*—as though the restrictive inflection could erase any competing claims on who he was.

. . . But it's not who you were? I finished for him.

He bit his lip for what seemed like a full minute. Sighed. I noticed that he was sighing a lot these last few minutes. Like he was shrugging off some kind of burden. Or shame. Or the weight of years spent without an ear to lean into. *How am I not gonna tell you?* he said.

He walked into his bedroom and returned with a leather valise. He set it on the wooden coffee table in front of us and unsnapped it. He pulled a velvet pouch the size of a tennis ball from the case, undid the drawstring, and spread a mound of uncut stones—diamonds, rubies, sapphires—onto the table. He padded to the small office he'd converted into a bedroom where Stormy slept, and pulled the door shut.

This is from a bad time. My wife doesn't even know, he said.

In the bedroom next to us, ten feet away, his wife, Elena, had just fallen asleep. The TV bitched *Desperate Housewives* through the wall. Stormy's toys were scattered across the living room carpet. Elena's law school books, flagged with Post-it notes, were stacked on the edge of the dining room table. There was nothing in this middle-class house that jibed with the case filled with surveillance gear, and the gems laid out on the table. Stefan studied the pile.

Tokyo is where everything went to hell, he said.

He didn't say anything for a full minute.

1

GIANT ROBOT!

In a second one of the two men falling from the sky will hit the ground first. One of them will get up and walk away and one of them won't. The street below is packed with Japanese kids with spiked orange hair and purple dreadlocks, drunken Western tourists—men, mostly—and U.S. servicemen fresh off the base at Yokota. The Japanese crime syndicate—the Yakuza—and the hookers are inside, the Yaks pressed against the walls, the willowy Japanese escorts pressed against listing Aussies or GIs, giggling directions to the pay-as-you-go hotels down Roppongi Street. Giant Robot! is the busiest club in Roppongi. Standing-room-only every night of the week. Tonight is no different.

When the asphalt fifty feet below stops them hard, it will be a miracle the men don't take out a gaggle of drunks looking to get laid.

————————

Sixty minutes earlier.

Stefan finishes his bowl of vinegared rice and fried egg at Shiba Park, on the edge of the man-made gorge overlooking the waterfall, and tries to figure out what the hell to do with the rest of his evening. Dana's at rehearsal, won't be home until eleven. Maybe he'll bum around for a few hours, pick her up outside the studio. There's no way he's going *in,* not after that time a few months ago when she'd gotten him a gig on the chorus line of her show and they'd dressed him up in a sailor suit—elephant flares, kerchief, Village People–style hat, the whole bit—and he'd had to wobble onstage pretending to know how to dance for two weeks. The real reason they'd hired him was because part of the routine had called for one of the female dancers to be tossed into the air and spun around, and that he could do. But he'd felt like an idiot, listlessly shuffling back and forth under the klieg lights to the canned disco sound track. His limbs would usually do whatever he told them. Grooving just wasn't one of his primary directives. No. He'll wait outside for her.

That leaves five hours to kill.

He sets the plastic bowl on the rock shelf and watches a young Japanese couple pose for each other at the manicured entrance to the waterfall. The boy holds his can of Calpico in the foreground, while the girl shouts, *Ichimaiue!—Higher!* from behind the camera's viewfinder. They're going for the optical illusion of the waterfall in the background filling the can in the foreground. Endless amusement. They'll take twenty shots if that's what it takes. Stefan's eyes drift. Ants hike the orphans of rice and swim in the sugary tamari left in his bowl.

Maybe he'll hit the dojo. He kneads the muscle deep behind his left hamstring and winces. Still no good. The 1996 K-1 mixed martial arts qualifying matches are just over a month away. A week ago—after getting out of jail—he'd hit the heavy bag hard and left most of himself on the mat. He'd overtrained, and now he can't lift his knee past his pelvis. He'll have Dana rub some Tiger Balm into it later.

Across Shiba Park, the Tokyo Tower does its Erector-set impression of the Eiffel Tower while the sun dips onto its spire. The waterfall is maybe thirty feet. Everything here to scale. Tokyo a neon, miniature city. At five-eleven, he's Japanese basketball forward material. The place is harsh and bright and has too many people. He hadn't given much thought to coming here. He hadn't given much thought to falling in love with Dana and leaving Liv and their baby, either.

Six months back, at Monaco's Sportsman's Lounge, Dana had left her table—walked right up to him, after an hour of eye fucking—when her royal date and her date's bodyguard had gone to the lavatory. She was bronze all over, with a small, square face and a pile of curls begging to be twisted around fingers, pulled, inhaled. An American, from San Diego, her voice thrummed sunshine when she pressed her number into his palm.

We should get together.

We will, he said, and she was back at her table by the time Prince Albert the Deuce and his bodyguard returned.

Stefan saw her every few days at first. Soon he was staying away from home every night. Liv, his longtime girlfriend, stood at the window of their flat, hollow-eyed, waiting for him to come home, to the life they'd built together and their baby daughter.

A Japanese gardener, in a short-sleeved Arrow shirt and pressed khakis, waves the pistol-shaped nozzle of his hose Stefan's way with a bow. Stefan picks up his bowl and walks down the path.

Liv is family. There's affection, but the passion has waned. His hunger for Dana reminds him of those cartoons where Yogi Bear smells a pie cooling on a windowsill and the scent-wave crooks a finger into his nostril, picks him up, and floats him into trouble.

He tells himself that Liv and their daughter, Mai-Sunniva, are better off back in London. The money he's managed to send them is better company than he could be right now, anyway. If he can fix his leg and take the tournament pot, he'll be able to funnel back even more.

As head bouncer at Giant Robot! he's paid well, but it isn't enough to start a new life with Dana, or fund his old life and three-year-old child in London. *Shit:* he hasn't picked up this week's paycheck yet. He'll stop by the club—just across the park on Roppongi Street—make sure his guys aren't goldbricking, maybe have a beer. That'll kill an hour.

By the time he gets to the club, the neon/booze/pheromone stew is in full boil. Japanese techno and U.S. hits that haven't been hits in the States for at least a season bleat into the night air from the PA system. He climbs the side stairwell, his leather sandals thwacking against each rung. When he's not working, he looks like some kind of Euro-hippie: blousy shirts, designer jeans, sandals, a few braided necklaces.

At the door, he hangs back. Checks out Grove—the Australian bruiser—makes sure he's letting in two girls for every guy. Grove nods his way. Stefan slides into the throng of people. Everyone is drunk, or nearly so. It's practically an edict. There are signs posted all over the club, on each of its three levels: *All those without a drink in their hand will be ejected.* Water does not count.

He finds one of his other guys, a white South African named Sylvester, dragging a Teutonic-looking teenage boy out of the ladies' room.

But I had to piss! the boy pleads as Sylvester marches him out. *So do we!* the queue of Japanese women screech back.

The bartender—a rail-thin Japanese guy with a shaggy haircut, satin shirt, and skinny tie—lines up a row of shots on the bar.

At the other side of the room, a glass breaks. Then another. Sylvester is back, at Stefan's side now, leaning in, yelling over the music, *Fuckin' doffies have been at it for a while.* Sylvester jerks his head in the direction of the crash, and both men cross the floor. Stefan checks his watch as he elbows his way through the bobbing mob. Still plenty of time to grab his paycheck from the office upstairs, grab a Sapporo, then head toward Dana's studio. Not gonna get stuck here on his night off.

The Yak barks into the semicircle of his crew at the far end of the bar. Showing off. The Yakuza and his buddies are barely into their twenties. Low-level. Not old enough to have reps or handle their liquor. They wear high-necked collars and long-sleeved shirts to hide the sleeves of black ink marking their family. The club—like many joints in Roppongi—has a sign on the front door prohibiting tattoos. The Yak making all the noise weaves and shouts some joke or story or something at his crew. Funniest thing they've ever heard.

At their feet, a harried cocktail waitress scoops up chunks of broken glass into her tray with a cocktail napkin. Sylvester goes over to the Yaks. Stefan kneels next to the cocktail waitress.

He raises her by the elbow. He turns her hands over in his. No cuts. *Leave it,* he says, and motions to the bar-back to get a broom. He watches Sylvester lean into the Yak who was doing the yelling. Firm but respectful. Nobody wants static from the Yaks. The Yak—all of five-seven, the build of a bantam fighter—rocks back and forth on his heels, grinning over his beer bottle at his buddies.

There is nothing more dangerous than a young drunken Yak. Except six of them. Stefan knows this. Instead of having Sylvester just bounce the guy, he pulls the hulking South African aside and says *Lemme talk to him.*

Stefan and the Yak trade kindergarten Japanese and pidgin English until the Yak nods at him and waves for his buddies to follow. The Yak seems to know the score, fun is fun, but things have gotten a little out of hand. No need for cops and heat. Maybe it's time to try their luck somewhere else. Plenty of clubs in Roppongi.

He'll walk them past the second-floor open-air balcony to the stairwell overlooking the street. A nice roundabout route. Enough respect so the Yaks don't feel like they're getting the bum's rush. He's glad that the guys seem less amped as they reach the balcony, the small talk working. He notices the Yak putting down his beer as they pass a table. Ignores it. A meaningless detail.

He's behind, the Yak and his buddies ahead. The Yak stops short. The distance between the two of them closes, the Yak winks to his buddies and in a wide-arcing pivot grabs Stefan by the belt and tosses him over the railing. Stefan's left hand reaches out for anything solid and locks on to the Yak's belt buckle. Now both men are over the side and Stefan spins the Yak midair and uses the Yak's body to absorb the impact. The hit sounds like a balloon pop-ping. Stefan rolls off the Yak. World swirling. He breathes, long and deep, until he's sure he won't pass out.

He steadies himself on all fours. Looks over at the Yak. He's not moving. He reaches to turn the boy around when he feels a hand on his back. He whips around, Grove standing over him, *Get the fuck outta here, go.*

A crowd now. Pointing up at the balcony, hands over their mouths. A girl faints into her date, eyes fluttering. Grove lifts him to his feet, *Guy was drunk, fell off the balcony, you weren't here . . . go!*

The Yak's buddies clang down the stairs. Stefan backs off from the scene, into the crowd.

A block and a half down, he hails a taxi in front of the Don Quixote department store. No one is following the cab. That's all that matters. He wonders if he can trust Sylvester and Grove not to sell him out. His father used to say that enemies are friends you haven't tested yet.

Seventeen minutes later he gets out a few blocks from Dana's studio in the electronics district of Akihabara. He walks the long way around, past the canyon of TVs and stereos, before ducking into a yakitori shop across the street from the studio. He takes a seat with his face to the door so he can see whoever comes in. Still two hours until Dana gets out. He orders a few sticks of grilled okra so the owner won't bitch. Doesn't eat them. The adrenaline crash is brutal and the smell of burning meat and cigarette smoke churns his stomach. His shoulder thumps from where it drove into the boy's scapula.

The kid is okay . . . it was him or me . . . the kid is okay. He fights it, but rests his head in the crook of his arm and falls asleep on the counter.

He comes to with a jolt. Checks his G-Shock. Rubs his eyes. A puddle of drool on the bamboo table. *Stupid*. He can't let his guard down like this. Good way to go back to jail. He remembers the stony Yaks he'd shared yard time with and shudders. They wouldn't be half as welcoming if he wound up there again. Not after what he'd done to one of their own. Those motherfuckers maim *themselves* when they fuck up. Whatever they'd do to him after he'd killed one of their own would be long and slow and immune from the guards' intervention.

Ten minutes later, when Dana emerges from the studio, he hoists her gym bag for her and groans as the strap settles onto his shoulder. She asks him if he's hurt his shoulder training. He mumbles yeah. She hurries to keep up with him on the walk back to their tiny apartment behind the Nagayato Elementary School in Ebisu-nishi.

At home, he tells her what happened. He doesn't want to—but she knows something is up when she gets out of the shower naked and gets no response. When he tells her, she is less surprised than he would have imagined. Then again, he's been out of jail less than two weeks. For breaking a rich Iranian tourist's nose at the door when the coked-up asshole got pushy.

This kind of shit just finds you. Dana shrugs. He tells her his whole life has been this way.

Nobody says it, but they both wonder if this is some kind of payback for what they've done. He has a family. She tells him he has to leave Tokyo. *Now.* Just out of jail, his word won't be worth much. *Maybe the guy's okay,* she ventures. *You take off for a while and come back when things cool down.*

The phone rings.

It's Grove. *Cops came,* he says, *asked about you, we all told 'em it was your day off.*

Dana looks over at him. *Well?*

And the guy? he asks Grove.

The line is silent.

Bile singes the back of his throat. He hangs up. No choice but to trust that Grove and the other guys will keep their mouths shut. You don't wind up a bouncer that far away from home unless you've got something to hide. Besides, he's heard enough war stories from all his guys to have them extradited to any number of countries.

Stefan looks down at his hand. It's shaking. The scars and fat knuckles start to blur. He thought he was better after leaving the life, but the shake is worse than ever. Everything is worse.

Stupid fucker shouldn't have tried to toss him over the railing. He got what was coming to him. Jesus, what was he . . . eighteen . . . twenty? No more than twenty.

He's spent his life doing things other men wouldn't do but there was always a line. Everybody usually got to go home and fuck their wives or hug their kids after. This is different. It doesn't matter that he's the one who got up and walked away. His end on the asphalt outside a shitty club a just punishment for all the things he's done.

Stefan rolls his clothes into his rucksack. Fishes a T-shirt from the laundry hamper and starts to pack it, but Dana begs to keep it. *It smells like you,* she sobs, hugging it close. As he kisses the salt from her cheeks and tells her he'll meet her as soon as he finds somewhere safe to land, he understands that it is not just this night he is running from. There were others. Nights spent behind a mask, a gun, or deep below the waves. He was not born to be this. He was *made*.

Punishment, reckoning—those things will come later. Right now, Tokyo isn't safe.

He's got to get out.

II

STARRED AND CROSSED

n 1964, black American Roye Templeton and Norwegian Ebba Boyesen—both students at the University of Copenhagen—met and fell in love.

Copenhagen was a beatnik paradise. From the university's five-hundred-year-old main entrance, it was a fifteen-minute walk east to the Strøget, a kilometer of red and gold stones laid into starbursts, a less hip Carnaby or Bleecker Street, a never-ending flow of bodies flanked by cafés, clubs, hot dog carts, and boutiques. Roye Templeton, twenty-one, was doing a year abroad at the beginning of his master's in philosophy, hanging around the Three Musketeers jazz club in the middle of the strip with his nose in a book and a joint in his mouth.

Roye was long and lean, his nearly opaque skin wrapped tight around muscle and bone. His hazel eyes set wide across his face—

some Cherokee there—his lips thick and vaguely feminine amid the hard lines of his jaw.

Roye was quiet and kept to himself. There was little in his blank stare and arched eyebrows that invited conversation. He couldn't be bothered to waste oxygen on people he deemed past hope of enlightenment. In his mind, that was pretty much everyone.

Roye's father, Furman L. Templeton, was the director of the Baltimore Urban League, and had successfully led the campaign to integrate Baltimore City's public school system in the 1960s. His mother, Irene, was a public school teacher. Roye was a disciplined scholar from a good Negro family and would succeed. That's just how it was.

Ebba Boyesen, twenty, had seen Roye around the university. There were few Americans and fewer blacks and those two things wrapped in the same package one tended to notice. Ebba was a Scandinavian beatnik pinup girl, eyes the color of breath in winter, a heart-shaped face propped above her standard-issue black turtleneck. Her family had deep roots in Norway, blood ties going back to the 900s and Olaf the Holy, the guy who brought Christianity to Norway at the end of a sword. Ebba's mother, Gerda, was a prominent psychotherapist, and Carl, her father, was a wealthy businessman and dilettante composer of music for film and cabaret. Ebba was going to marry a millionaire. That's just how it was.

In the fall of '64, a friend of a friend introduced Roye and Ebba at the Three Musketeers. Within minutes, talk turned to Kerouac and Kierkegaard and pretty soon Ebba and Roye were fighting. They got off on their differences—physical, cultural, dialectical. Ebba thought Roye was the most beautiful man she'd ever seen, and Roye, he had eyes, too. From that day on, there were only the two of them. He expounded his theories on socialism (*for it*), God (*against*), from beneath a nimbus of marijuana smoke. Ebba was a teetotaler. Roye was her self-appointed guru, her savior from a life devoid of sensuality and risk.

Grandma Boyesen got wind of the love affair six months in. In April, she showed up at Ebba's apartment just after dawn.

You are to pack your things and come back to Norway. Right now.

Ebba slammed the door in her face. There was a rustle at her feet as an envelope slid beneath the door. The letter was from the secretary of the king of Norway—the king's seal at the top of the page. It read: *By law, you are a subject of Norway, and as such, you are hereby not allowed to leave Norway until you are rightfully twenty-one years of age.*

Ebba was twenty.

She and Roye walked to the Hotel Terminus in the center of the city, where Grandma Boyesen was staying. Ebba told Granny that she and Roye *were in love, this is forever, I'm not going, nothing can tear us apart.*

Grandma B sat bolt upright. Listened patiently. Then told her, *That is not possible. You are not staying here with this black American drug dealer.*

Grandma B had him on the black American thing, but while Roye smoked a hell of a lot of dope, he was not, in fact, a dealer. Grandma B thought Roye was a dealer because a friend of the Boyesens—Marc—had gone to visit Ebba at school, where he'd gotten into some kind of existential debate with Roye, and *lost*—so he ran back home and told Ebba's mother that Roye was a militant Zulu dealing major weight and endangering her daughter's life. Marc had recently begun having an affair with Gerda, so it was decided that Grandma B was the best representative to rescue Fay Wray from Kong.

Roye and Ebba went back to Ebba's apartment, packed, and Ebba left with Grandma B on the ferry to Oslo the next morning. On the sixteen-hour ride over the North Sea, Ebba sat with her back to her grandmother, and began—knit one, purl one—a black scarf for Roye.

The Boyesens took Ebba to their mountain house just outside Oslo, where she knitted and sulked and refused to eat for two weeks. The house was spacious, and her parents had relegated her to what amounted to a private flat on the lower floor, where she was all but left alone. In a place where the sun didn't set long enough in summer for sleep to breed common sense, Ebba had an idea.

Turned out, it was easy to hide Roye in the flat. No one ever checked on her. She got her food from the kitchen during off-hours, came and went as she pleased. They lived on omelets and bad poetry and discussions of life and death and art. They made plans to be married. They made a game of hushed whispers when footfalls sounded near their door, reveled in walking freely through town, in almost getting caught.

Once, Ebba's father, Carl, saw Roye and Ebba in a clinch just outside the house. Later, Carl clucked and grinned mischievously at his daughter. *You find a new boyfriend? That was quick,* he quipped. His silly daughter—in love, now over it—had already moved on to someone more appropriate. Carl had only seen Roye from the back, bundled up in a scarf and floppy woolen cap.

After a couple of months of hiding out in the Boyesen compound, Roye grumbled, *This is no way to live.*

Ebba agreed. On the eighteenth of June, 1965, the day after

her twenty-first birthday, Ebba and Roye hopped a ferry back to Copenhagen. Roye and his few friends took up where they left off—minus even the pretense of attending classes—smoking pot morning noon and night.

Soon, needles flashed. Heroin was now part of the Copenhagen scene. Roye—and of course Ebba—abstained, but their world of cultivated boredom had soured. Hard to have dialectical debates when the straw man is on the nod.

Roye was brilliant. There was no denying that. Wrestling with Kant twelve hours a day was not for the unenlightened. But Roye was also intractable, resistant to new experiences. On holiday in Málaga, he wouldn't go in the water over fear of sharks. Ebba tried to tell him that the last time someone saw a shark in the Mediterranean was never ago. He still didn't go in past his ankles. When Ebba took him skiing in Norway, he balked at the bunny slope. She tried to give him some pointers, but he slung the skis over his shoulder, trudged off the hill, and wouldn't talk to her for days. It wasn't that she'd shown him up—he just couldn't abide not having control over his surroundings.

At bottom, Roye was a fairly parochial Southern boy—he'd formed and fixed ideas about the world early and held fast to them. Men and women had roles. Men were leaders, thinkers, drivers of the household. Women were muses, vessels to be filled with their man's opinions, books, albums, babies. Ebba had been groomed to marry well, sure, but upper-class Scandinavian women were somewhat more free-spirited than the feminine ideal Roye had imagined for himself.

For a while, Ebba accepted the role Roye expected her to play. She made pancakes and served beer to the black-clad mob splayed across Roye's living room floor. Most of the crew were Scandinavian, but a few were American. The American kids' ranks were thinning, though, with every week.

Sometimes, in broad daylight, Yankee boys were seen being dragged down the Strøget by U.S. Military Police. There was a U.S. "police action" starting in Indochina. Back home, American boys were starting to get called up. College deferments lasted only until they didn't. By '65, college or no, on U.S. soil or no, if you were able-bodied and it was your time to go you were going. The last place Roye wanted to go was Vietnam. There was only one thing to do.

In the summer, he joined the U.S. Navy.

Roye knew that if he was drafted, he'd go into the army as an infantryman. He'd heard from the unreliable expat underground that the navy wasn't going to be deployed in the Southeast Asian theater, so he figured he could cruise on a boat for a while, out of harm's way, then sail back into graduate school via the GI Bill. Ebba stayed in Norway, and Roye left for the States in November.

On some level, Ebba was relieved. Friction between the two had been mounting, and now the navy was going to end their battle without her having to fire a shot. Freed from her recent emancipation from her life of privilege and status in Norway, Ebba was shaping up to be a different kind of woman: one with an open-ended curiosity about the world. A belief in the mystical. The holistic. A hippie.

Two months after he returned to the States—just before he reported to boot camp—Roye wrote Ebba, told her he couldn't live without her, and asked her to come to Baltimore to live with his parents. She was twenty-one years old. Despite her feelings of suffocation, she'd never been so needed by someone, body and soul.

The tension between first love and forging an identity of her own became unbearable. No matter her misgivings at the imbalance of power in their relationship, the letters, and the abject display of vulnerability of a boy about to ship off to war, broke her. She decided freedom could wait.

Ebba arrived in Baltimore in the winter of '66, and moved into Roye's family's house, at 1502 McCulloh Street, a three-story West Baltimore brownstone in a black neighborhood hanging on to its middle-class status by bloody fingertips. Roye's father, Furman, liked her. Thought Ebba was exotic, cute. Roye's mother, Irene, thought she was too light—in skin tone and substance—to be paired with her son, who was destined for—on a black, bourgeois Baltimore scale at least—greatness.

The house on McCulloh Street was soul-deadening. After a lifetime of the elegant, spare harmony of Scandinavian design, Irene's riot of competing wallpapers—three different patterns in the living room alone—and the plastic taint of everything from the sofa to the linoleum were Ebba's first, lasting, impressions of her new home, and land.

After a few days, Roye's parents told him that despite what he'd learned overseas in smoky cafés and beatnik flats, unmarried Negro boys from good families didn't share beds with Norwegian flower children. So Roye proposed. His parents filled out all the paperwork and the young couple signed. Interracial marriage was against the law in Baltimore, so they were married in D.C. at the home of a black judge—a friend of Furman's—on February 16, 1966. The ceremony was cheerless and efficient and took five minutes.

Roye was a natural loner—one of only a couple of kids from his neighborhood to make it to college, never mind Europe. Circumstance conspired with temperament and they saw no one, went nowhere. Ebba sulked and begged to see some, or any, of America, but Roye was content to stay within the walls of 1502, facedown in a pile of Sartre.

In May, Roye departed for boot camp. Ebba's life now revolved around Irene's clockwork domestic schedule. The pots had to be scrubbed daily at nine, the rugs beaten at eleven, the sheets washed at two. The days ground on, time within the house on 1502 McCulloh a measured drip of Mr. Clean, Pine-Sol, Palmolive.

That fall, Roye got one and a half days off from boot camp. One Saturday, October 15, 1966, venetian blinds slashing Indian summer sunset across their bodies, Ebba and Roye made Randall Stefan Templeton.

III

PRODUCT OF
THE ENVIRONMENT

Stefan was born on July 15, 1967. For his first two years, the family lived together briefly, at the Naval Station Great Lakes, where Roye was commissioned from '66 to '69, in the northern Chicago suburbs, but mostly Ebba cared for Stefan at the house on McCulloh Street, alongside Irene and Furman.

Roye left for Vietnam in April of '69. The navy was no safe haven. Stefan was almost two years old when mother and son left for Europe three days later. Ebba was done with the house on McCulloh Street, with cars of rednecks yelling *nigger lover* as they screeched by, with the menace of the American ghetto.

They arrived in London, where Ebba's mother had begun the Boyesen Institute psychotherapy practice at 15 Redington Road, in Camden. Gerda—now split from Ebba's father—was renting the house and practicing her hybrid version of Reichian/Jungian psychoanalysis on London's open-minded elite. There were Kundalini erasures, out-of-body experiences, LSD seminars, time travel, past lives, trances, chakras and auras and primal screams and encounter groups. Sean Connery was a regular—his 007 character had started to creep into his own identity, and he needed exorcising. Ebba floated through every therapy, a trainee practitioner as well as a patient.

All the exploration of feelings and healings wormed its way into Stefan's toddler consciousness. He stroked the head of the middle-aged woman who blacked out after a debilitating hypnosis session. He howled along in stereo support with the millionaire industrialist undergoing primal scream therapy. Nap time was him in a corner while everybody else meditated. The mantras, the drone of the *ooohms* around him like nursery rhymes. Three-year-olds are usually concerned with their own immediate gratification. The *I* more important than the world around them. But before that bit of normal, natural selfishness was allowed to take hold, Stefan was imprinted with the notion that providing comfort and aid for one's fellow man was a necessity.

Aged three, Stefan walked with Ebba past the Crown & Goose on Delancey Street, Camden Lock. An old man was passed out on the sidewalk in front of the pub. Ebba veered around him.

Momma, you have to help the man . . . he's sick.

He isn't sick, he's drunk. Come on.

You go in there, and tell them to get a car and take him to hospital.

I'll do no such thing.

Stefan jerked his hand from hers. *Then I will help the man.* He plopped himself at the curb next to the man and patted his head. The drunk groaned. Ebba groaned. She walked into the pub and told them to call an ambulance and Stefan sat there and she sat there and nobody went anywhere until the ambulance loaded the drunk and the siren *hee-hawed* down Delancey.

He couldn't have articulated the sentiment, but if those rich fucks navel gazing on silk throw pillows and velvet divans back at Redington Road deserved saving, then so did this guy.

He was acutely aware of the absence of his father. When Stefan was almost five, Ebba was having breakfast with her younger sister, Mona—when she looked over and saw Stefan flipping through *Life* magazine. She crossed the room to take it from his hands but got to him too late. He was studying the picture of naked, napalm-bombed Phan Thi Kim Phúc, her arms frozen in a black and white pose somewhere between crucifixion and a grotesque inquiry: *why?*

Stefan looked up at Ebba. She froze. He returned to the magazine. Flipped through the pictorial.

After a beat— *Is this Vietnam?*

Yes.

Poppa is in Vietnam.

Yes.

He shook his head. *My poppa don't kill the children in Vietnam.*

No.

My poppa help the children in Vietnam.

Yes.

He shut the magazine. Crawled into her arms. Balled his fist and punched her shoulder. *I will borrow my momma to the children of Vietnam.*

Roye got out of Vietnam in late '72. He immediately joined his wife and son in Ibiza, on the hippie trail, where Ebba was supporting herself making jewelry and practicing from her grab bag of healing arts. She had taken a break from Gerda's Boyesen Institute— her therapy and her training were exhausting—and the chill of

London. Roye met his family in Ebba's little flat by the Café del Sol, off the twisty, whitewashed alleys of Paseo de Vara de Rey.

The Roye she got back wasn't the Roye who'd left. The brown, lean twenty-five-year-old she'd said goodbye to had returned a hollowed, yellow spectre. 'Nam had added a rust of paranoia to Roye's steel. Ebba had to wake him by gently touching his toes. Anything more invasive—a kiss on the cheek, say—could land her on the floor. Matchbooks and cans of Coke had to be checked for booby traps. Many nights she'd awaken gasping for air, Roye's hands around her throat, Vietcong come to kill him in his dreams.

But still, they were happy. Stefan scooting around pencil-thin alleys on his tricycle, days at the beach, evenings at the Café del Sol. Stefan was becoming a water baby—fearless below the surface of the waves—and attending kindergarten along with all the other Spanish kids. He was fluent now, in Spanish, English, Norwegian. A chubby, caramel toddler.

And the boy loved his guns. His weapons of choice were a pair of Hubley cast-iron Texan Jr.'s—long-barreled, anchored by white plastic grips emblazoned with black steer horns—loaded with D-3 fifty-shot caps. He kept his rigs slung low in faux leather vinyl holsters, able to clear the repeaters from a square stance in the time it took a peseta Roye tossed to hit the floor. *Git 'im Stef—Charlie's under the stairs—git 'im.*

There were expats and tourists to keep the therapy and jewelry in demand, weed and acid to blunt Roye's visions of the jungle. But after a year of unwinding, Roye decided that it was time to go back to the States. His father had died, Irene had moved into a high-rise downtown, so the house at 1502 McCulloh was empty. He could resume his postgraduate philosophy studies via the GI Bill, and the family could settle into a normal routine. He would leave at the end of the summer, get situated, and Ebba and Stefan would follow right after Christmas.

A fine and reasonable plan, except for one thing: there was no way Ebba was moving back to Baltimore.

Roye left and December came, and Ebba called to tell him she was staying in Europe, in London. Stefan was doing well, and she had returned to her studies. No sense disrupting things. She told him she'd come to Baltimore after the New Year for a visit at least, during a break from her classwork. Soon, the letter came from Roye's lawyers: he was filing for divorce. Roye told her to send Stefan for Christmas. Ebba was afraid to go. Afraid she wouldn't be able to remain committed to her studies and her newfound freedoms back in Roye's orbit.

Armed with his trusty six-shooters, black cowboy hat tied tight around his chin, spurs clanking into a PanAm 747, Stefan— accompanied by Ebba's brother—was returned to American soil. On the eighth of January, 1973, Roye called Ebba and told her that if she didn't return to Baltimore and assume her role as mother and wife, Stefan would stay with him. Roye's anger fed upon itself and things moved quickly: a week later, another letter from the lawyer. He was filing for sole custody.

Baltimore as a home was a death sentence as far as Ebba was concerned. But maybe there was a middle ground. She visited Roye and Stefan that February, and stayed for two and a half months. Roye was making a meager income as a philosophy professor at the University of Maryland at Baltimore County. They lived— briefly—as husband and wife, and Stefan was enrolled at School 66, Mount Royal Elementary, in a tony white neighborhood ten blocks east. Ebba had dutifully researched the best public schools in the area, and Mount Royal Elementary was a haven in that otherwise bleak section of West Baltimore. Eleven blocks east, 66 was not Stefan's zoned school—that would have been the much rougher Booker T. Washington Elementary, right around the corner from McCulloh Street—but Ebba had charmed the school faculty into accepting the boy. The school, located in the wealthy white enclave of Bolton Hill, was somewhat integrated, and had an excellent reputation for a public school.

His transition was difficult.

Stefan had never played with children before. Nursery school in Ibiza had been short-lived, and in London he had spent his time perched at the feet of a bunch of privileged semi-adults working through their psychic distress.

School 66 was a rumpus of kids scrambling through the wood-chip pile at recess, Wacky Packages cards traded with Wall Street fury, enmities and alliances going back a year or so ago to nursery school. Stefan had an accent like some bastard out of Dickens, and freaky duds off Carnaby Street.

He was also the only mixed kid at 66.

Chants of Oreo abounded. Fists, too. They didn't give a shit about his toy "lorries" and they didn't want to share his Toblerone. His six-shooters weren't much of a defense, and he couldn't fight. He was soft and trusting. A mama's boy. Ebba fretted over Stefan's lack of friends and his delicate nature. He spent most of his time with his GI Joe action figures, reading comic books, or watching his favorite TV program—*The Undersea World of Jacques Cousteau*. He spent hours in the tub, pretending his GI Joe was diving for treasure or fighting sharks in the bottomless sea. But he was his father's son, too. And Roye had brought back something from Vietnam—something besides rage, nightmares, paranoia.

Moo Duk Kwan—a sub-style of the fighting system Tae Kwon

Do—means "School of Martial Virtue." The navy introduced Roye to Tae Kwon Do, and he stuck with it after his discharge, quickly progressing to black belt, and from there, opening a small school in Baltimore's ritzy white Bolton Hill. Classes were held in a small church in the 1300 block of Bolton Street, frequented by housewives, some of Roye's philosophy students, and a hodgepodge of early adopters of the martial arts craze sweeping the country, courtesy of Bruce Lee and the dollar Kung Fu double features chopping and socking their way across ghetto movie screens.

Ebba asked Roye if he'd teach Stefan Tae Kwon Do.

He's gotta ask to do it, Roye told her. *Not you.*

When Ebba asked Stefan if he'd like to give it a try, the boy flinched.

It's dangerous, Momma. They punch and kick each other. I don't want to be hurt.

So she took him to art classes. *Boring.* Dance classes. Fucking mortifying. A multilingual, racially ambiguous outcast in a tutu? She may as well have drawn a bull's-eye on his ass.

This is not something for a boy to do, Momma.

Then she took him to watch Roye train a class at the dojo. *You see, Stefan? Your poppa is dancing, just like the class I took you to, but these are strong men.*

Stefan was terrified.

You won't be hurt, darling—it's just steps, like dancing for boys. But you must ask your poppa to show you.

Stefan watched the session—the stretching, the meditation, the high kicks and crisp strikes and the snap of the cotton gi's— petrified, transfixed.

Poppa, he asked that night after dinner, *will you show me the Tae Kwon Do?*

From then on, Stefan went with Roye to the dojo every Saturday morning and three nights a week, his tiny frame wrapped in a gi, stubby little fingers and toes aping his pop at the front of the class. Back at home, in the damp of their basement, there was more of the same. Knuckle push-ups, jumping jacks, *Keeeyas* shouted at the end of each kick or punch.

The discipline rounded out some of the therapeutic mysticism he'd been infused with in Europe. If he'd been taught to be in touch with the spiritual energy flowing from auras and chakras since birth, now he was forging a connection with his body. His knuckles grew callused. Tiger Balm took the place of baby powder.

At school, he remained isolated. Ebba took him on long walks through Bolton Hill looking for children in backyards or in parks. Even as a foreigner, she knew that the prospects for finding play-mates for her polyglot, racially murky son were better among Bolton Hill's liberal aristocrats. She knocked on the doors of the houses where kids' voices spilled into the street, and told the be-mused parents that her son wanted some *fellow children to play with, and would very much like to come in.*

Ebba was making sure Stefan would be okay without her. If it came to that.

By now, Roye had started in with how a wife and mother's place is in the home. Ebba nodded blankly during his lectures, but was secretly bound and determined to finish her therapy training back in London that spring. She had a plan. She would steal Stefan.

Stefan's passport was U.S.-issued. She'd always wanted him to have dual citizenship—but in Norway, citizenship was conferred via the father. Stefan was American on paper, where it counted for international travel. Roye had locked the boy's passport in a strong-box. Stefan wasn't going anywhere unless he said so. Ebba fretted and plotted how to get the document. Roye was no dummy and she was a lousy liar. She offhandedly asked one night, over dinner, if she could take a look at it, *Just to see what the picture looks like.* She wasn't offhanded enough. Or maybe Roye had noticed her bloodied fingernails, chewed to the quick with worry. He grilled her and she broke. Once Roye realized Ebba wasn't going to stay at 1502 McCulloh for good, he kicked her out.

For the next year, she came back for long visits of a month or so and on holidays, staying with hippie friends she'd made in Bolton Hill. Sometimes Roye would let her see Stefan, sometimes he wouldn't. Depended on his mood. On whether it rained that day. On some mysterious logarithm of rage and spite.

Ebba just as often stood outside on the sidewalk, Stefan pressed against the front window, not having seen his mother for two or six or eight months, Roye telling the boy to *get away from the window and be a man. She wanted out, so she's out,* his father said, snapping the curtains shut.

In the months between visits, Stefan trained in the dojo, but took the beatings from both the older white kids at school and the black kids in his neighborhood without comment. He was terrified. He tried to find another, safer way home, but he may as well have been looking for a chillier route to hell. McCulloh Street was McCulloh Street. Unless he was airlifted in and out, he could expect more beatings. Stefan was just as frightened of his father. Of his opinion. He took to stuffing his bloodied shirts into his backpack on the way home. Roye would have expected more of his son. The blood and the muggings just another example of how soft his mother had made him.

At six, he was a latchkey kid, and kept his house key on a plain dog tag link chain around his neck. The West Side black kids went through his pockets for lunch money every day, but the chain looked worthless. It was his amulet. Sinister fingers never ventured that far north. As long as he had his key, he could get home.

Sometimes he saw his mother: up ahead, on a Baltimore street, a blonde glimpsed from behind. He would follow, streaming mute tears, or break from his father's grasp and run toward her, tugging at her skirt until she turned around, looked down, the stranger wondering why the strange brown boy was clutching her leg and calling her Momma.

When he was six, Stefan got his wish. Roye was working two jobs—driving a truck as well as teaching at the university—and figured maybe it wasn't such a bad idea for Stefan to live with Ebba. The boy was always moping about, crying for her. From a practical standpoint, she could spend more time with him than he could.

Stefan flew to London by himself, and moved into Ebba's tiny communal squat on Acton Lane. Living with his mother was insubstantial. A flurry of "happenings." Perhaps most significantly: there were *no men*. And Stefan was now as much his father's son as a mama's boy.

He attended West Acton Primary, and fared no better there socially than he had back in Baltimore. West Acton was a community nursery/elementary school, a squat, barracks-like structure off Noel Road. Just like back at 66, Stefan got As and Bs. Just like back at 66—he got his ass kicked every day. The pallid, stodgy boys piled on him from the beginning. They called him a wog and told him to stop sounding like *such a Yank*, but he wouldn't drop his Hs or lose his six-guns for anybody.

It was starting to dawn on him that however many places he'd lived—Ibiza, Norway, London—he was an American at heart. There had been little permanence in his life so far. His travels in Europe were rootless, and Ebba's influence somewhat esoteric. Roye and the house on McCulloh seemed to be made of sturdier stuff: brick and iron and set in stone. His father represented solidity, and a kind of toughness that Stefan romanticized as quintessentially American. Roye was a rugged individualist, a warrior—had even fought for his country. Not so far, in the boy's imagination, from the men on cinema screens who wielded six-shooters in Monument Valley, or lobbed grenades in Guadalcanal.

Stefan missed his father, and as a sort of tribute claimed "American" as an identity. But that identity was defined more by Roye's absence than any real affinity for land or culture. He damn sure wasn't British. The kids could mock him all they wanted. He talked the way he talked because he'd been places these yobs had never been. He'd bounced on 007's knee in a West End townhouse, been run down and beaten by gangs on Baltimore's West Side ghetto. He spoke three languages and played chess and knew bits of the Bhagavad Gita, while his thick schoolmates had never been past Westway. Had never experienced anything more exotic than tikka masala.

I am American, he told his mother one day. *I have a house and a school, and I shouldn't live like this.* The days in the dojo, the house on McCulloh Street, the beatings, the small-mindedness of Baltimore—at least there had been a routine. A discipline. It was time for him to break Ebba's heart, too.

When Stefan got back to the States in January of '74, the city stuck him in his zoned school—Booker T. Washington Elementary. Compared to School 66 and West Acton, Booker T. was like

Attica. One hundred percent black and poor. Not exactly the kind of place a light-skinned kid just off a plane from London would feel at home. His first day, when it came time to do the Pledge of Allegiance, Stefan just sat there. He didn't know the words. In English class, the harried, morbidly obese teacher told everybody to *set down*. Stefan—pompous, elitist adults his primary company for much of his young life—felt obliged to tell the black lady wrangling future ex-cons for fourteen K a year that *objects are "set" down—people must "sit" down*. He spent the next three hours in the principal's office.

When he got let out for lunch, he went to the bathroom to wash his hands. He looked over at the black boy next to him at the sink. Smiled. A fist smashed into his nose. There was so much blood streaked down the white shirt Ebba had given him that they had to send him home before recess on his first day.

He was back in the dojo as soon as he'd returned to Baltimore—ass whippings and all. At least there was *order*. His body had missed the repetition and the release. He ascended to purple belt quickly. There were no other children in the class, so Roye had him spar full-contact with adults. Wanted him to learn to put together combinations—*no such thing as one punch, one kick*. Stefan remembered the forms—the patterns of kicks, blocks, strikes—and settled back easily into a training rhythm with his pop.

Three weeks after his arrival, Ebba followed. She was horrified to find Stefan languishing in one of the worst schools in the city. Roye was overwhelmed with work and not inclined to intervene—*This is where they want him to go, what do you want me to do about it?*

Ebba stormed into Booker T. and snatched him out of homeroom. She walked him the eleven blocks east to Mount Royal

Elementary, 66, and sat him in a chair outside the principal's office while she went in and had a few words with Mrs. Francis, the hefty, efficient, always grumpy lady who ran the place.

This boy out there, he is the grandson of Furman L. Templeton and he belongs here, where you know him and he knows you and he can learn something.

Fuck the paperwork and the zoning, Stefan was back at 66 that afternoon.

Mother and father were civil, but cool. Ebba made once- or twice-a-year pilgrimages to Baltimore to visit Stefan, and she was grudgingly allowed to see her son, but never allowed inside the house. On one trip, she bought Stefan a golden retriever puppy—Tug—to provide unconditional love in her absences. Roye forbade it. He'd gotten a German shepherd named Quasimodo while Stefan was gone. The dog was everything the Germans had bred it to be. Loyal. Watchful. And liable to take your hand off if you were not a member of the immediate household. Stefan was heartbroken when Roye told him he couldn't keep Tug. Quasimodo was dismayed as well. Tug would have been delicious.

Stefan spent holidays and every summer overseas with Ebba, wherever she wound up: Morocco, Monaco, Ibiza, London, Paris. Her therapy career was starting to take off—her mother, Gerda, had founded something called "Biodynamic Therapy"—and Ebba had ascended to full practitioner status, making some money at last. When he visited his mother in the winter of '76, on a ski trip to the Swiss Alps, he looked up for a moment from hooking his bindings.

It's changing me.

What is?

The training.

Jesus. The kid was becoming as earnest and severe as Roye. There were no knock-knock jokes or funny faces anywhere in him. But Ebba had to admit that she could see the change in his bearing.

On one Baltimore visit, she'd seen Stefan take his purple belt test. After the class—all adults—had completed the forms section of the test, it was time for the board-breaking portion. As every examinee went before Roye and smashed either a pine one-by-six or their hand, Stefan hung his head and breathed deep, soberly awaiting his turn. Ebba wondered what she'd gotten her son into. Stefan looked over. As calm as a capon in a henhouse.

It's an optical illusion, he said. He made a slicing motion with his hand. *There's nothing between my hand and the ground.* Then he went up and broke the board and got his purple belt.

Psychologists say you're pretty much who you're going to be by eight years old. By then, Nature and Nurture have done their best or their worst—the rest is just connecting the dots.

Roye didn't give a fuck if his son could tell whether somebody's chakra was out of alignment, as long as the boy knew how to protect himself. Baltimore was rough and the Vietcong had taught Roye how to prepare for an enemy. There were guns everywhere in his home. Under desk drawers—a palm-sized .25 Beretta; in kitchen cabinets—a nickel-plated Smith & Wesson .38; in linen closets—a snub-nosed .38; and in nightstands—a Ruger .357 magnum Security Six.

Despite his training and his access to artillery, Stefan did not find the courage or the confidence to strike back against the almost daily beatings. *Payback* would have required rage, and he couldn't muster rage on his own behalf. He'd been taught to give up the self, to see the world as collective humanity. Despite the magnanimity of his worldview, he was lonely.

Thanks to Quasimodo's snarling presence, any other pets—or friends invited over—were out of the question. In the spring of '76, a litter of kittens—five of them—wriggled through the chain link fence at 1502, snarfing the leftovers in Quasi's bowl once the beast had been let back in the house. Stefan set the fuzzballs up in a little cardboard box, and raced home to play with them every day after school. With his dangled scraps of Oscar Mayer bologna, they'd clamber over in a chorus of mews.

Some of the boys in the neighborhood would lope through the alley, jeering at Stefan and his *pussies,* from beyond the fence. They'd never climb the fence to do anything about it. They knew that a crazy-ass dog—and a silent, menacing, six-foot-something motherfucker—lived in the house with Stefan.

Stefan found the first head just inside the backyard, where the cardboard box was wedged against the garage. They'd decapitated the others as well, some of the bodies flung into the neighbor's yard, their heads batted down the alley like bloody powder puffs.

He didn't know who'd done it. Picking out inhumanity in West Baltimore was like giving out speeding tickets at the Indy 500. As he scooped up the kittens' matted bodies—*Clean up that mess before the rats get them,* Roye said—something whispered to him that it *was not all right for others to determine life or death.* That decision had to come from somewhere else. Not God—he'd learned from his father, nose jammed in *Thus Spoke Zarathustra,* that God was dead—but a just, merciful being here on earth, with the power to defend the weak and avenge the wronged.

A few days later, he was walking home, through the Bruce Manor projects on Eutaw Street and the derelict park that separated Bolton Hill and the ghetto.

Gimme your money, bitch.

There were two of them. Usually there were more. One was jet black, with a short bush and lips hung so heavy and thick that the pink underside showed through. The other one was round, a light brown pear of a boy with sleepy eyes and chicken pox scars. Stefan knew the drill. He hung his head and let them turn out his pockets. It'd be over soon enough. They stripped his backpack off. One of them smacked his head.

All you got is lunch tickets?

Stefan shrugged.

Uh-uh, the other one—the pear-shaped boy—said. *What's this?*

He grabbed the chain holding the key around Stefan's neck.

The first kick caught the darker boy in the solar plexus. A backfist into the pear-shaped boy's cheek and Stefan pivoted two roundhouse kicks in a 180 combo, the darker boy down, sucking air into emptied lungs, as Stefan wrapped his forearm around the other boy's carotid artery and dug his other thumb into the eye of the pear-shaped motherfucker. He'd gone for the key, and Stefan would have this boy's eye—not for malice, or revenge for the days of beatings at the hands of pasty limeys and dusky niggas unable to see beyond their neighborhood, not for the mother and father who couldn't bridge the gulf between a world browned by color-blind love and the cannibal reality of man versus man; not even for the kittens—no, he'd have this boy's eye because there would be *reckoning* from this day forward, meted out by someone with the pain and perspective and *power* to punish all those who trespassed. Stefan looked around him. At the darker boy, crawling away, on all fours. At the other boy, eyes fluttering at the edge of unconsciousness. This was neither good, nor bad. Right, nor wrong. It was *just.*

He tucked his key into his shirt and walked home.

IV

SAFE EUROPEAN HOME

y the summer of 1979, he'd filled out. Puberty and years of training had lengthened and chiseled him. He'd mostly skipped the gangly, oddly pitched, eruptive-skin phase. His features—always vaguely porcine—had come into symmetrical relief. His brow was a thick ridge over eyes flecked with gold and moss, his cheekbones perched high, his jaw as set as a terrier's. And there was something in his bearing. For the last three years back in Baltimore, he'd become sort of a West Baltimore playground legend. After a few fights—some in the hood around McCulloh Street, some on the playground at 66—word had spread:

Don't fuck with that Bruce Lee nigga . . . I saw him take out five motherfuckers at once. . . . Five? Shit, I heard the whole eighth grade at Booker T. came down after school to kick his ass, and he knocked them niggas out like duckpins, bam, bam, Hiiiiyaa!

Much of the talk was hyperbolic, some of it apocryphal. But some of it wasn't. Stefan had become—if not exactly feared—then respected. He walked ramrod straight, met and held every eye cast his way. He'd started to love the walk home through the projects— the reverential calls of *Hey, Stef-an! What's up, my man?* It had been years since he'd been jumped by corner boys. Another life.

At school and around the neighborhood he was affable and generally liked. But he didn't have many friends. His experiences were so singular that it was hard for other kids to grasp the quirkiness of his childhood. Though some of the generational touchstones were the same for many of his peers—child of Vietnam vet, divorced parents—the manifestations loomed larger in Stefan's case. None of these other vets had prepared their children for war. None of these other kids had traveled alone across oceans, between parents. And none of these other kids were mixed. Unlike them, he belonged wholly to no one: race, country, father, mother.

Stefan caroused and played and engaged, never fully committing to youthful escapism. At home, his father supplemented his chores and homework and training: *You know what a straw man fallacy is, Stef? No? Gimme two pages after dinner, double-spaced.* By now, Roye was teaching philosophy full-time at the University of Maryland at Baltimore County, and made no academic distinction between his students and his son. The war he was readying the boy for would be fought on two fronts: physical as well as intellectual. Stefan was an avid reader, though he read for the acquisition of knowledge rather than for enjoyment. The *Hagakure* held more allure for him than *The Phantom Tollbooth*.

His travels and newfound physical prowess made him cocky, aloof. Kids found that a little of him went a long way: they were both awed and put off by him. He was bored, bemused by them.

Their concerns were of the everyday variety: skipping classes, who liked whom, trading Now and Laters for Bubble Yum at recess, who went to Kings Dominion on the weekend. He couldn't care less. He'd ridden camels in Morocco and speared squid in the Mediterranean. What the fuck did recess have to offer him? To him, his classmates were ants in a farm, scuttling this way and that in their sealed glass universe.

All those formative years of beatings and fear of his fellows had been replaced by righteous indignation and *the ability to do something about it*. But there had been a cost.

As the longtime recipient of violence, Stefan had become conditioned to the anticipatory rush. With no one left to fear, he *began to seek out* the adrenaline spike. He walked through the projects at night. When he saw a gang of corner boys or potential stickup kids ahead of him, he made sure to walk through their midst—leaning hard into every shoulder that didn't make way—instead of crossing the street. If there was going to be trouble then it was up to them. But he made sure to be in the wrong place at the right time. He would never again change direction, or alter his path for anyone else. Nothing would be off-limits.

These bullshit tests of mettle were the only way he could get the adrenaline flow going again. He had a steady supply and a reliable pusher: by the end of the 1970s, Baltimore was in full decay. In the ghetto, childhood is measured in dog years. Soon, the fists and feet with which he bested his peers would be met by guns. At his size, with the rep he was gaining, no one was going to give him a pass just because he was only thirteen.

Roye could not help but notice the elevated menace in West Baltimore. The sound of gunshots was as regular as church bells; alleys were bleached nightly by Baltimore PD helicopter searchlights.

Though he'd kept the boy from his mother's softening influence as a tyke, Roye reckoned that some European civility could save Stefan from the streets. Ebba was doing okay with money by then. She could look after him for a while.

Mâcon, Burgundy. Autumn 1981. Daphodil—the grey mottled Selle Français—charges into the wood. Stefan presses his neck into the mare's coarse mane as chestnut branches rake across his back. Two hares—brown and rangy, tied at the feet—flop against either side of the animal as the field clears and the castle comes into view. He dismounts and yanks the rope to the dinner bell outside the pantry, the chime scattering doves into the sky.

Daphodil shakes her head and snorts into the low grass. Stefan pulls the hares free. William, the bony ebony cook from Martinique, opens the door to the pantry, grunts—*Ah, bon*—and taps out a cigarette. Stefan feels the cook's eyes on him as he closes his fist around the animal's sternum and squeezes the entrails onto the pavement. The orange tom who lives with the caretaker and his wife in the cottage next to the castle glides over and laps at the guts, ears pinned back.

Stefan slides the Chambriard folding knife Rene has lent him from his jeans pocket and thumbs it open. His mother's twenty-seven-year-old boyfriend has taught him how to hunt, this last year, and he casts half an eye around in case the young Frenchman is watching. Hates that he wants to impress him. Like Roye, Rene is impossible to please. Only makes Stefan try that much harder.

He slices almost to the backbone of the first hare and peels the fur. He'd like to dismiss all this *To the Manor Born* aristocratic education stuff as bullshit, but some of it is as tough as anything the streets back home had to offer. He'd always been around guns and knew how to use them, but he'd never put a bullet into a living thing. Rene had shown him how to use the .22 Ruger semiautomatic rifle (hanging now, John Wayne–style, in a leather holster at Daphodil's side), explained parabola, how to sight a moving target, and where to put the shot for a quick, humane kill. When Stefan wounded a hare or a grouse due to a rushed or misplaced shot, Rene shook his head and made Stefan twist the animal's neck until the twitching stopped. *You must not let it suffer. The meat is no good if the animal dies in pain.*

Rene also taught Stefan how to ride. He'd nearly broken two ribs the first time he got on Daphodil inside the polo grounds at the castle. Rene had smacked her on the ass as soon as Stefan grabbed a fistful of reins. Wanted to teach the kid a lesson.

The sharp-featured Frenchman was descended from nobility, a chevalier who'd inflated his status to viscount or baron or something, figuring nobody checked those details anymore. Rene did, however, have the virtue of a classical education. Stefan was aware that he had some Viking nobility in his own past, but it was theoretical. As much as he'd become elevated to a sort of playground god back in Baltimore, the skills he'd learned there wouldn't gain him admission to the courts and great halls of Europe. But the projects were no different from the polo field: neither would be off-limits to him.

The castle—Château de la Salle—is a few thousand yards off the A6, overlooking the Saône River valley in Burgundy. A serpentine gravel drive twists through the forest leading up to the tri-spired mansion, its stone facade covered in ivy. The cambered roof is tiled with terra-cotta shingles the color of dried blood. Griffins snarl from the parapets. A fifteen-meter pool juts like a teal flag from the end of a narrow walkway connected to the house. Another hundred or so meters of manicured lawn and all is forest, farm, vineyard.

Behind the massive oak doors, the domed ceiling of the great hall is engraved with gold-leaf stars. A snowy marble expanse lies underfoot. A baby grand piano flanks the small chapel by the library just left of the great hall. Centered at the end of the entrance hall, fronting the spiral marble staircase, is a half-scale statue of a seated Dante Alighieri.

The second floor hosts a warren of apartments, stone walls lined with patterned fabric, reserved for Gerda and visiting Boyesen Institute luminaries. The third floor and the attic-like fourth floor are where the paying guests stay, mostly wealthy Germans. In summer, the castle is home to 150 clients who spend dearly for the privilege of having Gerda, Ebba, and a handful of renowned lecturers tell them whether their spleens are storing negative energies from childhood.

Across the narrow tarmac at the end of the gravel road, just off the stables and the riding paddock, is the cottage house where Ebba and Rene live. Stefan isn't allowed in there. In June, he spilled chocolate milk in the living room and forgot to clean it up. Rene has banished him to the clock tower at the rear of the castle. A fourteen-year-old boy with his own residence in a tower in a castle in the heart of the French countryside. If this is punishment, it is not unpleasant.

The women in Europe are neither ugly nor shy. Fourteen-year-old Stefan and twenty-five-year-old William, the cook, regularly drive into Mâcon and pick up local girls—waitresses, university coeds—and bring them back to the clock tower. Stefan looks seventeen, maybe eighteen. Girls tell him he reminds them of a rising young tennis player—Yannick Noah.

Normally the scar tissue of teenage rejection turns to humility and anchors the ego. But Stefan has no such scar tissue. Women want him. They have wanted him since he has been aware of wanting them, and all he has to do is lie back. He oozes sexual entitlement. He's the walking, talking, strutting embodiment of Dizzy Dean's famous quip, *It ain't bragging if you can back it up.*

At fourteen, after a year here, he's fluent, but it's the caramel American exotica the girls dig. The rough hands and squared shoulders and Sugarhill Gang tapes he booms from his ghetto blaster back in his room. Women—beautiful, hungry—have been coming into his bed all summer long. He's lost count. He is half ashamed to admit that he can't remember a few of their names. But the memory of his first time lingers, a tangle of limbs and salt skin on lips and his heart thumping against his chest.

He had just turned thirteen.

When she walked into the room, the great oak door sighing closed behind her, he couldn't make out her face.

You want light?

She angled the lamp shade away, turned it on. Pulled off her cotton tunic. Her breasts jutted from her body, small cones bull's-eyed by puffy brown nipples. She slid out of her blue jeans. A shock of bush and the full scent of her, animal and sweet. She put his hand on her. Scrunched her face, her short brown bangs grazing her lashes.

You won't come inside me?

He shook his head. She licked her palm, wet herself, and climbed on top of him, wincing.

Ach . . . zu gross . . . She took all of him in, laughed, squeezed his cheeks. *Your mother would kill me,* she moaned.

The woman was Ebba's friend. Married. With a couple of kids. Before the summer ends, Ebba sees enough women and girls padding barefoot away from his room in the misty dawn to get used to it. She tries to tamp it down, but there's nothing to be done about it. She'd already forbidden him from swimming in the pool while there was an outdoor group session under way. None of the women could concentrate as he knifed through the water, or dried himself with a towel, shaking the black slinkies on his head dry in the sun. They'd snatch glances of him, jammed into blue jeans that wouldn't be out of place in a John Holmes movie, and suck air through their teeth.

Some of the husbands—fat Germans with sandals on over their socks—had complained. The husbands were the ones who paid. Just now, when the Boyesen Institute was gaining some renown, and the castle was full from May to September with patients in need of Biodynamic Therapy, was no time for Stefan to rummage through the clientele. It was bad for business. There was no excuse. Even if he was just a kid, he should know better.

The cook, William, stubs out his cigarette and takes the hares. They'll be tough, but good after a few hours' bubbling in wine and potatoes and leeks. Stefan walks Daphodil back down to the paddock and hands her off to Bernigault, the fourteen-year-old *pale-frenier.*

We ride this weekend? La Roche? the pale, smaller boy asks.

Sure thing, Stefan says. La Roche—the Rock—is famous among locals. A mini-mountain overlooking a brown and green patchwork quilt of some of the greatest white wine vineyards in the world, tilled rows of vines separated by understated, hand-lettered stakes: Pouilly-Fuissé, Chasselas, Saint-Veran.

Stefan usually sneaks Rene's Yamaha Enduro 125, with a girl, some smoky Morteau sausage, and a bottle of Mâcon-Villages to the Rock on weekends when the castle is overrun with Germans. He hasn't been since the end of summer, and it'll be fun to go with the snap of autumn in the air. Maybe they'll camp there, if Bernigault isn't too skittish. The *palefrenier* is shy, a bit of an outcast. But the closest thing Stefan has to a friend his own age. The stable boy goes to school with him, in nearby Lugny.

A year ago, upon his arrival, Ebba had put him in the Ecole Internationale de Paris for his eighth-grade year. It hadn't gone well.

Ecole Internationale was a ritzy boarding school in the southern Parisian suburb of Draveil, twelve miles from the center of the city. Stefan was part of the "American Track." English was the only language spoken. The school was made up of a bunch of rich kids from all over whose parents were diplomats, or bons vivants, or just sick of them. Stefan cruised along at EI until just before Christmas break, when some of the older kids decided to have a party. It had gotten out of hand. Someone had smuggled in booze, hashish. Only the upperclassmen had been involved, but the next morning the staff searched every dorm for contraband.

All Stefan had brought with him from Baltimore were a few changes of clothes, his boom box, his Tae Kwon Do gi, and a gift from Roye—a pair of oak nunchakus. While he was in class, the dorm-troopers took the nunchakus from his duffel bag and locked them in the contraband closet. When he got back to his room and noticed they were gone, he went to the administration office and asked for them back. The guy said no way, they were a *deadly weapon.* Stefan told him, *These are a gift from my dad, I use these to practice,* and the guy said, *Tough, they're school property now.*

Stefan shrugged, went back to his room, scooped his tapes— Police, Sugarhill Gang, Peter Tosh—and his gi into his bag, walked down to the contraband closet, kicked it off the hinges, grabbed his 'chuks, and walked out the front door. Taxi to Gare du Nord train station, transfer to Dijon, transfer to Mâcon, taxi to Château de la Salle.

Ebba and Rene were furious—EI wasn't cheap and there weren't many options for schooling around Mâcon. Rene enrolled Stefan at Collège Privé La Source à Lugny, a Jesuit school twenty-six kilometers west of La Salle. Stefan got on much better in the converted fifteenth-century abbey. The kids were locals, sons and daughters of vintners, *fromagères,* farmers. The student body and staff spoke no English. Stefan spoke no French. It was cultural immersion, which he preferred greatly to EI.

Collège Privé was rustic and provincial. Coffee and bittersweet chocolate sandwiched between slabs of day-old baguette for breakfast. Santenay Rouge, plummy and tart, cut with water, in tin cups along with supper. Mealtime at Collège was a holdover from some kind of monastic ritual, where kids were grouped around a massive table, and food was passed in order of rank, counterclockwise, from the most senior—the fourteen- and fifteen-year-old *troisièmes,* all the way down to the lowly eleven- and twelve-year-olds—the *sixièmes.* On his arrival, Stefan was thirteen, lowly ranked, stuck on the left-hand side, near the end of the rotation. Day one, a picked-over plate of scraps landed in front of him. Day two, after the lead *troisième* finished scooping his meal, Stefan reached over, took it out of his hand, and helped himself. Then he passed it *left,* to the bespectacled lower classman sitting next to him:

Bernigault.

Nobody tells us when to eat, right? he said to Bernigault. *We eat when we're hungry.*

Bernigault just smiled and nodded at the American kid passing food his way.

Bernigault returned the favor by teaching Stefan French, via Asterix comics late nights in the dorm.

On this September day, Stefan watches Bernigault brush the lather from Daphodil. Bernigault's father was a *palefrenier,* as Bernigault's children may very well become. A man's fate should be *made,* not born, Stefan reckons. Class and rank an unsettling notion to his American idealism.

That Saturday, Bernigault and Stefan take the horses across the fields and track roads west, into Solutré. They build a little fire and sleep on a slab of rock overlooking the valley, huddled under thick wool while the horses hang their heads. Stefan tells Bernigault about America, Ibiza, Morocco—all the places he's been in his fourteen years. Bernigault has never been farther than Paris, and the two plan an escape to the city for Christmas. They'll pretend to be cousins. Stefan will bring girls back to their hotel and make sure Bernigault gets one.

None of this will happen.

Soon Ebba will get pregnant. She and Rene will go to London to the Redington Road winter session of the Boyesen Institute, the staff will leave, and Stefan will roam the castle alone all winter, a young brown Hamlet. Rene and Ebba are so consumed with their new lives, they assume Stefan has gone back to the dorms at Collège Privé. Bernigault and the other local children return to school in Lugny, but Stefan can't be bothered. He stops going to school completely. He lives on what he can hunt, or the stockpiles of industrial-sized cans of food left in the castle's kitchen. He reads books by the pile every week, culled from the castle library. There's a hodge-

podge of mysticism, dusty tomes of European history and philosophy, even some German Stephen King left by clients. He reads
it all.

Still, boredom sets in. Absolutely fuck-all to do. No juice, no
excitement. For thrills, he walks the parapet at night. Buzzes hill-
ocks on the Enduro trying to catch some air. Takes to spending
nights alone in the woods. Nothing works.

V

WELL 'ARD

He returned to America at the end of the summer of '82. He'd asked Roye if he could come back, after painting a bleak—though accurate—portrait of his languishing education in Mâcon. Baltimore wasn't any safer, but Roye—an intellectual at heart—would rather his son take a bullet than become a dullard. Stefan's transcripts from Ecole Internationale and Collège Privé à Lugny may as well have been written in Mandarin, considering that Mandarin was about as widely spoken as French in 1982 Baltimore, so Roye had arranged for him to audit a semester at the University of Maryland at Baltimore County while city school administrators figured out what, exactly, Stefan's academic credentials amounted to. This had promised to take months. Roye enrolled him in his own philosophy classes—Philosophy of Sex, and Critical Thinking—to keep the boy sharp. Roye was a difficult instructor and there was no nepotism. Stefan was expected to grasp the basics of Derrida, Heidegger, and Descartes as well as any of the matriculating students. He had done well—except for logic, which confounded him—even though the classes didn't count for anything.

Roye and Stefan commuted to school together three days a week, trained the UMBC Tae Kwon Do team together evenings, and grew closer. Stefan was happy to be back in a world of discipline and order.

But UMBC was just a stopgap and both men knew it. Aware that city administrators would send him to his zoned high school— bloody memories of Booker T. Washington still vivid—if left to their own devices, Stefan lobbied to get admitted to Baltimore City College High School. City College was a merit-based public school. Academically, the next best thing to private school. Stefan traveled to the school near Baltimore's Memorial Stadium dressed in a silk suit he'd gotten in Paris, and proceeded to dazzle the principal and staff with premium, imported bullshit. He lapsed in and out of French. Grilled them about the rigor of their "curricula." Confided in them that while he'd thought about *remaining at university, where I'm studying presently*—he didn't want to miss out on the *experiences of his peers.*

He was admitted midway through sophomore year, into City's gifted and talented A track program.

He nearly caused a riot on his first day.

The women in Europe had responded to his looks by simply fucking him. The repressed American girls at City had no such outlet. There were rules about courtship, strict timetables: three weeks of making out followed by a season of over-the-clothes fondling, culminating with—after a respectable period of blue-balled stoicism—the remote possibility of an urgent, chafing handjob. Stefan walked into Mr. Jones's second-period history class ten minutes late on his first day, just after Christmas break. He was wearing his fitted European threads. He spoke in a deep whisper and walked like he owned the place. Girls practically slid out of their chairs. They'd never seen anything like him. They trailed him down hallways and shut up when he passed them clustered around their lockers in between classes. They *fought* each other over whom he might have just looked at.

Despite the attentions of the girls in Baltimore, for his first few months back, he was uncharacteristically nervous. Out of step. Here, all the black male faces he saw shared a single, glowering expression. A macho, cartoonish rictus in an attempt to instill fear or fend off predation. They were *hard*. Baltimore in the early to mid-1980s was Beirut for black men. Reaganomics and the flood of crack cocaine made hard times harder and guns were everywhere. Always a violent city—kids were now getting shot for their jackets, their tennis shoes, or looking at motherfuckers sideways. It was a bucket of ice water in the face after mist-dappled vineyards and Daphodil and falconing on the great lawn of the castle in Lugny.

To focus, he'd thrown himself back into his training with Roye. He was ready to test for black belt, but Moo Duk Kwan's bylaws stated that eighteen was the earliest age a practitioner was eligible for the rank. He trained for hours in the dojo, helping Roye teach the UMBC Tae Kwon Do team, and spent every night in the basement of McCulloh Street working the heavy bag. He'd rock the leather bag nearly horizontal, pine-snow falling from where the chains scraped the ceiling joist, as he snapped his inseam into the leather. When he leaned and bobbed in with a right hook, the bag retreated, then crashed back toward him, momentum stopped dead by his left.

He worked the bag for hours. No gloves. Up in his room, behind the bedroom door, attached to the wall, was a six-by-six square of leather-bound wood: a makiwara training board. The board was used to toughen the skin around the knuckles, and to focus the power of a punch. Fifty full-power punches from an inch away. Fifty from six inches. Fifty from a foot. Now the other hand. Start over. Do it wrong and you break your hand. Children below eighteen are never supposed to use the maki board: bones that haven't fully developed can be permanently damaged. He'd been using it ever since Roye had given it to him on his eighth birthday.

No matter how sharp and hard he was getting, he knew that it might not be enough. The streets vibed menace on every corner. Every once in a while there were announcements over the school's intercom relaying the news of a student's death by shooting.

We regret to inform you that Dontell Williams was killed this weekend during a robbery. Services will be held Saturday, at the March funeral home on North Avenue, at one p.m.

The stakes were deadly different than when he'd left. So he adapted. All of Roye's training had been in aid of *being prepared.* The Boy Scouts' motto, writ ultraviolent. He tested himself. There was a new tourist attraction downtown at Baltimore's Inner Harbor waterfront. It was a twenty-minute walk from the house on McCulloh, and once past the ghetto, it made for a pleasant evening's stroll through upscale residential blocks. There were always girls on the Harbor's promenade, throngs of teenagers from all over the city and county preening and strutting weekend nights. His favorite walks were these *night walks.* Baltimore so dangerous back then that certain streets were deserted, left to the hard cases. An odd paradox of danger and solitude. Like his nights in the woods outside the castle, just the creak of oak trees and the snort of deer in the dark.

Sometimes he'd pocket one of Roye's guns for a nighttime walk down to the Harbor, or around West Baltimore. Usually the palm-sized Beretta .25 auto. Not much stopping power but it could be stashed easily in a waistband or a sock. On the rare occasion when he knew he'd be hanging out near the Murphy Homes—the garrison-like projects on the West Side—the nickel-plated Smith & Wesson .38. Baltimore had just passed Detroit as the murder capital of the free world. Part of why he'd returned was the missing juice. The adrenaline. With the *pop, pop, pop* of gunshots outside his window Saturday nights, his blood was moving in the right direction again. But the attendant posturing and dimmed prospects of black American ghetto life held no allure for him. Proud to be a *brother,* he would never become a *nigga.*

Still, he copped bits from the urban style of the day and made it his own. In the mid-1980s, college basketball jackets were all the rage—brothers were getting shot every day for silver and blue satin Georgetown Starter jackets. Stefan thought the trend was ridiculous. So he saved up and bought a brown Starter jacket with an intertwined orange "SD" logo on the breast. He didn't follow baseball or football. He had no idea who or what the San Diego Padres were. He just liked the colors. Nobody was getting shot for Padres jackets, because nobody gave a fuck about the Padres. That was the point. It was *all* bullshit, so why not have some fun with it? When teenage black kids walked by and vibed ghetto elitism—*Man, what the fuck jacket is that s'posed to be?*—Stefan would shrug, boom, *Santo Domingo, brother!* and laugh all the way down the sidewalk.

At 1502 McCulloh, money was tight. When he realized that Roye wasn't going to be able to keep him in the style to which he'd become accustomed, he went out and got a job. Scooping ice cream or tearing movie tickets for minimum wage wouldn't cut it.

He loved the water. He'd been an exceptional swimmer since he could crawl. Self-taught. In and around the beaches of Ibiza, on holidays with Ebba. At the castle, he'd swum fifty, a hundred laps a day in summer. He had a brutish but effective stroke, and had landed a spot on City's varsity swim team. By his senior year, he would break the Maryland record for the 100-meter freestyle, coming in around fifty-six seconds and a few tenths. *Lifeguard*. That sounded like a cool way to make some cash.

As soon as he decided to become a lifeguard, he took every course the Red Cross offered in lifesaving. He completed the life-saving certification course at fifteen. Water safety instructor certification at sixteen—had to be eighteen for that one, but he made up something about losing his birth certificate. He took the paramedics training course at Catonsville Community College—they wouldn't budge on the proof-of-age thing, so he was only allowed to audit. With his dossier full of lifesaving certifications, he got an after-school job as a lifeguard at the only pool with a vacancy he could find, at Baltimore's League for the Handicapped, in the winter of 1984.

The League—up in North Baltimore, close to school, behind Memorial Stadium—was a vocational/therapeutic/social center for children and adults with severe physical and mental disabilities. Cerebral palsy, Down syndrome, muscular dystrophy. A far cry from the sunny, bikini-sprinkled country clubs he'd envisioned manning. At the League, most of his weekends and evenings after school—after swim team practice—were spent wading the length of the pool with paraplegics, quadriplegics, holding them close and letting the water rush over them, *You're swimming, Teddy . . . See that, man? You're swimming. . . .*

He'd carry the men into the toilets and peel their trunks over their knees so they could urinate before entering the pool. If there were accidents, he wheeled the swimmers into the showers and sluiced them clean beneath the spray. Some had enough use of one limb to learn a choppy doggie-paddle. He'd race them the width of the shallow end, using just the same limb they had access to in order to keep the match even. He always made the race close. Sometimes they won, fair and square. The League was underfunded. The pool was so overchlorinated that his hair went from black to rust. The swimmers broke his heart. He loved it.

He'd spent chunks of his life watching his mother and grandmother provide therapy, and sure, some of it was corny, but the power of that transfer of human energy had stayed with him.

And the money was good. Three hundred dollars a week before overtime. Almost as much as his dad made. He blew it on ridiculous ghetto wear—three-quarter-length lambskin jackets, suede Puma Clydes, gaudy leather coats—or obscure hardcover books— *The Mahabharata*, Mishima's *Sun and Steel, Ecce Homo.* He was extravagant with the few neighborhood friends he had—likely to toss a barely worn calfskin jacket their way, with an *I don't like the pockets* shrug—because he knew he'd gotten breaks none of them had, or would.

He worked as a lifeguard consistently through high school, and lettered in swimming and in cross-country. His SATs were decent—1370—and he had a 3.5 overall GPA. As usual, summers and Christmases were spent in Europe—Norway or wherever Ebba happened to be on the Continent.

His prospects after high school were hazy. He could have gotten a free ride at the University of Maryland, courtesy of Roye's professorship. Didn't really want to stick around Maryland, though. Way too parochial. He was offered a full swim scholarship at Texas

Christian University, but a couple things bothered him about the school, specifically the Texan-Christian parts. He'd gotten accepted at Vassar, and the American University, but they were expensive as hell. No way would Roye slide into penury because Stefan thought he was too good for UMBC or TCU. Whatever he decided— Roye had made it clear that by his eighteenth birthday he was either enrolled somewhere, or out on his ass.

By early July of 1985, he'd half made up his mind to quit the States and go back to Europe when a defensive end for the Baltimore Colts made up the other half for him. A housewife he'd been having an affair with was married to a pro football tackle. A black, hulking locomotive. His wife was a supervisor at the Community Fitness Center where Stefan worked winter of his senior year. Her husband was always on the road—the Baltimore Colts football team had relocated to Indianapolis the year before—and there was little danger of their getting caught during the season. The wife— Angie—was brazen. Got a kick out of coloring outside the lines. She'd let Stefan stay over, weekends at a time, take calls from her husband while she was fucking him—really pushed their luck. She'd even let Stefan borrow the guy's brand-new black IROC Z sports car. The thing cost nearly 15K—leather and chrome everything, cassette player, sunroof—tricked out and drag-ready. Stefan tooled around town in the sports car for days at a time, until one day, when he spilled his McDonald's fries between his legs, bent down to retrieve them, and got T-boned by a station wagon as he blew the red light. Unhurt, he managed to limp the IROC to her front door, where she'd stared mutely at the wreck for five minutes.

He's gonna kill me. She tapped the cracked fiberglass cowling. It fell off. *And then . . . he's gonna kill you.*

He left for Mâcon, and the castle, on July 22, 1985.

On the flight over, on a whim, he'd decided that he wanted to enroll in the University of Geneva's translating program. He had a facility with language, and the degree could lead to travel, adventure.

By then, Ebba had given birth to two little girls—the oldest, Veronique, was four, and Emmanuelle was barely a year old. Stefan told his mother his college plans, and took a train to Geneva to apply in person, with his freshly minted Baltimore City College High School diploma. Which was worthless.

He was informed that in order to attend U of G—or any decent university in Europe—he'd need something called an International Baccalaureate.

The IB was the equivalent of an associate's degree in the States. Two years' worth of classes to make up for the fact that American high schools' criteria for higher learning were Europe's idea of junior high. The best IB program was said to be at St. Selby's College, Oxford.

In early August, he interviewed with the dean, Margaret Scarlan—gave her the whole "grandson of educator Furman L. Templeton" bit. She'd never heard of him, but Stefan's diploma was legit and he'd scored 1370 on his SATs, so he was accepted. Tuition was almost twenty grand a year, half of which Ebba and Gerda were willing to cover. He was still short.

He knew his mother's cousin Gussie was flush—she'd just inherited 33 million kroner from her father—so he flew to Oslo to put the touch on her. Gussie, a small, compact woman, was a wreck. Her husband, Orsten, had somehow gotten involved in a business deal with a motorcycle gang from the neighboring town of Akershus. According to Gussie, they'd threatened to kill him if he didn't pay them off. More worrisome, they'd made kidnapping threats against Gussie's two young children. Gussie told Stefan he could have the other half of the tuition if he moved in for the rest of the summer and acted as the family's bodyguard. It was a cakewalk—no bikers showed and the summer flew by. Gussie paid the remainder due on Stefan's tuition.

St. Selby's College shared famed Oxford University's postal code, but was otherwise unaffiliated. In its student body, it wasn't so different from Ecole Internationale: a school for wealthy students, aged sixteen to nineteen, who needed some polish before they were eligible to enter the more esteemed universities of Europe. There were diplomats' kids, movie stars' kids, even some Habsburgs.

Stefan hadn't lived in England since he was six. Oxford, in the 1980s, was Thatcher's England: violent, segregated, ignorant. Eighty miles northwest of London, it was a big county of mostly working-class Brits, many newly unemployed. Since the early 1980s, the local British Leyland car factory had shed thousands from its ranks. Class resentment simmered. The locals drank their dole while the St. Selby's kids spent their parents' money securing futures as PMs, scions, CEOs.

While he'd been in the States, the U.K.'s youth had gone Goth and New Romantic. Girls had garishly dyed sideswept buzz cuts, boys slouched around in post-punk dusters and eyeliner. Stefan showed up two weeks late into the semester looking like an extra from *Miami Vice,* in a white blazer with the sleeves rolled up and a T-shirt underneath. He'd missed out on a housing assignment, so he stayed in the extra room of one of the professors in downtown Oxford until they sorted out a dormitory assignment. He was a poncey American wanker in a suit living off campus. For the first two weeks, no one spoke to him.

Late October. The Dew Drop Inn, a pub off the high street on Banbury Road. A dozen yobbos streamed by him, faces flushed red, reeking of lager and Embassy Regals. Abingdon United scarves tucked into Members Only jackets, scuffed Nike trainers, and skin-tight Levi's. He ducked his hands in his blazer pockets. The south England chill fussed his collar and gripped rigor-mortised fingers round his skin.

Up ahead, on the sidewalk—a cluster of people spread under a streetlight. Maybe five of them. Some standing. Some on the ground, bloody. He recognized a couple of them from school: Wilfred Chilangwa—a little Zambian guy with glasses—and Rusty Howe, a beige, freckled half-black Briton who'd been showing off earlier at the Dew Drop by breaking a pint glass with one hand. Both boys were down. Rusty's nose ran scarlet, and a Brazilian girl—the daughter of that country's minister of finance—was bent over Wilfred, asking if he was okay.

Stefan got closer, knelt on his haunches. *What happened?*

Those guys just beat us up. Wilfred pointed. *No reason.* He sat up. Brushed bits of gravel from the side of his face.

Stefan looked back toward the group of men. One of them gave the finger to a swarthy waiter lounging in the doorway of La Dolce Vita restaurant, the others lumbered in a phalanx between the median and the sidewalk. Rusty pulled off his shirt, balled it up, and tried to stanch the bleeding. Stefan stood. Cocked his head.

Hey!

Some of the yobbos turned around. Squinted at the dark guy—*fucking Paki, thinks he's well 'ard?*—in the middle of Banbury Road. *Wot?*

C'MERE.

They were drunk. Rivers of Tennent's down the local. He'd been drinking coffee by the pot. They came at him with a roar. Four or five leading the charge. Sloppy, wobbling like pool balls after a bad break. The first guy probably figured he had another few feet. The man reached back, balling a doughy fist when the side kick bent him like an arrowhead. No such thing as *one* punch— an uppercut snapped his head back onto the sidewalk as Stefan pivoted on the ball of his foot, a high roundhouse into the guy in the Pringle sweater on his left, his Adidas shell-head tagging the guy's cheekbone. A stupid, flashy move and Stefan knew it—high kicks don't have much power and leave you off-balance—but he figured he could risk it on these guys. Had been a long time since he'd been able to just let go. He danced back, torqued an elbow, missed. A fist stung the base of his skull, swarms of fireflies flickered and popped behind his eyes. He spun a back-fist into whoever was behind him, clasped his fingers around the man's head, pulled down hard and left the ground, his knee meeting the man's face in the air. The other guys started running, splitting down Mayfield Road, Stefan lobbing rabbit punches at the backs of their skulls and asking where they were going.

The Brazilian girl, Esme, helped Stefan get away as police converged. She ducked her head into his shoulder and pretended they were just a couple out for a walk as the police asked the St. Selby's kids *Wot 'appened?*

After the fight, he was like some hero on campus. No longer the dusky American in the summer suit. For starters, he'd fucked the suit so badly in the fight that he had to revert to his Baltimore ghetto-issue uniform of black Lee jeans, Champion hoodies, and Nike high-tops. To kids who didn't know any better, he embodied romanticized urban American decay: Travis Bickle and Run DMC and Fort Apache the Bronx.

A loner by nature, he made only a few friends at St. Selby's: Ricardo Alvarez, whose daddy was a high-ranking Colombian government official; Juan Camilo—another Colombian—a fervid anarchist, in the way only rich kids could afford to be; and maybe his best friend of the group, rakish Dane Peter Reichhardt.

Peter had been a teen actor in a 1983 movie by Danish director Bille August called *Zappa,* which had been a very big deal in Denmark. Peter's mother had died when he was four, and his father— Danish screen legend Poul Reichhardt—died just as the boy started at St. Selby's. Stefan had always gravitated toward boys who'd been raised by their fathers. These boys were more likely to peer around corners, prod hives. Mother bears kept cubs close. Fathers left their sons to their own devices, asking only that they reflect them, match them, fail to disappoint.

Danish tourists were always stopping Peter in the streets around Oxford, begging for his autograph. His mop of dark brown hair swept across his brow, he'd sigh and act as put upon as Princess Diana trying to take a stroll down Piccadilly Circus. Like Stefan, Peter was always bored, always looking for action.

Soon into his stay at St. Selby's, Stefan met a girl. Mathilde Tessier. Sloe-eyed and dark and thick-lipped. The kind of face you'd find smoldering over the shoulder of the leading man on an Italian movie poster. She was the daughter of a successful Parisian fashion designer who'd clasped her by the shoulders and told her upon her enrollment, *Bring back a lord.*

Seventeen-year-old girls live to piss off their daddies.

They met at the entrance to the school, just off the sharply planed hedges at the bus stop on the corner of Banbury Road and

Lathbury. Mathilde was riding her bike, about to swing onto Banbury, and Stefan was waiting for the number 2 bus into Oxford
City Centre. They noticed each other at the same time. He smiled
big, stepped into the street to say something—anything, it didn't
matter what, as long as she didn't ride by, ride away—and her eyes
went wide. The number 2 honked loud and screeched and nearly
pancaked him. He hopped back onto the curb and stepped around
the bus, the driver shaking his head and muttering, and crossed
over to where Mathilde had stopped.

Oh mon Dieu, je te croyais mort, she said. Then, correcting herself, *I'm sorry—I thought you were—*

—Dead? He laughed. *Non, et il faudrait plus d'un bus pour
m'empêcher de parler de vous.*

He had never been in love before. She was beautiful, smart, rich.
They soon became inseparable. They lived together at St. Selby's
after their first year, and during the summer at the Paris condo her
father had given her on Boulevard Invalides, a few meters from one
of Napoleon's former estates.

At St. Selby's, he neither failed nor dazzled. He studied biol-
ogy, history, international relations, comparative literature, and
German. He studied hard, but City College had prepared him for
nothing. He'd spent six years in the equivalent of high school. It
would be four more until he received his *licence* degree from the
University of Geneva. A lot of time behind a desk. The prospect
made his legs cramp.

At the end of their second, and final, year, in April of 1987, Peter
had the bright idea of a graduation trip to South America to visit
Juan and Ricardo.

It's crazy down there. We'll have a blast.

VI

LOTERÍA DE LA MUERTE

The trip hadn't started well.

The first day in Bogotá, all of Peter's luggage got stolen. Right off the conveyor belt at the airport. Peter hopped up and down and hollered, to no avail. Stefan called their buddy Ricardo, told him what had happened, and Ricardo's father called the airport. Minutes later, agents herded the boys into the customs room.

Your bags are gone, unfortunately. The room was packed floor to ceiling with "confiscated" property.... *What did you lose? A camera? Here we have Canon, almost new . . . you like Canon? Your bag, señor—it was leather? Here's a nice leather bag.* . . . Peter sauntered out of the airport like a winner from *The Price Is Right*.

They stayed in the seedy Candelaria section of downtown Bogotá, and proceeded almost immediately to go on a rip with Ricardo and Juan and a bunch of Colombian diplomats' kids. The boys cruised Candelaria's streets, terra-cotta slopes plunging toward the town center. In the Zona Rosa quarter, they hit the Black Label Club, a disco stuck in the London 1960s mold—mirrored ball, scattered tables, and a tiny dance floor—where they bought a bag of cocaine, as pure and white as an Amish schoolgirl, from the doorman. The coke was mostly just to offset the hundred-proof aguardiente. The fermented-sugar liquor burned going down, and it mashed the accordions and drums of the Vallenato music in the clubs into a circus dirge. When eyelids drooped and pulses waned, the cocaine sped the night back on hummingbird wings. For three days the wide-awake drunks ping-ponged between clubs: the Black Label, the Piperina, the Von Richthofen.

Colombia in June 1987 was a car backfire away from civil war. The revolutionary guerrilla groups FARC and the M-19 had joined together and only a flimsy cease-fire with the ruling government kept the country (sort of) stable. Two years prior, the M-19 had stormed Bogotá's supreme court building—the Palace of Justice— and taken everyone hostage. The Colombian army blew the building up with everyone inside. Negotiation, South American–style. In 1984, Rodrigo Lara Bonilla, Colombia's minister of justice— Ricardo 's uncle—had been killed by the M-19. Troops were edgy. Colombia was not the kind of place you wanted to start shit.

Peter was a good-natured loudmouth, the first quality diminishing and the second increasing depending on how much he'd had to drink. Somehow, after an all-nighter at the Black Label Club, he and Stefan and Juan the Anarchist wound up in the middle of Bogotá's town square, just across from the Palace of Justice. Juan procured a vintage finback Cadillac—anarchy was fine, as long as it had power steering—and they parked there to stretch their legs and to get away from the girl.

Sometime over the course of the night, Peter had picked up a Colombian girl he'd found crying outside one of the clubs in the Candelaria. He'd figured sad girls were always easy lays. But she never stopped crying. By dawn, outside the Palace of Justice, she'd been at it for about four hours. Nobody could figure out what was wrong with her. Or how to shut her up. Peter, frustrated at how he'd misread the situation—*How could a weeping Colombian girl outside a coke-filled disco not be a good time?*—went to take a piss, hoping the girl would be gone, or at least composed enough to dispense a blow job when he got back.

Stefan and Ricardo went over to marvel at the cannon hole— still there from the M-19 siege of 1985—in the door of the Palace of Justice. There were soldiers everywhere. Mostly indigenous Wayuu Indian conscripts, oval faces the color of aged leather, patrolling in clusters along the square. Stefan had just finished jumbling some Spanish small talk at one of the guards—he'd forgotten almost all of the Spanish he'd known as a child in Ibiza—when he saw the soldier's eyes dart from his.

Maybe a hundred yards away, a commander started shouting and waving his hands as dozens of soldiers swarmed the square, Galil machine guns locked and loaded, all eyes on . . .

Peter.

With his dick in his hand.

A drunken Peter—at Juan's anarchic promptings—had been convinced that it would be a profound political statement to take a piss on the statue of Simón Bolívar that lorded over the Bogotá square. Bolívar—"the Liberator"—is to South America what Martin Luther King is to black America, or Guinness is to the Irish. The commander was right in Peter's face, yelling, his hand on his sidearm, while Peter shook out the last few drops. Stefan raced over, hands clasped unthreateningly in prayer in front of him, and started pleading with the officer.

Mi amigo es muy importante, he said.

Ricardo chimed in, spun some bullshit about Peter's father being the Danish ambassador to Colombia, Stefan adding his earnest *Sí, sí, es la verdad!*

The soldiers ramped down a bit and the commander seemed on the verge of letting Peter slide, when Peter walked over to the commander and touched his finger to the center of the man's tie. When the commander looked down, Peter flicked his finger over the guy's nose.

The commander pulled his .45 and the soldiers all got on one knee and Ricardo and Juan and Stefan did the first thing that came to mind: they jumped on Peter and took turns beating and kicking him while he curled up in a ball and yelled *For fuck's sake!* The boys made a big show of disciplining their disrespectful friend—in the hopes that the commander wouldn't feel the need to—not stopping until they'd dragged Peter back to the Cadillac and shoved him in next to the girl—*still fucking crying*—and screeched off the wrong way down the street. Stefan decided that this wasn't the kind of vacation he wanted to be on. They were acting like what they were, drunken tourist kids.

The next day, Ricardo asked Stefan if he'd like to go up north, into the Sierra Nevada de Santa Marta. His aunt—an activist on behalf of the Arhuaco Indians—had funded a floating medical clinic for the Arhuacos living along the lower elevations of the Santa Marta range, and Ricardo had volunteered his help for part of the summer. It would be rough going. The mountain range reached heights of nineteen thousand feet in some places. Forests veined with rivers and ancient Indian civilizations were peppered throughout the clouds.

The Arhuacos didn't trust outsiders: lately, there'd been an influx of M-19 rebels and left-wing paramilitaries who'd come to harvest marijuana and coca leaves under the hidden canopy of their forests. Drug kingpins like Pablo Escobar were thought to be funding the M-19, or at the very least carrying out hits for them, in an attempt to destabilize the government, which had, of late, seemed to be on board with the United States' recently declared "War on Drugs."

Spread across the mountains in small villages, cut off from the rest of the world, the Indians were powerless to stop the armed gangs suddenly in their midst.

They do not like strangers, Ricardo had cautioned Stefan, while the guides rolled rifles into thick wool blankets.

They drove north, accompanied by Indian guards, until the roads ended at the rocky Spanish town of Pueblo Bello, the last non-Indian outpost. From there, the rifles and camping gear were loaded onto horses.

The narrow switchbacks ascended thousands of feet, into valleys as green as the Scottish Highlands. The Arhuacos stared warily from the edges of the tree line, cheeks jammed with mashed coca leaves. Stefan pulled faces at the kids and bowed and nodded respectfully at the adults. Travel had taught him that hands held in front of the body in a prayer pose were universally nonthreatening. So he did that a lot. His Spanish was for crap, and the Arhuaco dialect was based on an obscure language form called Chibchan, which happened to be the easiest word of the language to pronounce.

The older men with their long white robes and squared head-dresses looked like the bastard space children of the Aztecas and Parliament Funkadelic. Western gear was just starting to creep in. Men squatted in the dirt in front of thatched-roof adobes to weave hats, their rituals and dress unchanged for a thousand years. Except for maybe a Casio wristwatch or a pair of flip-flops.

When they reached the mobile clinic, Stefan and Ricardo camped with the Indians for a few nights. Stefan watched the medical workers dole out antibiotics and conduct rudimentary evaluations on the villagers. The four doctors, all Colombian, worked from a massive military-issue tent. They slept in smaller, two-man camping tents set off to the rear, or with the Arhuacos in their villages. Stefan had never seen humanitarian workers in the field. Their transactions were immediate, efficient. A kid losing fluid from intestinal parasites got a blister pack of amoxicillin and some electrolytes and the color rushed back into his face right there.

He'd taken almost enough courses back in Baltimore to become a registered nurse, but he'd never had to save a life. He told one of the aid workers about his training—swelling his résumé to include EMT certification—who the fuck was gonna check references two thousand feet above sea level in a lost civilization?—and asked if they could load him up with a mini–medical kit. He and Ricardo would be going deeper into the Santa Marta range to do some camping on their own, and if they ran across any sick Indians, they might as well be prepared. The workers gave him a Merck pharmaceutical manual, a small sack filled with antibiotics, and some antifungal creams. The kid seemed to know what he was talking about. And Ricardo's aunt was sponsoring the clinic, so it's not like they could say no.

Stefan was on a horse in the jungle, loaded with guns to fend off possible guerrilla attacks, and drugs to help the natives. It was the perfect combination. Excitement—danger—made even better by doing some good. He'd have gotten off on just the gun and the horse part. But if he was being honest with himself, what he got off on the most was the power. *He* had doled out justice on behalf of those who couldn't seek it for themselves in Baltimore ghettos and Oxfordshire streets. Now *he* could dole out salvation.

Also, he had read a lot of Joseph Campbell, and the air was thin at those altitudes.

They camped in the forests, or stayed with Arhuaco Indians along the small villages in the Sierra Nevada. There were no guerrilla ambushes. No sign of the M-19. The Indians welcomed them. They were impressed with Stefan's horsemanship. The Indians were surprisingly healthy, to a large extent.

Most of the illnesses were confined to the very old or the very young. Of those, infections were the norm. Mostly bacterial. Water contaminated with human and animal feces, brought about by poor irrigation and lack of sanitation. It was typical for a child with a severe bout of *E. coli,* or staph, to become dangerously dehydrated. Then, massive amounts of water—the same brackish water that had made the child sick—would be poured into him in order to rehydrate him. Without a way to stop the initial infection, the results were sometimes fatal. In a Santa Marta village, Stefan saw an Arhuaco boy, maybe three, so severely dehydrated that his eyes had gone yellow and sunken into the copper moon of his face. His lips were blistered and cracked, and his body could barely keep the weight of his head from lolling forward. Stefan used the age/weight dosage chart on the side of the Merck manual and split the Keflex pills into thirds. He made Ricardo hang out in this village for five days, not trusting that the villagers understood that the kid needed the full dose of antibiotics. His Chibchan was even worse than his Spanish.

Two weeks into the expedition, Ricardo was itching to get back to civilization, but Stefan was just starting to feel like more than a tourist come to chew coca and score hookers in Bogotá. Something had changed. When he came back down the mountains, some small thing had taken root alongside his constant need for adrenaline. He had gotten his fix, and managed to do a little bit of good.

After a month in Colombia, Stefan split from Juan and Ricardo and Peter. He could no longer be part of a group tour. The endless consensus building. Who wanted to go where, see what, eat what. He'd traveled alone since he was five. He could immerse himself in a culture more effectively without a gaggle of rowdy boys along for the ride.

Aw, man, this was supposed to be us, all the amigos, together! Juan complained, while Stefan jammed his gear into his rucksack back in Bogotá.

We've been together, Stefan said. *I've seen all of Bogotá I need to see. I get it: coke, señoritas, do it all over again.*

Yeah, sounds bloody awful, Peter snorted.

Where are you going? Juan asked.

Stefan just shrugged.

The plan was that they'd meet up again at the end of the summer in Manaus, Brazil, then sail the Amazon all the way into Caracas, Venezuela—blow it out one last time before going back to Europe. Stefan had gotten into the University of London at Paris's interpreting program. He'd decided against Geneva. He knew he could do a lot worse than having a beautiful girl who worshipped him and luxe Parisian digs. He and Mathilde would live together in her condo while he began his degree that fall. For the last two weeks of July, Stefan wandered around Colombia, snorkeling off some of the Caribbean beaches, trying to learn how to play guitar on a five-dollar acoustic he'd picked up in Barranquilla. His hair had spiraled down to his shoulders and he'd gotten as nut-brown as the Arhuacos.

He drifted toward the Venezuelan border, via Santa Marta, laden with a machete, the guitar, dusty campesino pants, and flip-flops made from hammock tissue and old tires. A wandering gaucho. At the Maracaibo border crossing, the Colombians told him it was a good thing he was leaving, since his visa had expired. He hadn't noticed. Proscriptions, rules, regulations, were meant to be gone around, over, through.

When he crossed into Venezuela, fifty yards away, the border guard took a liking to Stefan's machete. He'd bought the thing for twenty thousand pesos. It had been dull as a butter knife, but he'd worked the blade against stones around the lagoons in the Sierra Nevada and it held a pretty good edge. The guard helped himself— grabbed it right out of Stefan's pack roll. Stefan grabbed it back. The guard made another grunting lunge for the machete.

Stefan punched the guard in the face and booked back to the Colombia border, machete fast in his grip. The Colombians wouldn't let him back in. Expired visa and all that. On the Venezuelan side, a phalanx of guards stood slapping their batons into their palms, yelling at the Colombians to send the *gringo negro* back. A five-minute game of international monkey in the middle ensued. The Colombians took pity—or maybe just wanted to fuck with the Venezuelans—and let Stefan in, on the condition that he not pass

Go on the way to the consulate to get his visa straightened out. Then he could cross back into Venezuela via Cúcuta maybe, or across the river at Casuarito.

He returned via the Maicao road and caught a bus headed west across the pinched narrow end of Colombia, into the Caribbean beachfront town of Ríohacha. He checked into the El Miramar, a two-story hole with concrete beds and blankets made of mosquitoes. Place looked like a jail in a Sergio Leone western. Ríohacha was a grungy, middling port city. There were some fried hippie backpackers on their way to or from Venezuela, sailors, and not much else. Stefan called Ricardo, and arranged to meet up with him back in Bogotá in a few days, where the Alvarez family would get his paperwork cleared up. He ate alone in an open-air bodega next to the hotel that first night—roast fish with more bones than meat, local aguardiente—and plucked a pair of chords that were either lousy reggae or shitty salsa.

He picked up his key from the chambermaid—a tawny mestiza, maybe seventeen—at the front desk of the hotel around one in the morning, wagging a grin and the dregs of the bottle of aguardiente her way. The next morning, the manager knocked on his door, pissed that none of the rooms were getting cleaned. In broken English, he told Stefan that the girl's boyfriend was surely on his way to kill him, as several people had seen her go into his room. Stefan didn't give a shit about some jealous kid pulling an Othello, but one more jam with his dodgy paperwork and he'd be fucked. He'd just make sure he was out if and when the kid came.

He asked where the good beaches were, and the manager told him that the very best beaches were northwest—too far to walk—and besides, they were controlled by Guajiro Indians.

The Guajiros . . . they will kill you, señor.

He'd spent enough time with the Arhuacos to feel somewhat comfortable with whatever indigenous populations were out there. The innkeeper sounded like the parents of some of the white kids he'd known back in Baltimore. They'd forbidden their children from visiting the house on McCulloh Street because it was "too dangerous." Bullshit. He'd lived through it, and become better for it.

Stefan walked three hours northwest, chopping and slogging his way through dense mango groves and inlets, until Eden opened up before him.

Shallow water the color of an Aryan newborn's eyes, palm trees rimming the pool like lashes. A crescent-shaped cove of talcum powder underfoot. Just beautiful. A hundred yards away, a five-foot reef shark had washed ashore, soft white underbelly puckering in the sun. He tried to cut one of the diamond-shaped teeth from the beast, but his pocketknife couldn't manage—they were really in there—and his hands got all cut and bloodied so he left it be.

He stripped and lay out on his clothes, happy to just take in the sun and the aguardiente. He browned and dozed, nose or toe twitching flies off him as he slept. When he awoke, he wasn't alone.

Twenty feet to his left, a Guajiro Indian sat on his haunches, watching him. Another Indian was dumping fish guts from a bucket into the lagoon. The man sluiced the bucket and joined his friend. They were small and brown, bare-chested, baggy white pants gathered over their knees, hands under their chins. They weren't armed—that was good. Stefan waved the bottle of aguardiente— the stuff was better than an American Express card—at them. Smiled big.

In some places, a grinning naked man brandishing a bottle and beckoning two other men might raise an eyebrow. This wasn't one of those places.

The Indians edged over. In turn, each took small pulls from the bottle. One of the Indians spoke about as much Spanish as Stefan, and Stefan told him about how he'd just come from up in the mountains with the Arhuacos, giving them medicine. The Indian told him that their chief was sick. He rubbed his belly and grimaced, revealing a toothless valley of gum bordered by lonely canines. Then the Indian asked if Stefan could come back that night with some of the medicines and help the *jefe*.

Stefan checked the sky. If he left immediately, he could get back before the sun went down. *Sí,* he nodded, sliding into his clothes. The Indians smiled, nodded. They pointed toward a path cut through the palm trees on the other end of the beach. That's where Stefan should go when he returned. The village just through there. As Stefan started back toward Ríohacha, the Indian who spoke Spanish stopped him. He touched his hand to his chest and said, *Si tu corazón es fuerte.*

Corazón meant *heart* . . . Stefan knew that. Wasn't sure about the rest of the phrase. Probably some kind of salutation. Jesus, his Spanish had really gone to shit.

Three hours later, he blew by the hotel manager—*That boy was here for you, señor*—and beelined it to his room. He hopped into his Levi's and laced up his Timberlands. Grabbed his backpack with the blister packs of Keflex, the Merck dosage manual, and a few bottles of Pedialyte and bounded back down the stairs.

The hike wasn't as much fun the third time. The sun basted on a sticky film of sweat, and the aguardiente hadn't done him any favors. But he was on a mission. The healer healing in the jungles of a faraway land. He tried to remember the classes he'd taken at the Red Cross: systolic palpation, viral infections versus parasitic . . .

hadn't thought about this stuff in a while. He'd better not fuck up and kill the chief. That would not be good.

The light was fading. He jogged a bit to close the last few kilometers. Got into the same kind of trance he used to when he ran cross-country in some of the wooded fields around City College. Hummed the Police's *Synchronicity* to keep his cadence, just like he'd done at track meets. Goddamn if Baltimore was ever this hot, though.

He crossed over the mango grove as the light was going. He stopped. Something was wrong. The beach was *gone*. Waves chugged halfway up the trunks of palm trees that had seemed rooted in sand a few hours before. The tide had come in.

He could make out the path cut through the palm trees leading to the village directly across the water. Solid land there. He waded in, backpack held high over his head. It wasn't too deep, just up to his shoulders. A quarter of the way across and he remembered what the Indian had said: *tu corazón es fuerte . . . your heart is strong . . .*

No—that wasn't it—not exactly. *Si tu corazón es fuerte . . . Yes, your heart is strong.* The path through the trees just a hundred or so yards away now, black water warm, flexing its current. No . . . wait a sec . . . *si* also meant *if.*

If your heart is strong was what the Indian had said, it occurred to him, at the same time the first shark bumped him.

In the light the moon made on the water, fins thrashed around him. He remembered the Indian dumping fish guts into the lagoon. This must be a fishing village. Who knows how many villagers chummed the water before the sun went down. One shark nosed him behind the knee and he shipped water.

He looked straight ahead, the path the only thing in his field of vision. *If your heart is strong.* He trudged along. Sharks curious but not enough to mouth him.

He'd have to brush up on his Spanish one of these days.

The village had maybe fifty inhabitants. The dwellings were frame shacks lashed together with sticks and woven palm fronds, fronted by small porches overhanging the water. The chief was a small, bowlegged man of near fifty. He had a floppy straw hat and a greyed tank top over a proud bowling ball of a belly. Stefan "examined" him. Squeezed his adenoids. Felt his pulse. Shone a Maglite into his pupils. He looked okay. The chief didn't speak any Spanish. Just pointed to his stomach and grumbled. Christ: that could mean anything from indigestion to a perforated ulcer to fucking colon cancer.

He remembered the directive real doctors practiced—*First, do no harm*—and figured that applied to pretend doctors, too. So he gave the chief some Pedialyte. Pharmaceuticals too risky. They were too far from help if he turned out to have some kind of allergy to antibiotics. The chief made a face at the sugary, salty elixir, but drank it. The village kids kicked the empty bottle around like a soccer ball in the dark. Stefan stayed up with some of the men in the village, drinking local *chichi*—beer made from fermented corn. The Indian from the beach told him, by the crackle of the fire pit, that they were going to kill him when they came across him on the beach that afternoon, but they had looked into his heart and saw that he was good. Stefan smiled and thanked them.

He stayed with them for six days—fishing, checking up on the chief, and racing the local kids in impromptu swim meets across the lagoon. None of the stuff he gave the chief helped his stomach-ache, but the man grumbled good-naturedly and drank the few bottles Stefan gave him. The humanitarian mission was evolving into a pleasant bit of social anthropology, but his paperwork was bound to be ready soon, and he had to meet Juan and Peter in Manaus. He returned to the hotel, where the manager looked like he'd seen a ghost.

Nobody comes back after being with those savages.

Stefan bristled. He didn't tell the guy that he had, in fact, almost gotten killed. That was beside the point. Fucker needed to broaden his mind.

He had a belated twentieth-birthday party with the Alvarez family, who gave him a gold-plated shark's tooth on a leather necklace after hearing about his adventures with the Indians. The Alvarezes dropped him at the airport a few days later. They hadn't been able to fix his visa—but they'd gotten him a seat on a military transport plane to Leticia, at the southernmost end of Colombia. From there, he could take a river boat—a *recreo*—across to Manaus, meet up with Juan and Peter, and the trio would sail up the Amazon, into Venezuela, bypassing Colombian border control.

When he got off the plane, a man with short-cropped black hair and a DAS T-shirt, a member of Colombia's Department of Administrative Security—the secret police—welcomed him with a hearty smile. Then he handcuffed Stefan and dragged him off the tarmac.

The DAS routinely screened the passengers on short local flights: drug cartels often used them as courier routes. They rode the ten kilometers to Leticia's jail, a small cinder block compound just off the highway to the airport.

In the constable's tiny office outside the cells, the DAS guy riffled through Stefan's bag. He thumbed his passport. *You are sure you're American?* There weren't many blank spaces left. *You travel a lot.*

Stefan said *yes,* he was sure.

You're very dark.

There are a lot of dark Americans.

Yes. That is true. Eddie Murphy.

The DAS officer sighed. Led Stefan back to the cells. The three cells were filled—ten men deep—with Peruvians and Indians.

You know what the lotería del muerte *is?* the officer asked.

Stefan didn't.

You see how there are ten men, in space meant for two? Well, tomorrow, they will have the lotería de la muerte: *the lottery of death. They will draw straws, and whoever draws the short straw, the others will jump on him, on his stomach, until he dies. That way, there will be more food, more space.*

The men lounged listlessly, some sleeping head to foot on the floor, some watching Stefan and the officer.

If everyone is implicated, no one can be punished, the agent continued. Then: *So how are we going to settle this? This problem of your visa?*

Stefan looked at him. Unsure of the answer but ready to hazard a guess. *Isn't there some kind of fine?*

A fine could take care of this, it is possible, the agent agreed, leading Stefan back out to the office.

He took almost all of Stefan's money, the remnants of his graduation present. He drove him to the small port at Benjamin Constant, where Stefan would have just enough money to take a local boat across to Manaus in Brazil, where he could meet up with the boys along the Río Negro and sail the rest of the Amazon into Venezuela.

The banana boat he bargained his way onto was beat to hell, but there were berths up top, and bananas and cheap fish could be bought along the way. At least it wasn't crowded. The stocky

Swedish-Brazilian guy seemed nice enough, and spoke a little English. The small Peruvian with the yellow tank top and the long ponytail mostly kept to himself.

The speedboat's searchlight casts a full moon onto the deck. A bullhorn cackles from the black and tells the banana boat to cut its engine. The diesel sputters and sighs and dies. The Río Negro whispers against the banana boat as the speedboat drifts into the bumper tires. He jams his passport into his underwear at the sight of the spotlight and palms his knife. He passes the Peruvian Indian with the waist-length ponytail and bright yellow tank top, and the stocky Swedish-Brazilian guy he's shared a berth with for the last two days—and looks for a spot he can dive off the side from.

The cop from Colombia's Department of Administrative Security had warned Stefan to watch out for pirates. The DAS agent told him that floating gangs scour the Amazon tributaries looking for gold shipments culled from the mines along the rivers. Sometimes they move on if there's no loot, sometimes they kill the passengers. Stefan heads quickly to stern—there's a gap between the low canvas ceiling and the railing he can bail from—but the men from the speedboat beat him to it. There's no room to fight on the cramped banana boat deck, and if the pirates have bullhorns and spotlights it's a good bet they've got guns.

There are six of them. Ponytails and broken noses. They shove him back onto the deck as they fan out. The men are as big as he is—nobody under five-eleven, lots of muscle—huge for the Amazon. One of the men has an Uzi, the others have .45 autos.

They herd the half dozen passengers toward the bow and

start going through everybody's pockets. He has no money—the DAS has taken care of that—but one of them reaches for the shark's tooth around his neck and Stefan's hand locks around the man's wrist without thinking. His muscles remember the days when the only way he could get home was via the key around the chain. The man doesn't let go and neither does Stefan until another man— the one with the Uzi—jerks the Peruvian Indian out of line by the ponytail and yells for the rest of his men. Stefan loosens his grip and the man holds his stare for a beat before joining the others at the stern.

The men shout Spanish and Portuguese at the Indian but he doesn't understand. They beat the Indian, the thick, dull slap of bone and metal against flesh bouncing off the water into the trees. Sickened, Stefan lets the knife drop into the palm of his hand, the Swedish-Brazilian mestizo noticing, a headshake, Stefan easing the knife into the back pocket of his blue jeans instead.

Through the gap between the cabin and the stern, he sees the men bend, heave, the chant of *uno . . . dos . . . tres . . .* and his knees go to jelly as the Indian's body flops into the river. They've killed him, just like that, for whatever reason, or no reason.

The man who'd had his hand around Stefan's neck leans in and whispers something to the man with the Uzi, both of them looking his way now. The man with the Uzi nods, nods . . . *sí, sí,* and they come toward him, the slow turn of the boat bringing the Indian in the water into view, yellow tank top ballooned with water, sinking into the Río Negro.

The guy with the Uzi comes toward him. Holds out his hand. Stefan fills it with his passport. The one with the .45 hangs back with the others. The man with the Uzi raises an eyebrow.

You no American. Bullshit. You look like Indian.

No, I'm American.

Where from?

Baltimore—it's in—

—Baltimore! The man with the Uzi leads Stefan by the elbow portside. Leans in. *Let me ask you, my friend: you think the O's have a chance this year? They moved Cal Ripken to shortstop, when they know he's better on third—why would they do this?*

Uh—yeah. They might go all the way this year, though, Stefan bluffs. He's never seen a Baltimore Orioles baseball game in his life.

I think so, too, the man with the Uzi says. *Listen—your visa's all messed up. You're a good kid, traveling through this country alone. Anyone bothers you, you tell them Captain Caldeira, Brazilian Polícia Federal, says you're okay. You'll do fine.*

His men pass on either side of Stefan, the guy with the .45 saying *Lo siento* as he passes, all of them getting into the speedboat, the engine eggbeating the water.

The banana boat's engine turns over, and as the smaller boat edges away into the black, the man with the Uzi—Captain Caldeira—calls out from the bow, *Welcome to Brazil!*

VII

DIVER DOWN

He loops the hitch knot around the rusted eye hook and tethers the parachute lift bag to the slab. Black and green algae shimmy on the six-by-six mass of concrete. Schools of picarel give him the silver side-eye. To his left, Lacaze *thwumps* nails into the block anchoring the Christmas Tree—the nickname given to the ornately knobbed and valved columns of an undersea oil rig. Today, their assignment is to move small slabs of concrete from one end of the Christmas Tree to another. It's a make-work assignment, on a nonfunctioning mock oil rig. Stefan ties the inflated parachute bag—really just a big underwater balloon—to pieces of concrete, and the bag gives the masses lift and buoyancy so they can be moved by one man underwater. Lacaze is in charge of blasting the slabs with nails, and attaching the eye hooks where the lift bags will get secured.

After Lacaze gets the hang of the nail gun, they'll switch—

Stefan will take the gun and the Parisian will tie down and move the lift bags. Lacaze is a cheerless fuck, serious to a fault. Eats chow by himself, doesn't go out on weekends, probably doesn't even jerk off without logging it in his dive journal. Stefan can see, through his glass face mask, the man's brow split with a worry line as he hunches close over his work. Lacaze is managing the recoil as best he can, but the .357 caliber propellant used to launch the nails is shoving him around good. The current muscles the men this way and that, but the lead belts attached to each man's unisuit—an insulated, baggier version of a diving wetsuit, topped with a full face mask—keep them from straying too far. Their oxygen lines trail sixty feet up to the surface, where the support team monitors them from the quay. The Marseille sun is up there, too, above the old port and the fish markets and the yachts in the harbor.

The coffin-sized concrete block lifts off the seabed like a leaf on a summer breeze. The parachute lift bag is rated at one ton of displacement—enough ballast for one man to push the concrete through the water and set it down somewhere else. This drill, like all their drills at AIDP, is about repetition. Move this, nail that. Get used to manipulating tools and machinery through oversized Kevlar fingertips in the freezing depths. Skills needed for daily operations on a deep-sea oil rig or underwater construction.

The nail driver ripples the water with a boom and the gun spins from Lacaze's hands. Lacaze drifts back—there's a crack across the face glass of his helmet where the recoil of the gun has smashed into it. He tucks his head and tries to breathe in the pocket of his mask as his unisuit fills. He looks at Stefan and screams. The concrete slab drifts between the men, Stefan thrusting his fins, closing the distance, hooking his right arm through the webbing of the parachute and wrapping his left around Lacaze, a violent jerk—his shoulder separating from the effort—as the hitch knot comes free from the slab, the parachute rocketing toward the surface, pulling the men from below, Stefan expelling the air from his lungs to keep them from bursting as the chute breaks the water, catches air, and sends them crashing back to the surface.

He wakes up in the hyperbaric chamber—where dangerous levels of nitrogen in the blood caused by rapid ascent are replaced with pure oxygen—Lacaze across from him in a bunk, zonked out. He drifts in and out of consciousness. His shoulder—back in its socket—thrums. Hours later, he comes to in the infirmary. A nurse, a lanky guy from Lyon, watches soccer under a TV perched on the wall.

The nurse turns—*Don't shout*—ambles over to the bed. *You've had a decompression accident.* He touches his hands to his eardrum. *Crepitus.*

Stefan wiggles his jaw. Pop, snap, crackle. Sound comes back into range, a radio dialing through static. He rises, but the floor comes up to meet him and he grabs the edge of the bed before he goes down. In reality, he's only moved a few inches—not even close to making it out of bed. The crepitus has created gas pockets behind his eardrums, blown them, upended his equilibrium. He chokes down bile, sinks back into the pillow.

His Corsican roommate—Jean-Pierre—comes in.

Hey, man, how you doing?

Ah, fucked up.

Could be worse, eh? Could have been me. Jean-Pierre leans in. *Supposedly, they are coming to give you a commendation later. Exceptional bravery.* Jean-Pierre shakes his head. The corners of his mouth go south. *Templeton,* he says, *I recommend that you get the fuck out of here.*

Just south of the Champs-Elysées, in the Sixth Arrondissement, is the Boulevard des Invalides. The wide boulevard, one of many ringing Paris, is a perfect example of Georges Haussmann's late-nineteenth-century modernization of the city. Buildings are large and squared away, mostly free from Baroque embellishment, imposing due to sheer magnitude rather than ornamentation.

Mathilde's father bought her an apartment in the ivory, quarry-stone building at number 13, Boulevard des Invalides, where she and Stefan lived the fall after graduation from St. Selby's.

Mathilde was pursuing her dreams of becoming a fashion designer. Stefan had registered at the Paris branch of the University of London, but balked at the last minute. College was an abstraction. After dusty, adventuresome months on the road in South America, the idea of sitting in a lecture hall, gathering credits for some undefined *career*—or worse yet, *job*—seemed like a morphine drip. He didn't know *what* he wanted to do with his life, but he was beginning to think there was no degree for it. Besides—he was living the good life. They had a chauffeur, and maids, and wanted for nothing.

It was de rigueur for Daddy Tessier to fly them out to the family castle in Marrakech, the men lounging, drinking sweet tea and puffing hookahs, while the ladies harried the chefs and florists and browsed through silk in bustling stalls. There were courtside tickets to Roland Garros—Michael Chang versus Andre Agassi—weekends in Calvados for the running of the horses at Deauville, dinners at Au Fin Bec, talk of marriage. But that was theoretical, too. As much as Stefan loved Mathilde, his large stretches of free time weren't conducive to fidelity. It was Paris. He was barely out of his teens. Not unattractive. He slept with many other women—most damagingly, a couple of Mathilde's best friends.

Otherwise, he filled his days working out at the Body Gym near the Bastille. Oak floors tarred with sweat and salt, a heavy bag. The routine was comforting, but he was redlining boredom. His father had once told him, *All those who wander are not lost,* and he took it to heart.

In January 1988 he was working out at the Body when he felt eyes on him. At first he thought the guy was waiting for the heavy bag, but the man never moved in to queue. *Ah:* the older man—maybe forty, small-boned and hollow-eyed—was checking him out. Whatever. Didn't make a difference to Stefan.

But there wasn't so much a *hunger* coming off him, as *assessment.* After a while, when Stefan backed off the swinging bag, the man walked over.

You work out pretty hard.

Yeah, well, Stefan panted dismissively.

Catching the accent—*You're American?* Then Colonel Bertrand Virot smiled and asked the question everybody got around to asking him, wherever he was: *What are you doing here?*

An hour later, over foamy Kronenbourgs at the China Club, Stefan ran down his story. The older man seemed genuinely interested in Stefan's history and his plans for the future. Virot gave up little: he was a legal attaché in the French army, lived in the neighborhood, just around the corner from the cavernous, checkerboard-tiled China Club, on Avenue Ledru-Rollin. Unmarried, but left it at that.

A few beers in, he asked Stefan what he really wanted to do; why someone with his level of conditioning and intellect was a kept

95

man with no immediate prospects. Stefan leaned back in his chair. Laughed. If he thought about it, let himself dream, he really wanted to . . . kind of silly, really, but at the back of his mind, he'd always had a romantic notion—wedged somewhere between being a martial arts action star, or an agent with MI5—of being a deep-sea diver on Cousteau's *Calypso*. The TV series *The Undersea World of Jacques Cousteau* had been his favorite growing up, and though he wasn't a daydreamer, the salty divers flipping over the side of Zodiac boats, the *Calypso* bouncing over the chop, the shark cages and extraterrestrial seabeds, had always held a powerful allure. That fall, he'd even gone to the Cousteau Foundation's Paris offices, where the man at the desk had sneered, *Cousteau picks only the top graduate from the Académie Internationale des Plongeurs—impossible, for an American.*

Despite the man's dismissal, Stefan had written away to AIDP for an application. The Cousteau receptionist hadn't lied: AIDP was not only prohibitively expensive, but exclusive. Admission for the class 2 diving program was limited to a twice-yearly roster of just twenty-four men, with a strong preference for those with military backgrounds. He'd jammed the application in a drawer somewhere and forgotten about it.

Virot listened intently. When Stefan finished, Virot asked, *Do you still have the application?*

The next day, based on this brief meeting, Virot wrote him a letter of recommendation.

Marseille, the third-largest city in France, was a down-at-the-heels beauty. The main thoroughfare, the Canebière, was a bouillabaisse of junkies and hookers and Gypsies and expats. The salt-beaten houses piled on top of each other in the Panier section, above the old port, looked down on the city. High-rise tenements in the suburbs on the way to Toulon threw cement into the clouds across from the rugged natural skyline of Mont Sainte-Victoire.

About ten minutes' drive from the new port of Marseille—northwest past the gilded hotels and bistros fronting the harbor, and jutting off the main road, the Promenade Georges Pompidou—was the Port de la Pointe Rouge exit, which leads to a row of quays and the unadorned brick compound of the AIDP dive school on one side, and a reinforced wall of stone and cement bordering the Mediterranean on the other.

Stefan arrived by train at AIDP for his physical and mental evaluation. They sat him down in the hyperbaric institute inside the main classroom building, and told him to close his eyes. In the raised atmospheric pressure of the institute, they squirted ice water from a syringe into both ears, and spun the chair in a 360. Then they took a measurement of his pupils with a Maglite to gauge his equilibrium. From there, they took him around to the massive yellow diving bells—the underwater hyperbaric chambers—sealed him in, and dropped him down eighteen meters. They pumped oxygen into the bell to see if his blood could handle the excessive oxygenation without sending him into convulsions. Then he had to run for fifteen minutes on a treadmill; swim to a buoy in the matchbox-shaped inlet outside the barracks; and do some math. The math part was the hardest. He was pronounced an excellent candidate.

Afterward, he met with the director, Paul Menard, a thin-lipped, balding ex–French naval officer. They talked money. A short conversation, as Stefan didn't have any. Ebba and Gerda's Boyesen Institute was no longer the cash cow it had been until a few years prior. Ebba and Rene now had two young children to support, and after the coin they'd already shaken loose for St. Selby's, and Stefan's graduation trip, the seventeen grand for the course at AIDP was out of the question. Even if Ebba had had the money, she was furious that she'd just shelled out thousands of pounds for his International Baccalaureate, only to have the kid lounge around like a sultan this past year in Paris. Now he wanted to run off and join the *Calypso?* Not on her dime.

Commander Menard laid it out. One either paid in advance to go to AIDP, or accepted a year's assignment after graduation if the academy fronted the tuition. If the student declined the assignment, then he would be responsible for the full tuition.

Ça va?

D'accord.

When Mathilde found out he was going to Marseille for perhaps as long as six months, she broke it off with him. His latest "adventure," his inability to buckle down and pursue a career, his philandering, had all become too much. Stefan was remorseful, and made a halfhearted attempt—flowers and mixed-tape apologies— at smoothing things over, but his interest had flagged. He was content to start school unencumbered.

His first day at AIDP was July 2, 1988. Though not officially a military installation, AIDP was as rigid as the French Maritime. The students wore orange uniforms. Lights out at 2300. There was reveille—obscene, shrill, at dawn, or in the middle of the night— whenever the commanders felt like it.

Stefan's roommate, a heavily muscled twenty-six-year-old Corsican named Jean-Pierre Manueli, grumbled when the klaxon bitched at dawn the morning of their second day. *Let's see what the bastards have got for us, eh?*

Stefan liked him. Jean-Pierre was gruff, ex-navy. A self-exiled outsider. Corsicans positioned themselves as haughtily distinct from the Gallic hordes. Took pride in their separation when it suited them, assimilated when it didn't.

The barracks fell out quayside, where they shimmied into wet-suits and lead-weighted vests in the grey dawn. They would be running an obstacle course. Underwater. The instructors gave each diver a single shot of oxygen from a regulator, and the man dove to twelve meters, twisting through netting, hoops, and buoy lines on one breath of air. Some of them popped up halfway through, heaving and gasping. But most of them made it, Stefan included.

Afterward, their lungs ached like they were shot with pneumonia. The frigid sea popped eardrums and sent icy bullets into the brain. The romance of the *Calypso* would be hard-earned.

Half of each day was spent in the classroom, studying currents, tides, oceanography. First-aid, navigation, principles of undersea construction. Sextants and maps and radar sounding. The other half was spent in the water: scuba, diving bell, free dives. Free dives were the most dangerous.

Sometimes they would rouse the divers in the middle of the night and buzz them two nautical miles into the bay of Marseille. From there—wearing only a wetsuit, fins, twenty-pound weight belts, and a chronograph—they'd be dumped and left to find their way back to shore. If the water was calm enough—it usually wasn't—the men would swim back, bitching and joking about how it would serve AIDP right if all this tuition sank. Most of the time, it was too choppy and dark to see the other men, and you just swam, maybe for the lights between the spires of the basilica of the Notre Dame de la Garde on the left, and the glittering boats in the quay on the right.

If the weather was dour, the phosphorous glow from their wrist compasses was the only means the divers had of getting their bearings. Sometimes driftwood and fishing nets and discarded tires bumped them in the dark. Sometimes finned and muscled bodies from the deep bumped them, too. A few divers freaked out, the solitude too much, the disorientation too profound.

The groggy days in the classroom proved their worth. The science made it possible for the fitness to save them. Stefan loved all of it. He found the solitude of the water pacifying. He could concentrate on his body, and the way it moved through a shifting, enveloping organism. The way he could drift himself into a riptide, ride it laterally, use it to get himself to shore instead of fighting it and getting carried out to sea. The way he could dive, feeling where the pockets of water went from cool to warm, knowing there was a current there he could exploit. He read about barometric pressure, the rotation of the earth, and how you could tell by the earth's axis which way the waves would break. There was no mystery. Fear was a result of being unprepared. He'd already prepared for this: the swim back to the base from the rocky islands of Iles du Frioul, off the coast of Marseille, was no different from the walk across the projects to his house on McCulloh Street.

After dives, he went running. The other divers, sucking cigarettes and shaking their heads from exhaustion, thought he was stark-raving batshit. Why would anyone pile on *more* training? *Crahzee Americain 'awt-dog cowboy Sean Wayne mozerfuckair.*

He'd go seven or eight kilometers around the city, up to the St. Charles train station, past the Gypsy hookers with babies slung across their hips, past the tourists burned by sun and drowned by wine. Around the paved gravel and the fountains at le Parc Borély, all the way back to AIDP.

He was gonna go hard and get on the *Calypso*.

He was the youngest diver by at least five years, and one of only a couple with no military background. He made up for it by always being the first one in the water and the first one back. His only friends there were his roommate, Jean-Pierre, and an Australian guy named Ron, who'd been a commercial pilot in the 1970s. Ron was living on a yacht in the quay near the school, after years of flying betel nut from Papua New Guinea to Australia. Betel nut fetched a fair price in Australia, but not nearly as fair a price as the sweet, sticky Guinean marijuana bud he smuggled in along with the fruit. Ron had also been a diver, until he lost the two middle fingers on his left hand on a rigging cleat.

Weekends, Jean-Pierre, Ron, and Stefan sat among the sawdust at Les Treize Coins, in the Panier— "the Breadbasket"—quarter. The joint was a popular hangout among Corsicans. Euro/Afro pop blared in the front bar, and tagines wafted from the kitchen. It was at Les Treize Coins that Ron noticed Jean-Pierre's tattoo.

What's that? Popeye?

Jean-Pierre didn't smile. He turned his right hand over, hiding the silver-dollar-sized profile of a man, blindfolded, in black ink. Ron knew enough to let it go. He was a visitor—scarcely more than a tourist—and the palest guy in the room. After he'd gone, and the pastis had loosened the screws along Jean-Pierre's tongue, he leaned over to Stefan.

Do you know of the Sea Breeze?

Stefan shook his head.

The Bris de Mer—the Sea Breeze—was a Corsican organized-crime syndicate, with vaguely separatist leanings, operating out of Marseille. The city, because of its proximity to Spain, Italy, and

Africa, as well as its bustling port—the largest in France—was an excellent base. Drugs, booze, women—it all came through the port.

The BDM had hideouts and training camps in the Calanques— the soaring limestone mountain inlets zagging the east coast of Marseille all the way to Cassis. Its members were small and dark and scarred; the tattoos marking their hands depicted a Moor's head, in profile, a blindfold covering his eyes. The nameless Moor was an archetypal martyr who'd been shot by firing squad in the 1800s or something. The image was also the Corsican flag.

Stefan was fascinated by revolutionary movements. The former underdog couldn't help but root for minority populations. Jean-Pierre recognized the kindred spirit. The two of them would tongue-in-cheek hum the "Marseillaise" just before dropping over the side of a Zodiac for a dive, or engage the French divers in immigration debates about the influx of Algerians and Sub-Saharan Africans into France.

On Stefan's twenty-first birthday, after a day spent arc-welding pipes underwater off the Iles du Frioul, Jean-Pierre leaned over to him as the Zodiac zipped back to shore.

Put on some real clothes, meet me outside at 2300 hours.

Stefan was waiting outside the barracks in a crisp linen shirt and white jeans when Jean-Pierre pulled up in a brand-new black BMW M3. *Get in.*

They hit the Treize Coins, where there was a party under way. Luc—stocky, broken nose, jet-black ponytail—was three days home from prison, after doing a ten-year bid for double homicide. The Corsican had owned two nightclubs in Marseille. One night, two Algerians tried to extort protection money from him. They didn't see the tattoo of the Moor on his hand.

The bar was packed for Luc's homecoming. He and Jean-Pierre had friends in common, and when he heard that it was Stefan's birthday, Luc had all the whores dance on the bar, *like in the John Wayne movies, for our cowboy!*

Then, just before midnight, a Spectre M4 machine gun appeared from a back room, or car trunk, and Luc led the crowd outside and fired off twenty-one shots into the Marseille sky, *Bon anniversaire!*

Weekend nights, Stefan hung with the Corsicans, and some of the guys from the BDM. The BDM never let him in on the criminal aspects of their lives, but seemed to get a kick out of the younger man's infatuation with their lifestyle. They let him fool around with their exotic cache of automatic guns, and took him on a few shooting trips into the Calanques.

But for the bulk of those seven months in Marseille, Stefan trained as a class 2 diver. Class 2 divers had to have at least a hundred dives in open water—a percentage of those being mixed gas, or diving bell via an umbilical. He learned how to do repairs on underwater structures, various at-sea rescue techniques—there was the body of an old helicopter outside the barracks, which would be towed into the bay for the divers to practice on—and basic oil refinery maintenance.

He would learn some other things, too.

———

AIDP's director—Menard—and a diving superintendent come into the infirmary and pull up chairs on either side of him. The superintendent is the one who scooped him and Lacaze from the water after the accident. Tall and stooped, hawk-nosed and grey-eyed, and today, a smile. The room is empty. Lacaze is back in the hyperbaric chamber. He got the bends much worse than Stefan.

The diving superintendent leans in. *That was quick thinking today.*

Thank you, sir.

Menard suggests a commendation, and I agree.

Stefan is silent. Psyched: this will look good on his record.

A look between Menard and the superintendent. *There are some extra classes we think you should take, once you're up for it. Some more . . . extensive training.*

Stefan nods. If only the top two men get chosen for the *Calypso,* every advantage helps.

The chairs squawk as the men nod at each other, at him, rise, leave.

A week later, he's back in the water, ears stopped with cotton. A little slower, but not much. It's dusk. They've just finished a dive between the Calanque mountains—the wreckage of pirate ships at the mouth of the Mediterranean a good training ground when the instructors are feeling lazy. The divers can screw around underwater, get used to shimmying in and out of tight spaces, don't need much supervision. At the end of the day's exercises, the diving superintendent motions for Stefan to hang back as the other divers load into two Zodiacs and head back to AIDP.

A quizzical shrug from Jean-Pierre as his boat zips away, Stefan left in the third Zodiac with the superintendent and two instructors. They speed farther into the ocean, the towering V of the Calanques moving behind them. The instructors open a plastic Pelican case containing short lengths of PVC pipe, sealed at both ends. They all don fresh tanks, and dive, Stefan in the middle. One instructor carries the pipe. Another carries a spindle of braided electrical wire. Stefan lugs a nylon sack of shot weights. Helmet lights glow a field in front of them. This narrow mouth of the Calanques was one of the places the Germans came through when they invaded in '42. The French Resistance larded the seafloor with influence mines—metal disks triggered by a change in water pressure—many of which were still lying in state, lying in wait. There's little risk to anyone from these mines, as the straits aren't frequented by ships large enough to trigger them. The AIDP instructors detonate them sometimes, as a training aid.

The instructors point out one of the gently domed, silt-crusted mines, and attach a section of pipe next to it with the braided wire, anchoring the setup with some of the shot bags. They swim back to the Zodiac, unspooling the wire, tying the ends off—ground, positive, negative—to a motorcycle battery. They touch the ends of the charge to the battery terminals and the mine explodes in a flash of silt and a belch of surface foam. On the next dive, they hover above Stefan as he sets a charge on his own, hands shaking. A long way from his GI Joes in the bathtub.

In the coming weeks, after his regular classes, they take him to the rocky islands off the coast—Iles du Frioul, Ile de Riou—or to empty classrooms washed in fluorescence, and teach him about underwater munitions and demolition. They teach him how to gain a footing at the side of cliffs, how to plant mines, how to set transponders on submerged objects. He's learning stuff that's not on the books, not in the brochure for AIDP. A whole other education than the one he signed up for.

Let's talk about your tuition. Menard's office is small, antiseptic. His shelves hold maritime manuals listed by year, going back to 1974, and various certifications and commendations from the French navy. A woman with a long, equine face and four children of varying ages—presumably his wife and kids—sit on a tractor, in a field somewhere, the woman on Menard's lap, the kids draped over the tractor like monkeys. Stefan has been at AIDP for four months. Graduation is eight weeks away.

Stefan starts to speak, Menard stays him. *The placement with Cousteau, this isn't going to happen.*

Menard looks out the window. *The* Calypso *placement is for the top two divers.*

I've still got a few months to pull up my ranking. Hides the shock: thought he was doing better.

Menard gives him a patient smile. Fishes a cigarette from his pack. Extends it.

No, of course you don't smoke. He lights his Gauloises. *The question isn't your class placement. If you are not the best in your class, you are number two. But you are American. No American has, or will be, on the crew of the* Calypso. He shrugs. *Ever. I tell you this to prevent hurt feelings, and to decide what's best.*

Stefan sighs. Leans back in his chair. The tang of cigarettes makes him sick.

So what? I take an assignment somewhere for a year? Resigned. He'll work on an oil rig. Not romantic, but the money is supposed to be decent. Even after paying off his tuition he could still do okay.

Menard squints through the smoke. *No . . . we'll assign you somewhere appropriate.*

What does that mean?

Menard flicks a piece of tobacco from his lips. *That means that we won't let talent go to waste. We just want to make sure you're willing to accept your assignment. I understand disappointment, but we need to know that our investment is still sound.*

Stefan chews the inside of his cheek. Not sure how far to press the Cousteau thing. If anybody'd know his chances, it's Menard. And Menard says he's got no shot. He's stuck. Doesn't have $20,000 to pay them back. If they've got a job—any job—he needs it. He nods.

Menard smiles. *Okay then. Here is what we propose: after your class 2 certification is completed, we will place you with NATO for one year's duration, through the French Maritime.*

Stefan blinks hard. *The military?* It's not like the thought hadn't occurred to him. But he'd rejected the idea of his being recruited for military purposes early in the training: as an American, he figured he was immune.

No different from what you've been doing, really. Just formalized. There are posts guarding the strategic oil reserves, doing maintenance, security. . . . If you like it, there are worse careers than the military.

Menard rises. *But this can be worked out later. For now, pay attention, keep going. . . . This will work out for everyone.*

In the cafeteria, over chow, Stefan tells Jean-Pierre about his talk with Menard. Jean-Pierre wags his fork his way. *I told you to get the fuck out.* He shakes his head. *You fucked up . . . running all over the city after the day's work is done . . . gung ho all the time like some Navy SEAL . . . they figure, if it walks like a duck, my friend. . . . Your mistake, Templeton, was: you stood out.* Jean-Pierre pissed now, struggling to keep his voice down. *These bastards all come from that world. Cheaper for them to farm you out to NATO than to have clothed and fed you in their navy for three years. Wake up!*

It makes sense. He can't deny the logic of it. Most of these other guys have already done their service, and this is their segue into the private sector. He's come in—younger, needier—a civilian with an aptitude for this stuff. At their mercy.

He wonders if Colonel Virot made a backdoor arrangement

with AIDP. Maybe the whole thing was a setup from the beginning. He doesn't want to be in any man's army. He has a hard-on for the toys, the stakes, but at the end of the day, the life of a cog doesn't appeal. He's more comfortable alone.

He saw what the military did to his father. Maybe the war hadn't split Ebba and Roye up, but it coated whatever differences they had in jungle rot and Agent Orange. He'd been the beneficiary of his father's paranoia, but hadn't inherited it. The world was an expansive, wondrous place that needed exploring. Service had walled Roye in, made him fearful, angry. And the ulcers. In 1985, just before Stefan left for Europe, Roye had been laid up in the Baltimore Veterans Hospital with bleeding ulcers. Doctors suspected Roye's exposure to Agent Orange may have been the cause, but there was no proof. No recourse. The dilapidated facility was filled with hollowed men from wars long gone, who had left the best parts of themselves in foxholes.

This will not be the life for him.

At midnight, one month before Stefan completes his class 2 certification, Ron pulls his salt-eaten white Porsche 911 cabriolet up to the gate. He flashes his headlights twice, and Stefan scales the chain link fence, his duffel slung around his back. Ron drives him to the St. Charles train station, where the Australian presses a hundred francs into his hand and gives him a two-fingered wave goodbye.

Stefan climbs the hundred steps, past the circling Gypsies and sleeping backpackers. A pair of French police side-eye him, turning instead to an Algerian junkie on the nod. The junkie rolls down a couple of steps, crashing into a stray huddled against the cold. The dog twists and gnashes, ears pinned, eyes wide. The junkie moans.

Stefan fishes the money from his pockets and stares up at the departure board. There is a train leaving in eleven minutes.

VIII

THIS IS THE LIFE

The entrepôt—a squat white behemoth of a warehouse—is next to a train station. The rear of the station—facing the west side of the entrepôt—is surrounded by tall fencing, perched atop a slight incline. Trains earthquake past the small station twenty-four hours a day, but stop here only from seven a.m. until nine p.m. This is good. It is now one in the morning, with nobody around to hear the explosions. Except Jack.

Jack is parked up the hill, outside the station, in a dark blue Ford Sierra station wagon. The plates belong to an Opel Corsa somewhere across town. He presses his binoculars to his face and scans the entrepôt. Too dark to see anything. Should have night vision goggles. He told them they should have night vision goggles, but night vision goggles *cost money, and if they had money, they wouldn't be here in the first place, would they, so shut the fuck up and keep an eye out.*

He twiddles the knob on his walkie-talkie. *How's it going?*

Stefan snatches the walkie-talkie at his waist. *Jesus Christ, Deutsch!* How many times does he have to tell that asshole: *Speak only German over the radio?* In case anyone picked up their frequency, it'd sound like the job was being pulled by Germans. In Stefan's case, with one year of German he'd taken at St. Selby's, an autistic German.

Sieg Heil! Jack crackles into the radio. Mike turns the alarm key on the metal box outside the entrepôt's employee entrance half a turn and the red light clicks twice and goes green. The guy from Securitas—a low-level security guard with the company they'd paid $300 for a copy of the alarm key—hadn't bullshitted them: it's the real thing. According to Mike, the guard had promised them there'd be at least 600,000 kroner—roughly $100,000—in the entrepôt.

Off Stefan's nod, he and Mike flank the double door's seam, crowbars jerked in opposite directions until the deadbolt clears the frame and they're in. Mike picks up the army rucksack and the two of them stride double-time past the staff lockers, into the warehouse now, Persian rugs and mod carpeting, past the high metal shelving units stacked with boxed china and cutlery, toward the sturdy door at the rear of the warehouse marked *Privat*.

Stefan jams the serpent-tongued flat end of the crowbar into the jamb and pops the door open. On the left of the management office are two wooden desks, one cluttered with a telex machine and an electronic typewriter, the other anchoring a Compaq 386 computer, cursor winking green.

Along the right side of the room is a row of waist-high filing cabinets, topped with phone directories, potted plants, and office workers' vacation photos.

Next to the cabinets, separated by the water cooler, is the safe.

A Chubb model—stout, white—wrapped by a stainless steel band around the face. There are options for both key and combination access.

They will use neither.

Stefan jumps onto one of the filing cabinets, twists the face off the smoke alarm, and pockets the 9-volt backup battery. Mike hefts the rotary hammer drill and the length of extension cord from the rucksack. Stefan pulls out a hammer and a quarter-inch center punch. He lines the tip of the punch with each corner of the safe, in the hair space between the door and the frame, and rear-ends the punch with the hammer. The only mar is a pebble-sized dimple, but that's enough. Mike switches out the water cooler's plug for the drill's. He lies on the floor and presses the bit against the first dimple, and the carbide whirs.

Stefan pulls the rest of the kit from the rucksack: two World War II–era gas masks—cheap, army/navy store vintage—a handful of blasting caps, and a bath soap bar of gelignite. The putty-colored explosive is a more stable form of nitroglycerin, easily moldable and not likely to make your head migrate from your body if the car hits a bump.

After a while, *Take over, yeah?* Mike rises, shaking out his wrists. Fishes an apple from the rucksack and chomps. The drilling is slow going—only the top left corner is done—and they've already been here two hours. They've gotta be gone by sunrise—0530 at the latest. It is three a.m. Stefan crouches on the floor and starts drilling.

Metal shavings curl from the second top corner seam as the bit bores slow and steady. He knows he can't go above 2,000 rpm with the drill—metal on metal smokes and burns out the bit if you push too hard—but they're running out of time. He leans on the drill and squeezes the trigger and now the bit really moves. And snaps. *Fuck me . . . gimme another bit,* he says, unscrewing the bit with the chuck.

Mike swallows a mealy bite of apple. Shrugs. *There is no other bit.*

The walkie crackles, *Train's coming if you wanna go.* Jack's been out there for hours, bored shitless. At least he's remembered to speak in German.

Stefan doesn't answer him. Just stares at Mike. The guy is unbelievable. Made such a big deal about being a pro and knowing what he was doing and he brings *one* fucking bit. When Stefan had asked about whether they should use a borescope—a fiber optic rod that could be inserted into a single drilled hole in the safe, so they could line up the tumblers on the lock gate and open the thing— Mike had snorted, *This ain't fuckin'* Rififi—*we'll blow the thing up and go.*

Both men stare at the safe. The plan had been to drill holes in the four corners of the frame, where the bolts engage the door, and pack the gelignite into the quarter-inch openings. *Boom,* the door would separate from the frame, and somewhere in the neighborhood of a hundred grand would give itself up to them. With only two holes drilled, and no spare bit, they'll have to improvise. Stefan unwraps the film from the gelignite. It has a tacky consistency and a florid, saccharine odor he can't quite place. Wait a minute . . . *marzipan.* That's what it smells like: sticky sweet marzipan paste. He breaks off a half-inch chunk and squeezes marble-sized globs of putty into the top drilled holes. It'll have to do.

He crimps the electric leads from the blasting caps into the gelignite and unspools the twenty-five-foot wire across the room. Crouching behind the office desks, he cuts the ends of the braided wire—green positive, red negative—careful to leave a few feet of extra slack, a trick he remembers from AIDP: always give yourself a few extra feet to fuck up when planting munitions. Farther away is always better than too close. Just now, he wishes they'd brought a bigger spool. Twenty-five feet is pretty fucking close to the charge. They'll have to be in the room with the safe when it goes off.

They leave the offices, fifty feet of orange safety lights guiding the way, until they get to a cul-de-sac loaded with oriental rugs and carpeting samples. They load up on some of the rugs and lug them back into the office. Mike fills an empty trash bin with water from the cooler, and they soak the rugs through. They cloak the safe with the sodden wool. Stefan opens the windows in the offices, so there's somewhere for the expanding gases to escape once the charge goes. Mike turns one of the desks on its side, so the flat surface faces the blast, and they sit behind it in the dark, a half hour, forty-five minutes, until Jack calls with the signal: *Another train coming, if you wanna go,* over the walkie.

We're good on this end, Mike radios back.

This is it.

Stefan hands Mike a rubber cap from one of the blasting caps and each jams a cap into his jaws: if your mouth is shut during an explosion, the change in air pressure from the shockwave can burst your lungs.

HÖREN SIE?—Do you hear it?—Jack yells into the walkie, excited now, finally something to do, and Mike and Stefan slip their gas masks on, the end of the positive lead in Stefan's hand, the lantern battery in his lap, *ES KOMMT!—It's coming!* Jack squawks as the train barrels into the station, louder, louder, can't hear anything over the steel wheels on the tracks and that's the idea, as Stefan touches the lead to the terminal.

He was a quitter. At great expense to his family, he'd gotten his IB—with the intention of going to university—but had wound up at AIDP instead. And he'd left there, no closer to being part of the *Calypso* than any yob walking the street. After taking the train from Marseille to Paris, and then a flight from De Gaulle to Heathrow, he'd arrived in London with one goal: he needed to prove to himself that he could finish *something*.

In London, while staying at Acacia House—now the headquarters of the Boyesen Institute—he chucked his pride and asked Gerda for a small loan. He may not have graduated from AIDP, but he'd amassed over a hundred hours of dive time in his diving log, which could provide a foundation for a career as an oil rig worker. Not as glamorous as the *Calypso,* but a way to use the skills he'd worked so hard to acquire.

There were two formal certifications divers needed before they were eligible to work on deep-sea rigs: the first was the Certification Scheme for Welding and Inspection Personnel—the CSWIP—offered as a one-week course at the Falmouth Oil Exploration port in Cornwall, England, which he took and completed in November 1988. Second, all workers in the deep-sea oil industry had to pass a firefighting and rescue program in order to be eligible for employment. Oil rigs were vulnerable to hurricanes, tsunamis, explosions, and structural breakdown. Every member of the crew had to know how to evacuate the structure in the middle of the ocean, and how to administer first aid and rescue out at sea.

The industry-standard offshore firefighting and medical training course for divers was held in Aberdeen, Scotland, as part of the

Robert Gordon Institute of Technology. By now, Stefan was almost out of the money his grandmother had given him. He bullshitted his way into a reduced tuition, in exchange for acting as translator to a group of Spanish waiters who were taking the course so they could work in the kitchen departments of rigs. His Spanish was still lousy, but even though the Spaniards had scratched their heads over most of his "translations," he sounded like Cesar Romero to the Scots.

Some of the RGIT training was old hat for him, but some of it was new. During the five-day program, the students performed downed helicopter simulation rescues and floating-fire extinguishment drills—all in the frigid chop of the North Sea. The Mediterranean drills at AIDP were a holiday compared to the bone-chill of Scotland.

For their medical training, the students worked shifts at the casualty ward at Ninewells Hospital, in Dundee, assisting doctors and nurses in triage. They did sutures, tracheotomies, and dissections on cadavers, the highlight of which—besides the medical knowledge obtained—was the salami incident. One afternoon, a group of the students gathered in the morgue to observe a cadaver dissection. The morgue tech, a block of a Scot, glared sternly around the room.

Aye, let's have at it, then.

He leaned over the body on the metal slab: an old man, blue-grey and swollen, half-opened eyes the color of weak tea. The corpse had a foot-long autopsy incision from his navel to his pubis. Most of these divers were ex-army—hard and unfazed.

A lot of men kinnae handle this, makes 'em boke, the tech said, reaching into the cavity. His hand made a squishing sound as he rooted around for something. One of the divers yawned.

But that shouldnae stop ye from getting the proper nourishment, the tech continued, as he pulled an—obviously planted—Saran-wrapped salami sandwich from the corpse's stomach cavity, unwrapped it, and ate it. One of the divers blacked out, hit his head on the metal table, and knocked out two of his teeth. Legend had it that the tech did that bit every year, until some poofter complained to the dean.

Stefan received his Medical Training for Divers and Off-shore Firefighting certification and returned to London with all the requirements met for an entry-level position on an oil rig. All he needed was a job.

Norway was the third-largest oil producer in the world. Gerda no longer lived in her apartment at 6 Hjelmsgata, a neglected two-bedroom midway up a cobbled street in Oslo's posh West End. She told Stefan he could live there rent-free, in exchange for fixing the place up a bit.

Except for playing bodyguard to Gussie's kids, he'd never lived in Norway as an adult. He was Scandinavian, in name and blood, and the prospect thrilled him.

There were very few blacks in Norway. There's a myth that Scandinavian women become ravenous nymphomaniacs at the sight of any man with dark skin. Only it's not a myth. He was not lonely. The girls and their attentions helped him become fluent, quickly, in Norwegian. He immersed himself in the culture: read Ibsen and Heyerdahl; drank aquavit; went to bathhouses.

But the work thing was a problem. He was still an American citizen. He had no employment visa. Ebba had told him, years earlier, that she couldn't get him Norwegian citizenship because it was passed patrilineally. And she had been right. Except that the laws had been changed during the early 1980s, to allow *either* parent to confer citizenship—as long as the application was made before the

Ebba Boyesen, Stefan's mother, circa 1969. Ebba met Roye Templeton in the beatnik paradise of the University of Copenhagen in 1964. Deeply in love, she followed Roye back to his hometown, Baltimore, where Stefan was born. For a Scandinavian flower child, segregated Baltimore was a less than idyllic home.

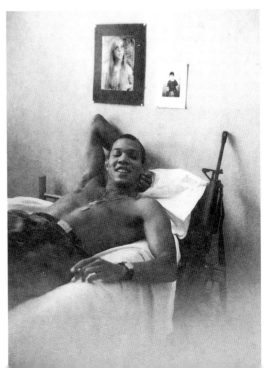

ABOVE AND RIGHT: Roye, Stefan's father, Vietnam, late 1969. He served for three years, but the Vietcong haunted his dreams for many more.

A rare photo of the family together: Roye, Ebba, and Stefan, fall 1967, Baltimore. Roye would leave for Vietnam in 1969, and nothing would ever be the same.

Roye and Stefan, father and son, 1969, at the Naval Station Great Lakes, Chicago, just before Roye left for Vietnam.

ABOVE: Stefan, Ibiza, 1971. Mother and son lived a carefree existence in the Mediterranean hippie haven until Roye joined them in 1972, just out of combat. The family tried to pick up where they'd left off, but everything, and everyone, had changed.

LEFT: Stefan spearfishing for squid on one of his visits with Ebba, somewhere in the Mediterranean. Still a mama's boy, but an adventure jones was starting to take hold.

RIGHT: Ebba and Stefan on an adventure in Morocco, circa 1976. Stefan spent holidays and summers with Ebba, who was the opposite of his disciplined father.

BELOW: The author and Stefan, Baltimore, 1979. With his thousand-yard stare and squared shoulders, Stefan was now a feared playground legend, polyglot, and badass in training. The author was not.

Château de la Salle, Burgundy, where Stefan spent his early adolescence. Here he learned to hunt, shoot, and ride a motorcycle. He was a French aristocrat with some of Baltimore's west side still in him.

Ultimately, the castle was a lonely exile from the experiences of his peers. He went from boy to Renaissance man in a few short years.

Stefan in Valledupar, Colombia, 1987, running medical supplies to the Guajiro Indians. The trip was supposed to be a graduation blowout with friends, but he quickly grew bored with the party scene. He volunteered for the promise of adrenaline and a chance to do good.

Diving with the Académie Internationale des Plongeurs, Marseille, 1988. Stefan trained with the men from whom Jacques Cousteau selected the crew of the *Calypso*.

Stefan training at the dojo, Oslo, 1991. From his adolescence, the dojo was his refuge and point of connection with his father.

LEFT: Skiing, Nordmarka, Norway, 1992. Stefan connected with his maternal roots while living in Oslo in his mid-twenties.

RIGHT: Liv Thulin, a Norwegian country girl when Stefan met her, and Mai-Sunniva, Stefan's daughter with her.

Stefan taking a break during a gems-for-antibiotics swap on the Burmese side of the border with Thailand, 1996. After the events of the Gib, Stefan put his full skill set to use. He knew gems, he understood military theory, he knew how to hustle, and he needed to help.

Chiang Mai, Thailand, at the Lanna Muay Thai training camp, 1996, working out some of his demons. He needed to make things right. Do penance. In the dojo, where he'd always found the truth.

Monk at the Chiang Mai wat, 1996.

Stefan, cleaning the wat as part of his penance, Chiang Mai, 1996. He trained in Muay Thai during the morning and scrubbed the holy structure in the afternoon.

Stefan with the monks of the Chiang Mai wat.

Crossing into Thailand from Burma on a gems and antibiotics run, 1996. Some adventure and some altruism. Unbeknownst to Stefan, he'd spent his life training for this work.

With Paramedics for Children, in the wake of Hurricane Mitch, Honduras, 1998. He had come full circle from his days running antibiotics in the Sierra Nevada over a decade earlier.

With his wife, Elena, 2000.

In the Abyei province of Sudan, 2007. Now firmly in the disaster relief world, Stefan traveled to aid the world's most volatile region, where he was convinced traditional NGOs had failed.

Meeting with leaders of the Sudanese People's Liberation Army, south Sudan, 2007. If civil war was coming, Stefan was determined to be on the right side of it.

Stefan with Sudanese boys,
Agok village, 2007.

Stefan and David near the contested border between north and south Sudan, November 2007. AK-47 courtesy of the SPLA. Security courtesy of the SPLA and Stefan Templeton. Thirty years later and not a damn thing had changed.

child's eighteenth birthday. Ebba had been unaware of this change. Stefan was twenty-one. It was too late.

He'd always had pretty good luck with skirting formalities, but the immigration officials at the Oslo foreign police office weren't having it. If he stayed longer than six months in the country, he was an illegal. He decided to go over their heads and mailed a letter to King Olav V:

> *I am the only child of an Afro-American/Native American father and Norwegian mother. Until the age of six I lived with my Norwegian family in Scandinavia while my father served as an officer in the U.S. Navy in Vietnam. My parents soon separated after my father's return. In the divorce proceedings my father was automatically granted custody by a U.S. court, on the grounds that I was a U.S. citizen; my mother was only granted weekend visiting rights. Having been informed by the Norwegian embassy in London that Norwegian law did not recognize descent from a mother, my mother had no legal recourse and no one to turn to. I therefore spent the next twelve years of my life living alone with my father in Baltimore, Maryland, each year punctuated by two visits by my mother and occasional trips back to Europe. Five days after my eighteenth birthday I left the States to study in Oxford, England. I have not lived there since.*
>
> *You may detect an undertone of bitterness in this letter, it's true; as I sit here I cannot help but feel indignant, appalled of the injustice of a law which would affirm a father's claim for his child's citizenship and deny a mother's solely on the basis of her gender.*
>
> *I am also a son of this country as much as any child is the son*

of one of his parents. I am undeniably, irrevocably linked to this country. I could well speak of summer hikes in Nordmarka, sailing in Oslo Fjord, hunting in Telemark, Sunday skiing up to Ullevalseter and Trivann and Jul Fester with my family and friends.

I suspect that there are many such legitimate cases such as mine. I realize that this letter will probably have no effect whatsoever on my case, as the Norwegian immigration authorities will probably refuse any case such as mine regardless of the circumstances, as they would wish to avoid setting any legal precedent for immediate granting of citizenship to an adult. Apparently only a warmhearted king's will can do that. Nevertheless I submit this letter as a statement of intent.

Sincerely,

Randall Stefan Boyesen Templeton

The Boyesen surname was an inspired touch. He'd never used it before, but the name had a legacy and cachet in Norway, and every little bit helped. While he waited for a response from the government, he found work as a backup diver for a couple of Oslo-based companies: Dacon AS and Scandive AS, subsea contractors that specialized in maritime rescue and oil rig maintenance. The work was cold and rough and piecemeal—sometimes he'd get three calls a week, sometimes three a month. With so much free time, he signed up for a semester-long shipping course at the Norwegian School of Management, and that, along with his IB from St. Selby's and some smooth talking, was enough to land him a job as a junior broker at Bery Maritime—a brokerage specializing in large-tonnage dry goods. Stefan slapped on a suit and tie and tried his hand at the young executive lifestyle. He made a few small sales—coffee, bauxite—bought himself a used candy-apple-red Daimler Vanden Plas, and supplemented his income with the occasional dive.

In late winter, he met a girl.

Liv Thulin, sixteen, was a wispy country girl dreamt up by the Norwegian tourist board. White hair, blue eyes, and lofty, freckle-kissed cheekbones.

Liv and some friends were sitting in Olsen's Café, in the West End, finishing off a bottle of claret, when one of them noticed Stefan at a table playing chess. He'd become a regular at Olsen's: the heat worked better there than at his apartment.

One of Liv's friends leaned over and said, *That's the guy I was telling you about,* and went over and asked Stefan to join them. There was some talking and twirling of hair and flaring of nostrils, Stefan zeroing in on Liv right away: she was the most beautiful girl he'd ever seen. He leaned back in his chair and gave a pretentiously low-key account of his life to the girls, but mostly to Liv. An hour later, a girl walked in. Lithe and tall and looked like she'd just stepped off a catwalk. Stefan's date for the evening. He gave Liv a wistful smile and his date a be-there-in-a-sec nod. He said his good-byes, met his date at the door, and started out onto the sidewalk. As the door shut, he caught it with his foot—*Hang on, I forgot something*—walked back over to the table and whispered to Liv, *I'll be back in an hour, if you'll wait for me. Please . . . wait.*

It was tacky, and cocky, and if he *hadn't* shown up eighty minutes later, she may well have left.

Liv was a simple girl, overwhelmed by the attentions of this worldly guy every woman seemed to want. She lived with her mother in the outskirts of West Oslo, in a working-class neighborhood near the Hovseter metro. That first night, he mostly talked and she mostly listened. He told tales of faraway places and adventures; she corrected his Norwegian.

He walked her to the metro, along the cobbled streets, scrambling for a way to prolong the night. *Wait,* he said—*tell me a fairy tale.*

She stopped, paused, screwed up her lips—nearly killing him dead—and told him that *There was once upon a time a king who had a daughter. She was such an awful fibber that you couldn't find a greater liar anywhere. So the king made it known that if anyone could outdo her in telling fibs and could make her tell the truth, he should have her for a wife and half the kingdom into the bargain.*

There were many who tried. All and sundry would be glad to get the princess and half the kingdom, but none succeeded.

There were three brothers; they were also going to try their luck. The elder two set out first, but they fared no better than all the others. Then the youngest, the Ashlad, thought he would try. He set out for the giant palace and met the princess outside the cowshed.

"Good-day," he said.

"Good-day," she said in return. "You haven't got so big a bull as we have! Look . . . And we milk into great big casks."

The Ashlad replied, "Let me tell you . . . I climbed right up to the clouds the other day and there I felt the North Wind resting. I felt stranded as I hovered there in the wide open, but a warming wind kindly let me down. I landed in a fox's hole—the nest of your mother and your father I think it was! You didn't know your mother gave your father such a blow that plenty of figs dropped from his hair!"

The princess shouted: "Father never grew figs in his hair!"

By that the Ashlad won her!

Stefan laughed, hard and unforced, even though he hadn't really been listening. The whole time she was talking, he'd been watching the way her jaw curved into her throat, how she couldn't look at him while she was speaking; he was in shock that a sixteen-year-old girl had such a pull on him. He hadn't fancied a girl her age since he was twelve.

At the Briskeby tram station, he took off his watch, a chunky, silver diving Tissot, and put it around her wrist.

I love this watch, he said. *And I need it back.*

She smiled, getting his drift. *Then you will have to come for it.*

She worked as an assistant at a potter's studio in the West End, right by Olsen's Café. She was working there, firing the kilns the next morning, when he came for the watch.

They took walks in the Nordmarka forest every Sunday, skied the cross-country trails around Oslo all winter, picked wild strawberries and blueberries in summer. They lived together almost from the beginning. Liv's single mother was liberal, and Liv was headstrong, and that had been that.

He'd always identified as an American, but Liv, and Norway's reflection of his mother, felt like home on a cellular level. He was tempted to call Roye, tell him about the girl, about how the son had fallen in love with a girl in much the same way the father had. But he didn't. Stefan was not the type to stay in touch.

He absorbed everything he could about Norway's culture, in a frantic attempt to catch up on all he felt he'd missed. He spoke only Norwegian, and learned Bokmål, a highly formal, upper-crust dialect he'd gleaned from studying the works of his favorite writer, the doomed, self-proclaimed "anarcho-nihilist" Jens Bjørneboe. His *The Silence* was a rumination on Europe's colonization of the rest of the world, and the damage caused in the name of crowns and countries. It meshed perfectly with Stefan's diffuse, post-adolescent revolutionary streak. He dug any people who fought back against impossible odds. Roye had grounded him early in the philosophy of black power—Frantz Fanon, Stokely Carmichael—as well as the European classical tradition—Nietzsche, Schopenhauer, Russell. Bjørneboe added the syncretic benefit of a cultural tie to his new homeland.

Besides afternoons of chess, he dabbled in marble sculpting, painting, and jewelry making. He stayed after work, with Liv, in the pottery studio, and chipped pieces from stone, until some of his abstract shapes began to make sense to him. He cribbed amorphous shapes from Matisse, Henry Moore, Knut Steen, looking for a style. He hunched over fishing wire, and strung beads into necklaces for hours on end. The act of *creation* did not torture him. The act of being a *creator* was what propelled him into the studio. He would take something harder than flesh and blood and make what he wanted from it.

He was not a *quitter*. He was a seeker. The more he knew, the more he mastered—even superficially—the more of the world he would have access to. Plenty of guys were lovers or fighters or thinkers. Few were *all* of those things.

King Olav V turned out to be a hard-ass, and denied Stefan's request for citizenship. He could only live in Oslo for six months at a time, legally. There was a way around this, as Copenhagen was an overnight ferry ride, or a seven-hour drive via Sweden in the Vanden Plas, away. Every few months he and Liv would pop over the border for a quick holiday, and then back, so he could get a fresh stamp on his passport.

Bery Maritime was shaping up to be a middling, barely reliable source of income. And his co-workers found his arrogance and cockiness off-putting. He was a low-level junior broker, but brought an American, Gordon Gekko–style aggressiveness to the gig. The Scandinavian method of salesmanship was laissez-faire, *You buy if you like, but if not there is no problem, my friend . . . would you like some herring?* Stefan called potential clients three times a day before lunch, cornered them at bars, questioned whether they had the vision, the foresight, the *balls* to make their mark on the bottom of a check. He was tolerated by his peers, but not liked.

They were just *waiting* for him to fuck up.

He made some money on the side, at Olsen's, where he'd camp at the end of the banquette along the wall and hustle chess for money. A bored local journalist happened to be drinking there one night and thought it was somehow newsworthy that this black American/Scandinavian was the neighborhood chess champ. The reporter wrote a blurb in the *Dagbladet* about Stefan, a human-interest, local-color puff piece. In the article, Stefan had described his occupation as a "broker" for Bery Maritime, omitting the "junior" part—an upgrade his colleagues used as evidence of his self-aggrandizement. The article made its way to upper management, and he was let go for "misrepresenting" his status.

As of summer 1990, he did not have the legal ability to work in Scandinavia, he was in love, and the few freelance dives he was being assigned were growing ever more dangerous. Typically, he had to lay fiber optic cables in the North Sea, or install anti-submarine detectors, which worked on some magnetic principle that disrupted your internal organs and killed you instantly if you activated them in the wrong sequence.

In September, Scandive buzzed him on his beeper and told him to report with his gear to a strategic oil reserve storage facility in Bergen. He met up with his occasional dive partner Svein—a middle-aged Norwegian who dove part-time while working on his master's in economics—in a parking lot next to a mountain. There was a fifty-foot staircase built alongside the mountain, punctuated by a steel door. They flashed their ID cards at the surveillance camera outside the door, and the lock clicked open.

Inside, drilled into the rock, was a spiral metal staircase, twenty feet down, and then another steel door, another flash, another click, and a storage facility the size of six football fields lay open before them. It was like the hidden lair of a super villain. Inside the hollowed-out rock were hundreds of thousands of metric tons of refined crude oil. Stefan and Svein dragged tanks and dive gear and wetsuits into the facility. There was not a drop of water to be seen.

A foreman, in jeans and a blue oxford, came over. *Great, we've been waiting for you.*

There may be a mistake, Svein piped up. *We're divers. I don't see any water.*

No mistake, the foreman said. *Follow me.*

The men walked through a maze of pipes. Cut into the leveled rock floor were the petroleum holding tanks, sealed with five-foot-diameter manholes. The ceilings were covered in soot. The fumes were dizzying.

You guys got radios?

Yup.

Turn them off. The foreman stopped at one of the holding tanks. A violent arc of soot slicked the wall above the tank. Svein tapped Stefan and both men looked up at the same time and noticed a manhole cover, twenty feet above them, jammed halfway into the rock ceiling of the mountain.

There was a little bit of an explosion, the foreman said. *About a*

half hour ago, so we need you to go in and check for magnetic interfer-
ence, or leaks . . . before it sets off a chain reaction.

Below them, down a steep ladder, was the holding tank. An
ocean of light sweet crude. Petroleum haze shimmied in the air and
singed their lungs. The foreman coughed hard, eyes tearing from
the stench, and waved them off to their work.

An oil dive. That was the job. He'd never dived into oil before.
In water, you could freeze, drown. But this shit was poisonous.
Impenetrable. Explosive. He hoped his dry-suit could withstand
the corrosive bath, but he wasn't sure. What if it ate through? They
hadn't prepared for this. He wavered on the edge of the tank.

You sure about this? he asked Svein.

We're here, Svein said and shrugged, lashing nylon cord through
the dinghy's grommets. *Help me with this,* he said, handing Stefan
an end of rope. Fear and doubt were existential concerns. The rope
needed to be tied. Before there was another explosion. There was
a job to be done. At its completion, they would be paid. Stefan
pushed everything but the motion out of his mind.

They lowered themselves, and a dinghy, into the black. Svein
dove, in a sealed dry-suit, along the perimeter of the tank, checking the seams with a spark-proof flashlight. The biggest danger
was another explosion. The oil fumes were a sneeze away from
igniting—even static electricity could set the thing off. Barring an
explosion, the toxicity of the stuff was lethal. Both men breathed
through tanks, even Stefan in the dinghy above the surface. Stefan
was the lineman, holding Svein at the end of the nylon rope. Svein
had discovered a leak on one of the valves and worked on switching
out the gasket. Stefan's gloves started to slip. Svein was sinking. Oil
has no buoyancy—the rope had to stay taut. Stefan couldn't get a

grip. The oil made the rope slither right through his neoprene gloves. He wrapped the rope hard around one hand. It was no use. Svein was drifting farther away, into the muck. He needed a better hold. He unsealed his glove. Did the same with the other. Using his bare hands, he wrestled Svein back toward the surface, the rope slick as mercury.

When he got home that night, a fever came on hard and fast. He started vomiting. He looked at his hands wrapped around the toilet and noticed that they were swollen to twice their size. The oil had seeped into his skin and poisoned him. It was a week before he could stand without help. Liv nursed him through it, sure he was going to die. She knelt at the side of the bed and made him promise not to dive anymore. It was too risky, the pay was lousy. They'd find another way to survive.

His second night back at Olsen's, ten days later, still weak and shaky, he set up the chess pieces on the marble table and nursed an aquavit. Across the room, a biker, in cheap racing leathers and a cut-off jean jacket vest, accused the waitress of keeping his change when he'd asked for it back. The waitress told him to look in his pocket—she'd just handed it to him—but the guy was drunk, and as she leaned over to tell him again he smacked her across the face. A man at another table rose, shoved the biker. The biker put his fist between the man's eyes, once, and the man fell back into the banquette in a jumble.

Stefan swung the biker by his ponytail through Olsen's plate glass window. A group of customers clustered at the window and watched the biker get up, dust himself off, yell something incomprehensible to the skies, and stumble off.

Stefan went to apologize to the owner, a chubby guy with silver hair—but the man waved him off. Said insurance would cover it, and if he had been younger he would have done the same thing.

Then, *I have some friends, they own clubs. . . . Do you need a job?*

He worked mainly at downtown clubs like Rocky's and the Sinn Mark Bar, sometimes at the Waterfront. He enjoyed bouncing. And the money was okay. Cash, under the table, in the thick of Oslo's nightlife. A keeper of order. For one of the safest, cleanest cities in the world, club security was a heavy gig. Scandinavians drank to a nearly Irish degree. Every once in a while, he got to jam some violent drunken cocksucker, relieve some pressure, the whole thing sanctioned.

He hadn't trained in a long time: the dojos in Oslo were a joke. Bouncing belligerent Vikings was a good way to stay sharp. He learned a different style of fighting in Oslo, losing a lot of the flourishes inherent in Tae Kwon Do, paring things down to their simplest components. Street fighting. Against people too high or blotto to know when to stop. Already proficient, he got *efficient.*

Since he never got home before four or five in the morning, his days were free. Twice a week, he taught self-defense at a gleaming fitness center called FitnessXpress, downtown. Before his class one day, an aerobics instructor bounced over to him. The man was fit and chirpy, a Nordic Richard Simmons.

I hear you're American! the instructor lisped in Norwegian, blond bangs tamped beneath a pristine blue headband, tangerine spandex suit shimmering. *Can I talk to you?*

He motioned for Stefan to come over to the huge window overlooking the parking lot. The guy told him that he needed help applying for a U.S. visa, so he could go to Las Vegas for an aerobics competition later that year. Not only did he not speak English, but he was having some problems with his paperwork.

What kind of problems?

The guy looked around, rocking his knees back and forth in a cardio-wiggle. *I'm a convicted felon.*

Twenty-nine-year-old Mike Nortveg had not only been the 1988 Norwegian national aerobics champion, but at the age of six his mother had locked him in a closet for an entire year, causing a national scandal—and psychological trauma—after which the press had branded him "the Wild Boy of Oslo," due to the degradation of any and all of his social skills. He was made a ward of the state until the age of seventeen.

When he was nineteen, he and a buddy attempted to rob an armored car from a Husqvarna motorcycle, Mike spraying the car with a submachine gun, Geronimo-style, from the back of the bike, until the car stopped. Mike and his accomplice sped into the Lillomarka woods with about 50,000 kroner, only to get turned in by an acquaintance a week later. Mike was sentenced to three years in Oslo prison. While there, he learned safecracking, how to defeat alarm systems, and lock picking, under the tutelage of the older cons. The judge at his sentencing had recommended he learn a trade.

When his bid was up, he was released into an unknowing populace, where he'd discovered his true affinity: aerobic fitness. He and Stefan had a long talk that day, and every day after their classes were over. Mike clucked about how hard it was for people *who hadn't been given a fair shot* to survive in Oslo. *There are ways, though,* Mike had hinted, that first meeting, *for men of enterprise to prosper.* Stefan had brushed him off. He wasn't a crook. Sure, times were hard. But he wasn't that desperate.

Soon after meeting Mike, Stefan met Jack Sananes. Jack was in his early twenties, a quiet, bookish sort, who sometimes played chess with Stefan at Olsen's, after sheepishly turning out his pockets, *only for fun, okay?* Jack was thoughtful, played well, and seemed in need of a friend. He was a commercial pilot by training, but for reasons he wouldn't go into, no longer flew. He was a polyglot, just like Stefan. They would flit back and forth between languages, *biskop sju; chevalier sept; checkmate!* Like Mike, he'd done time in prison. At the time of their meeting, Jack seemed like a sweet little guy who'd made some bad choices and was down on his luck.

Mike and Jack—two lost, broke, and broken souls—met Stefan just as he found himself out of work, and struggling to keep his promise to Liv not to risk his life doing the only thing he could legally do in Scandinavia.

One night in mid-January 1992, Stefan came home from a shift at the Sinn Mark Bar, shoved his weekly pay—the equivalent of $200—into the metal box under his bed, and woke Liv up with a kiss only to have her tell him that she was pregnant.

His mind raced. He loved her. That wasn't a question. Wanted her to give him a baby, a basketful of them . . . *but now?* There was no way. They had nothing. A lousy time for her birth control pills to fail. Only they hadn't.

I stopped taking my pill.

Why would you do that?

Remember when you got sick . . . from the oil? she said, gathering the sheets around her. He noticed that she wouldn't look at him. He knelt on the floor next to the bed so she'd have to meet his eye. *I knew then . . . that the way you live . . . one day you wouldn't come back.* She finally managed to look at him. *And I knew I would have to have something to remember us.*

He squeezed her hand.

He loved her.

Would do anything for her. But they had no money. And nothing on the horizon suggested any promise, anytime soon. Life was about more than just themselves now. There would be a baby, helpless and needy.

They were fucked.

At FitnessXpress a few days later, he waited for Mike outside his aerobics class. Almost left a few times. *What the fuck was he thinking?* Made it to the sidewalk before he turned back around and went up again.

You said something about making money, he said to Mike as spent housewives panted by them in the aerobic studio's doorway. *Was that real, or bullshit?*

Mike smiled.

———

Blue flames afterburn through the safe, through the carpets, across the room, and past his ear. The pressure wave churns his insides as thick grey smoke fills the room. The echoes of the explosion die down, a warbling coming through now, louder—Jack, on the walkie—*What the fuck was that?*

Stefan and Mike drag what's left of the carpets off the safe. Because they'd only managed to drill the top two bolts, the top of the door has peeled away from the frame, but the bottom is still anchored securely. There has to be equal pressure on every side of the frame in order for the door to open. Mike raps on the metal. Shrugs. *The job's sunk. Let's get out of here.*

Stefan breathes hard. His hand is shaking. He didn't want to come here, doesn't want to be here, but the only thing worse than doing this awful thing is leaving with nothing. Mike had promised him there'd be money here. The guard had told him so. The guard had come through with the alarm key; the layout, the office, was just as he'd said it would be. Everything up until now added up to the money being here. It *had* to be. The money from bouncing was not enough to raise a family. Liv is home, pregnant, ankles swollen and on bed rest.

It's up to him to take care of them.

There's another train in forty-five minutes.

Mike's incredulous. *No, it's impossible.* He starts shrugging and pointing out the illogic of it all, stopped by a thick brown finger against his sternum:

We're doing it. Nothing's blown.

There are two extra blasting caps, and they still have three quarters of a stick of gelignite left.

They fetch more rugs, load the drill holes with a quarter of the explosive, wire the cap, wait for the train—4:09 in the fucking morning now—set it off, and it's Krakatoa North. The smoke clears, and this time . . .

. . . the door's still locked.

But. They can rattle it a *bit*—it's definitely expanded. The bottom bolts still holding up, though. Chubb makes a decent safe.

Mike sighs. *See? The job's blown.*

FUCK THAT! Stefan screams, spittle and sweat fogging his mask. He pushes Mike out of the way, squeezes the entire block of gelignite into every seam in the safe—the thing's fucking oozing explosives.

Umm . . . what are you . . . ? Mike starts, then thinks better of it, dragging the other desk in front of the overturned one, as Stefan plops the last blasting cap into a blob of gelignite like a candle on a birthday cake. They don't even wait for the train. There's no time.

131

This time, blast shoves them back against the far wall, the desks slamming into them half a second later.

Out in the car, Jack blinks at the sound as the ground hiccups. He looks around and wonders if he should just start the car, get the hell out of there, and try Finland for a few months.

Stefan and Mike unpin themselves and stagger toward the safe. The rugs have melted into a wet goop. But the safe is wide open.

Even in the dark, they can tell that the door's been blown off. The reason they can tell, even in the dark, that the door's been blown off, is because of the glow in the air, from maybe $100,000 worth of burning embers, the entire contents of the safe, going from orange ingot to ashen snow as it dissolves into the soup. He reaches out and snatches the floating corner of a krone note, like a firefly on a summer breeze. It is a 200 note. The money had been there. Packed snug and bundled and waiting for them. Now there is nothing left. Just vapor and smoke and the charred remains of what had been a bad idea to begin with. Failure, at even something so ignoble, burns the back of his throat. Up until now, he's quit everything good he's ever tried. He can't even do *bad* right. A failure at fucking up. About more than ego, though. A failure at providing for his family.

You done now? Mike asks, packing up the gear.

Yes. He is done.

For now.

IX

THE GIB

Norway's version of 911 was 112. That was the number that flashed black on the grey screen. The third page in as many minutes. Had to be Mike.

Stefan had steered well clear of Mike for the past few months. The man bristled with manic, dangerous energy. He'd already done time and didn't seem to care if he went back in. The two hadn't spoken much since the bungled job at the entrepôt. Stefan had retreated somewhat—sunk into a depression. Conflicted between the sense of failure he'd felt—they'd performed like amateurs, no better than smash-and-grab thieves from off the corner—and the rush. They'd come *so* close. The money right there. If it hadn't been for Mike.

Stefan was sure they'd left the job with nothing because he'd let the supposed pro take the lead. That couldn't happen again. Other people could make mistakes. If he was going to jail, it wouldn't be because he'd left the details to someone else. *No.* He wasn't going to jail. No sense thinking like that. Success was a matter of planning, nothing more. Like diving: check your tanks, your equipment, *before* you get wet. Come back every time.

Having failed in the attempt—he felt compelled to see *if* he could do it. He replayed the gig over and over. Tweaked the details. *Next time* would be different. Nothing left to chance. He flushed with shame for even considering a *next time.* His ego hounded him, though. He'd risked his family for nothing. Had to come home with *something* to square the books.

He had these thoughts mostly on bad days. Days when he'd come home after bouncing at the Sinn Mark or Rocky's stinking of tobacco and ears ringing with lousy techno. A sea of rich cocksuckers gliding past him at the door like he was nothing. Every once in a while he got to toss one of them—or worse—but they went on with their lives, and he went on with his.

Liv noticed how he kept hitting the mute button on his pager. *Anything important?*

Nah. He shrugged. *Some bullshit.*

He refused to let Mike ruin their evening. Whatever he wanted could wait.

The first night out for them in a long time. An art opening for the sculptor Knut Steen. Floating through the gallery, they were a young, exotic, bohemian couple rubbing elbows with some of Oslo's brighter lights. Professionals, academics, artists. This was the life they wanted for themselves. For their baby. He would make it happen.

Five months after giving birth and the purple hollows under Liv's eyes had finally begun to fade. Sixteen hours of labor. And then those first few days of dread: Mai-Sunniva's windpipe had closed twice during the night and they'd had to rush her to the hospital. The doctors thought it was cystic fibrosis. Mercifully downgraded to asthma after a swarm of needle jabs and sleepless nights outside the emergency room. The steroid shots they'd started giving her seemed to be working—they no longer had to sleep in shifts. After all the stress and the worry, Liv's mother had demanded they get out and do something, just the two of them. She'd watch the baby. The night a gift of freedom. The wine and cheese and languid marble shapes made them feel like part of the world again.

But Mike was in trouble. Stefan knew it. Their agreed-upon code for alarm was 112. Liv's mother would have just used her phone number if there was a problem with the baby. As much as he tried to push the sonofabitch from his mind, his conscience dragged the blond albatross back and slung him around his neck. He felt like he had *two* kids now. Mike just as helpless. Maybe *less* sensible. Stefan still felt responsible for him. Even after his fuckups at the entrepôt.

There had to be a reason his pager kept thrumming against his waist. Maybe he'd hit the pay phone outside the gallery. Just make sure the guy wasn't at the end of a gun or in jail somewhere. He could ruin his evening worrying about the fucker, or just deal with it—probably nothing anyway. He'd be back at the party before Liv got out of the bathroom.

What is it? he said into the phone receiver.

I have a job tonight, Mike said, voice brittle and hyped. *I don't know if I'm gonna be safe without you, man.*

Two hours and some change later, Stefan was in Løkka, making Mike run it down for the fifth time. The only reason Stefan was even listening—against every shred of sense and discipline and morality in him—was because *this* plan hinged around a different mark: the score was a dope dealer.

Stefan had seen the type slither through the doors of the club every weekend. More money than they could spend in a lifetime. Adding nothing to society. He couldn't even get citizenship so he could support a sick infant. Some people made their own luck. He would make his own justice. Reparations. Frantz Fanon and Malcolm X and Jens Bjørneboe would approve.

Yes. He could take that motherfucker's money and sleep soundly. Stealing drug money wasn't stealing. It was reallocation of wealth. Venture socialism. As Mike laid it out, Stefan justified the score to himself until he was in a self-righteous froth. Shit—danger aside—there was no legal downside. It's not like a dope dealer could call the cops and bitch about how somebody'd stolen his drug money. This was just the kind of score his adrenaline jones needed, and his wallet required.

But *tonight?* He needed more time. Planning removed some of the variables that put lesser motherfuckers in jail. They didn't even have time to get the crew together.

We have the crew, Mike said. *You, me, and George.*

George? Stefan had never heard the name. And he didn't work with people he didn't know. At least Mike was a known entity: a psychotic, impetuous, known entity. Mike told him that George was an ex-policeman who'd opened a suntanning salon in West Oslo. Business was lousy. Mike was one of the few clients the place had. The men had gotten to talking, George floated the name of a wealthy drug dealer he remembered from his days on the force, and . . .

At the eleventh hour, Mike had had wiles enough to know that they were in over their heads. He'd gotten spooked and called Stefan. *I'm asking you as a friend.* Guy really knew how to push his buttons. The appeal to friendship was one of Stefan's Achilles' heels. He had few friends, and his nomadic nature kept him from maintaining the ones he'd made. But once in his orbit, a friend could count on his loyalty to an improbable degree. It wasn't that he'd forgotten or forsaken the friends he'd made over the years: life was too short for phone calls, and how could he have condensed all that he'd done into a postcard, had he been inclined to write one?

George was thick and ruddy, a squared face carved from the Caucasus. He wasn't happy to see Stefan and Mike pull up at the supermarket parking lot in Akershus.

George, meet Alex. Alex, George. Stefan had demanded that Mike call him only Alex from then on out. He was sorry he'd given Mike his real name, but from now on, anyone he met in the life would only know him as Alex. He and Liv and Mai-Sunniva were each other's world. He had too much to lose. *Alex* was just a name—in honor of the character in Anthony Burgess's *A Clockwork Orange*—that nobody could tie to him or his family.

Mike told George that Stefan had experience at this kind of thing—and that they needed a third in case they ran into anything heavy on the job. After some huffing and puffing, George laid it out: the job was to break into the drug dealer's home. A few hours over the border in the western Swedish suburb of Karlstad.

Stefan asked him how he knew the guy was holding cash and George just said, *'Cause I know. The guy used to live in Norway, and he's only gotten bigger since he moved. It'll be worth your while if we let you in on it, Alex.*

George huddled with Mike, sketching out the plan, and that's when Stefan disabused George of a momentous delusion.

George? Shut the fuck up. I'm in charge. You got a piece?

George gave a nervous laugh. Mike gave him a shrug letting him know that this was how it was, unless George wanted to do something about it.

Yeah, I got a piece.

Lemme see it.

George pulled a Beretta .380 from the small of his back.

Stefan held out his hand: *Give it to me.*

Fuck you, George said.

Bye. Stefan shrugged.

He was halfway out of the parking lot—*Fuck this, he was out of the life anyway, didn't need the troub*—when Mike ran over and palmed George's Beretta to him through the driver's side window of the Vanden Plas.

He's cool, man—whatever you say . . . just go home and get your gear and meet us here in an hour? Okay? He's gonna go with or without you, and I need you there, man . . . watch my back.

———

Karlstad, Sweden, is a small city, four hours southeast of Oslo. Maybe sixty thousand Swedes on the Klarälven River delta. There's a bustling port, a massive municipal hockey rink, and orderly rows of stave-roofed brick homes. A few kilometers inland is Sandbäcks-gatan, a green hamlet of square Legoland houses tucked into woods.

Mike and Stefan took the Vanden Plas, behind George in his Passat on the E18. The house was a two-story chalet at the end of a long driveway. There were few other houses within sight, and at three a.m., no lights. Just three men in the dark and cold, steam jetting from the nose slits in their ski masks, black gloves moving fast.

Mike disabled the alarm by attaching two alligator clips to the phone line outside the house. This made sure the electrical circuit wasn't broken when the contact point—the door—was opened. If the circuit didn't break, the alarm wouldn't go off. Then he flipped through his rings of bump keys until he found one for the deadbolt on the front door. He'd learned how to make bump keys in prison. You just took the key to a particular brand of lock—there were only a handful used for most residences—cut each groove to its deepest setting with a file, inserted the key into the corresponding lock, tapped the end with a rubber mallet, twisted, and Open Sesame! With six or seven bump keys, you could open 80 percent of the doors in Europe.

It would occur to Stefan later that a drug dealer should have had more than a single deadbolt and a rudimentary alarm.

It took them a moment to get accustomed to the dark. Shapes began to emerge. The living room was crammed with Danish modern and the walls were covered in framed black and white landscapes. The owner had a good eye. Off the living room was a wide staircase of wooden planks. They took them single file, standing on the far edges of the wood to keep it from creaking.

Stefan opened the master bedroom door just as the man in the bed switched on the bedside lamp. He put his foot between the man's shoulder blades and cocked his .45 next to his ear.

You hear that? he asked. The man nodded and stopped moving. The woman next to him was awake now, a sharp intake of breath, eyes wide, lots of white, as Mike flex-cuffed her, moving her to the side of the bed, her feet on the floor.

No, no, what do you want?

Stefan shushed her, cuffed the man, and put him on the opposite side of the bed.

What do you want? the man asked him.

Then George said something strange: *Where are they?*

They. Cash was usually referred to in the singular. Norwegian and Swedish are different enough that the moment came and went mostly unnoticed, until later, when it was too late to do anything about it.

Leave us alone, the woman whimpered, and Stefan motioned for Mike to help him sweep the house. They left George to watch the couple.

Mike and Stefan checked the clichéd locations—behind framed pictures, in desk drawers—as well as the unorthodox—the freezer, the toilet tank—and were just about done with the upstairs when they heard the crackle of electricity and the screams.

Stefan was through the bedroom door and had kicked George's knees from under him before he could use the cattle prod on the woman again.

I'm doing you right here, Stefan said, jamming his .45 into George's ear.

Alex, Mike said, *be cool.*

I am cool, Stefan said evenly, *but I'm still doing him.*

WHATAREYOUDOINGWHATAREYOUDOING? George ducked and covered into the deep shag.

Shut up. Then to the couple on the bed—*Please excuse him, that shouldn't have happened.*

The woman was handsome, perhaps forty. There were two welts on her bare forearm from the prod. The man—the drug dealer, Stefan reckoned—was in his late forties, thin and balding, with a concave chest, the skin slack around his jowls. Pretty milque-toast for a dealer. Looked like a systems analyst.

Don't leave us here with him, the man begged.

Stefan sat on his haunches in front of the woman, making him-self smaller, less of a threat. He patted the edge of the bed. *Come over here, sit by me.* He put two fingers on her wrist and checked her pulse. The electricity from a prod could induce cardiac arrest in some people. Last thing they needed was a murder beef—drug dealers or no. She was a little arrhythmic, but settling down.

Where is it? he asked.

Downstairs under the credenza, with the videos, the drug dealer said.

He motioned for Mike to check it out, then flicked his knife from his holster and cut the woman's flex cuffs. He duct-taped her hands and feet and tossed the roll to George so he could secure the man. George ripped off a length with his teeth and started to tape the man's mouth. Stefan grabbed his arm and shook his head. Fucking amateur. The tape-over-the-mouth thing was for the movies—in real life, people panic and die when their airflow is obstructed. These two could yell all they wanted out here in the middle of the night. With some sweat and some elbow grease they'd be able to free themselves in under an hour.

Mike appeared in the doorway, holding a metal strongbox. Big smile.

Stefan sent Mike and George in the Passat with the strongbox: no way was he—a brown guy in a flash Vanden Plas—gonna trans-port the take back over the border.

They met up just after dawn at George's suntanning salon in West Oslo.

Mike and George let him in the back door, and Stefan followed the two of them into a room with a tanning bed opened like a giant razor clam, the lockbox sitting right in the middle of it. The gunmetal-grey box banged and twisted from their attempts at opening it.

Where's the money?

Money? Mike asked, flipping the lid. He pulled out plastic sandwich bags of peridots, sapphires, rubies, diamonds. An emerald pendant as big as a baby's fist. Stefan looked from man to man, wondering if he should kill them both, leave them in a tanning booth turned to high, until the smell roused the neighbors in a few days.

The job was for cash in hand. Jewels required selling, putting yourself out in the black marketplace, giving people a face—if not a name—and waiting.

Fuck you, Mike. You lied to me—

This is just as good as money!—

—fuck you. This is on you. Call me when you get my cut. You burn me, I'll come find you and kill you.

Stefan brushed them aside and left. He was furious the whole drive home. All he'd done was answer a page, but once again, he'd done something horrible, and once again he had nothing to show for it. He needed the money. Living in the most expensive city in the world with no papers, no work visa, no degree.

He calmed himself. At least this time, they'd gotten *something* of value. So what if the stones had to be sold? Not his problem. Even a couple of morons like George and Mike could find a way to make some cash from the take. He'd see a cut—Mike knew better than to cross him.

As the sun came up, he leaned over Mai-Sunniva's crib and stood there, listening to her breathe. She was getting better, her lungs pink and clear and doing their job. *Mai-Sunniva:* still getting used to the sound of it. It had taken them months to name her. They'd decided to wait until they'd gotten to know her, so they could give her a name that fit. Tried out Irene, after his grandmother, but this baby, green-eyed and gummy smiles, was no Irene. Finally, about two months after she was born, they'd settled on Mai-Sunniva, after a tenth-century Irish princess who'd fled to Norway and been martyred in a cave. They dug the mystical tinge of her name. She was a new creation, as they were in their union. A pink, glorious mutt.

It had taken her long enough to join them. Liv had had three false labors, back and forth to Ullevål Hospital until the doctor, a diminutive woman with cropped hair and chewed eyeglasses, sat them down.

Go home, she'd admonished. *Drink a bottle of wine and make love.*

They'd followed doctor's orders and Liv was in labor two hours later. The little girl was born early on the morning of September 13, 1992.

———

He wobbled—had to hold on to the crib before passing out. All he'd eaten was the plate of hors d'oeuvres at the party, and the adrenaline spike from the job left a hole in his belly. He made a six-egg omelet and fell asleep at the table with the fork in his hand. By the time he got out of bed it was dark again—five hours of daylight this time of year—and he made his way to the kiosk on the corner for some juice and some aspirin.

Waiting for the man to sort the change from his purchase, he swigged long from the juice, bringing the bottle down now, eyes catching the black bold of the evening edition of the *Aftenposten.*

*Massive Jewel Heist . . . Special Investigation . . . Grade-A Case . . .
Well-Known Antique Dealer and His Wife . . .*

Below the headline, above the fold, was a massive close-up color photograph of the emerald pendant, taken in happier times.

An antique dealer. An ordinary citizen. Not a drug dealer. No security. It was a home invasion, straight up. Whatever code he'd thought he had was a joke. He was a common criminal. His hands started shaking.

He paid for the paper and read it as he walked to the car, scouring the text for leads. According to the report, there were no suspects. He tucked the paper under his arm and raced home, half certain the police would be there waiting for him. A cop patting down Liv while someone from the state pried the baby from her arms. The people he'd been trying to provide for ruined, because of him.

There were no police waiting for him. Liv was home, watching TV. The baby was asleep. He spared Liv the drama of all that had happened. Left the newspaper jammed next to the driver's side seat. He'd read the article so many times he'd memorized every word, each pixel from the photos ingrained into his memory. The more he knew, the less panicked he felt. Information was tepid comfort. He started to calm down. His hands still shook, but the tremors were less severe. His mind applied some logic to the practical—as well as moral—position he was in.

Roye had taught him well. Had trained Stefan to question everything. He had rewired his conscience into what he'd rationalized as "situational ethics." For every terror his conscience raised in him, there was a soothing counterargument: *How could he have known the couple weren't drug dealers? If one acts badly—in good faith—is he absolved?* Lots of "if a tree falls in the forest" bullshit. What was he going to do? Break back into the house and give the jewels back? Turn Mike in—some poor, twisted sonofabitch who'd spent his childhood locked away in closets and prison cells? Kill him? No. He could wallow in guilt, or adapt. What was done was done.

Two days after the job—a little over fifty hours since he'd answered the page—Stefan called Mike. There was so much heat over the stones, he needed to know that Mike wasn't trying to unload the stones in a jewelry store or pawnshop. According to Mike, everything was cool.

Are we burnt?

No, Mike said. *We have a buyer for the stones, and we have a meet.*

Good. Page me when you get my cut, asshole.

Er . . . it's not that simple. With Mike, nothing was. *It's out of the country.*

How far out of the country?

And you know I only speak Norwegian. . . .

What about George?

Nope, Mike tsked, *another country bumpkin like me.*

Where? Stefan sighed.

All you have to do is drive down with the stones, pick up the money, fly back. So simple.

Where? Stefan repeated, temple throbbing.

Gibraltar, Mike chirped. *It's warm there!*

He could have told them to fuck off. Walked away with nothing. *Again.* But if he left it to them, they would blow it. Sell the stones to the wrong person, bring the heat down on all of them. At least if he decided to do it, there was a measure of control. He could even cut them out of the deal if he felt like it. He probably wouldn't—it had been their score—but it would serve them right if he went all in for himself.

Call me when you've got the car, and a time and a place for the meeting. He started to hang up the phone when he heard Mike's voice buzz through the receiver.

Come again? Stefan asked.

I said, already done. Mike explained that George had a sideline, in addition to robbery and suntan purveyance: George ran a stolen car insurance scam.

George and some cohorts worked with Scandinavian car owners who couldn't keep up with their car payments, or who wanted a newer automobile. The owners arranged for their late-model cars to be "stolen" by George's associates. Then the associates drove the car to one of a network of chop shops in Europe, where the car was sold whole, or for parts. The rightful owners of the car were reimbursed with either a new car, or for the car's full value by their insurance company: *provided the car was reported stolen within forty-eight hours.*

Stefan would have two days before the car they gave him was reported to the police. Europe—tip to tip—in forty-eight hours.

The buy was set for Monday afternoon.

It was Saturday morning.

When he got home, he told Liv he was leaving on business. She didn't ask about the specifics and he didn't offer any. He knew that if he got busted, they'd go after her. If it could be proven that she knew anything about what he was doing, the state would take the baby away. Liv was a simple girl, uncluttered by means, ends, and where the money came from. Stefan, in his self-imposed role as life-giving hunter, had decided that there would be no part-time jobs for her, no day care, no state support. He packed a duffel for the trip and swallowed some Unisom. He'd need all the rest he could get in order to drive straight through with no breaks.

A demonic howl introduced Metallica's "Enter Sandman."

He blinked in the dark. The digital display read 3:56 a.m. Liv was in the corner of the room, holding the baby, Mai-Sunniva crying to beat the band. If she cried hard enough, it could bring on an asthma attack. Then they'd have to sit with her in the hospital again while the doctors gave her steroids. Liv nodded at the ceiling. A party. Stefan sighed, rolled his feet over the side of the bed, wrapped on a robe, and shuffled upstairs.

Big yawn while he waited for someone to answer the door. Gotta be up and on the road—sharp—by dawn. Remembered what it was like to party all night. Now he's the grumpy old man asking the neighbors to keep it down. Kids grow you up fast. A sleepy, sheepish grin at the guy—young, buzz cut, buzzed—who opened the door. Metallica and hashish tang and the clank of beer bottles and the hazy blur of a party in the background.

I'm sorry, man, I've got a newborn baby downstairs . . . just wondering if you could keep it— The door slammed in his face on the *down* part. Stefan cocked his head and stared at the door for a beat. As he climbed back down the stairs, the volume cranked clockwise. Bass rattled the floorboards.

He pulled a T-shirt over his head, laced his boots, grabbed a screwdriver.

Just forget it, come back to bed, Liv said, rocking Mai-Sunniva. He laughed. Took the stairs to the basement, unscrewed the cover to the fuse box, and disconnected the power to the top floor apartment. He'd just go back up there and tell them to keep the fucking music down and then he'd turn their power back on.

This time five guys answered the door. The guy who slammed the door in his face stepped into the hallway. His hand moved at his waist. Maybe just to gesture, or scratch his nose—but the outcome was no longer in Stefan's control. Muscle memory and reflex took over, the guy slammed into the panel of the neighboring apartment's door, wedged into the caved wood like Pooh in the trunk of a tree. One of the guys in the doorway stepped into the hall and Stefan side-kicked him back into the apartment. He pulled the guy from the splintered door and kicked him down five flights of stairs. *Told the sonofabitch his baby was trying to sleep . . . whatever happened after that not his fault . . . people think they can fuck with you, that there are no consequences, but life was all about consequences . . . motherfucker should have thought of that before he slammed the door in his . . .*

On the ground floor he looked down and for the first time noticed that the guy had gone to jelly. Then, something else clicked. He stopped. Like coming out of a trance. He knelt, checked the guy out for injuries. As though he'd come across this beaten man on a street somewhere and couldn't help but help. He ran his hands under the man's shirt. Felt like a few broken ribs. Liv peered out from the second-floor bannister. He told her to call an ambulance.

After the ambulance carted the guy off, the police came. Luckily, some of the neighbors backed up Stefan's story—*loud drunken party, five guys against this one man—just had a baby*—Liv in the background cooing the helpless creature, the louts from upstairs still drunk and incoherent. The cops signed off on Stefan's version, which was good, as there was a Heckler & Koch submachine gun, a .45 auto, and two bars of gelignite in a footlocker under the bed. By the time they left, it was dawn.

Time to drive the length of Europe with the stones.

He'd made only one request of Mike: an inconspicuous car—no flash. He would be transporting the most sought after stolen property in Scandinavia in a stolen vehicle, and he was brown.

Mike and George greeted him outside the tanning salon with a brand-new, fire-engine-red Audi S4 sport sedan. He could have taken the Vanden Plas—but it was a pretty flamboyant ride itself, plus, he'd registered it in Gerda's name. Too risky. And George's Passat was a real beater. Might not make the trip. It was the Audi or nothing and the clock was ticking.

He insisted on stashing the stones himself. Mike handed him the double-sandwich-bagged bundle, and, for the first time, he got a sense of just how big the take was: there were fifty-six top VVS—the gemology rating for stones of flawless clarity—1½- to 2-carat brilliant-cut diamonds; a 30-carat aquamarine; a small fistful of rubies and sapphires; and the emerald pendant—25 carats surrounded by fifty diamond points. He undid the rear door panel and taped the bundle to the outside of the speaker.

At seven a.m. Sunday, he tossed his rucksack into the back seat and roared out of the snow onto the E6 heading south. He'd brought with him a full gallon of water, an empty gallon to piss in, a thermos of coffee, a loaf of bread, and some dried sausages. In an hour, he was on the Frederikshavn-Göteborg ferry to Denmark. He passed through Denmark by late afternoon, and reached the German border by suppertime.

He almost made it.

The German guard at the Flensburg border control checkpoint came out of the booth, waving another guard over. The first guard circled the car, while the second guard's eyes darted between Stefan's passport and Stefan. He kept his hand on the shifter so they couldn't see it shake. He could slam the shifter into reverse, J-turn out of the lane, across the median, and back over the border. He'd ditch the car and bail into the woods along the E6 before the Norwegians could rally and give chase.

The first guard flashed a look at the second guard. They flanked the Audi. He wished he'd told Liv to stay with Jack, who'd recently moved to Copenhagen in an effort to kick a nasty heroin habit. He remembered the guns in the apartment, and the plastique under the bed. Even if Liv didn't know about the gems, there's no way she could explain the rest of it away. They would charge *her,* too. Then they would take the baby.

Is this your car? the first guard asked.

No. It's a friend's.

Well . . . I'm afraid you're not going to be making it into Germany this evening.

Stefan gripped the shifter, slid his foot onto the accelerator. He'd need to get the rpms into the 30,000s in order to beat the Germans to their phones, their guns. *Ten thousand . . . fifteen thousand . . .*

The first guard backed away from the car and pointed at the Audi's tires. *Those tires are not allowed on German Autobahns.*

He backed off the gas and stuck his head out the window. *Fucking hell:* the Pirellis were studded with nails. In Norway, the roads were covered in snow for so much of the year that most cars had studded tires as a matter of course. But they'd churn the soft asphalt of the Autobahn. He almost laughed, just to release some tension.

The second guard returned his passport. *You'll have to turn your car around and go back, we cannot allow you to proceed.*

It was hard finding an open auto parts store near the Danish-German border on a Sunday evening. He pulled into a gas station, where a lone elderly woman manned the register and half eyed a footie match on a Casio portable TV. He told her he needed tires and she said she'd call Bob. A pickup filled with a Danish farmer in his sixties pulled in about twenty minutes later.

You got 250 kroner? Bob asked.

Stefan handed Bob the 250.

Bob put the Audi up on the lift. *You don't need new tires,* he said as he took a pair of pliers and pulled out each nail. When Bob finished, forty minutes later, it occurred to Stefan that it might not be the wisest course of action for a black American in a screaming red sports car loaded with stolen gems to reappear at the same border crossing he'd just been turned away from.

Bob—is there another way into Germany? Those guards at Flensburg were real assholes.

Bob drew Stefan a map and Stefan crossed over at Padborg, ten miles east, crossing into Germany by midnight. He needed to make better time than this. The owner had forty-eight hours in which to report the car stolen—but that was the *maximum* window. There was every chance that the owner—whoever he was—would get a case of the jitters and call the car in after thirty, twenty-four, fifteen, or even eight hours. A routine stop wouldn't be so routine after that.

A hundred seventy-five kilometers per hour all the way through Germany, stopping once for fuel in Köln, crossing over at Strasbourg into France and the A6—twenty-four hours since he'd left Oslo and he was in the Pyrenees.

On the French side—at the Col d' Ares near the Spanish border—the traffic slowed to a stop, a long queue of cars snaking back from the checkpoint. He got out, stamped the needles from his legs, and looked down the road.

Shit.

Cars—hoods and trunks open, panels ripped from doors and hatchbacks—lined up in front of the guard booths. The owners pacing, smoking, while German shepherds sniffed their vehicles' interiors. He got back in the Audi. The mountains below too narrow and jammed with cars for him to turn around. The queue crept forward too relentlessly for him to climb into the back seat and take the jewels from the panel. A single guard—obviously the one in charge—was selecting which cars got searched and which cars got through. As Stefan neared the man's sight line, he did something he'd learned back in the projects when confronted with anyone who'd get in his way: he pulled off his sunglasses and stared hard into the man's eyes.

Vámanos, allez! The man waved at his car, directing him around cars in mid-search. Only someone with nothing to hide would have been so brazen.

The four hundred miles from Seville to Marbella lasted all day. Twenty-eight hours in and still not there. He assumed the car had already been reported stolen. He was dealing with Mike and George. If they told him he had forty-eight hours, the safer bet was that he had twenty-four. Shit, the safer bet was that it had been reported *last* week. There were no safe bets when it came to those two. He used freight trucks' slipstreams and put lots of asphalt behind him.

Thirty-three hours after leaving home he pulled into the parking lot off the quay at Gibraltar's marina. He looked out at the edge of the Rock of Gibraltar to his left, and the azure straits to his right. It was quiet, aside from some late-afternoon maritime activity along the marina.

He needed to wash his face, take a proper stand-up piss, and call the number of the buyer Mike had given him. Most important, he needed to off-load the stones and put them somewhere safe—he didn't know the buyer Mike had set him up with. There wasn't much in the way of cover—just a barren car park, a public marina, and that big dumb rock.

Twenty minutes later, a deep Norwegian voice answered the

phone. Said he'd meet Stefan at the Queensway Quay Marina in fifteen minutes. He'd do the thing they do in the spy movies: carry a newspaper so Stefan could recognize him.

The sun felt good and hot—he'd forgotten how much he'd missed it over the few years up north. Stefan saw the man first. Watched him for a few minutes to make sure he was alone. Short, lean, somewhere in his forties, dressed in jeans too high on his waist and a pale blue linen blazer. His white hair made a game attempt at full coverage, stripes of ruby tanned scalp visible through the wisps. The man ambled leisurely up and down the marina, not the least bit surprised when Stefan walked up.

Hey . . . Stefan, how's it going?

Stefan didn't blink. *My name's Alex.*

Okay. Whatever you say. The man shrugged.

Maybe he could send him over the railing before anyone on the marina noticed. How had this guy gotten his real name? Had Mike given it to George? Maybe it was a setup. But Mike liked breathing in and out and knew better than to burn him.

The man stuck out his hand. *I'm Ödd.*

Stefan didn't give a fuck. *Where's the money?*

What money?

Stefan got into the man's space, crowding him against the marina railing. *The deal is: you give me the money, I give you the stones, I go bye-bye.*

But . . . Ödd stammered, *we don't have a buyer yet.*

Stefan eased away from Ödd to let himself fantasize about whether he'd rather take one of Mike's front teeth, dislocate his elbow, or just keep the stones and give Mike and George fuck-all.

You're supposed to leave them with me, and I'm supposed to deliver the car . . . then I'll find a buyer and sell them . . . that's the deal, Ödd said.

Stefan snapped back into focus. He'd nearly gotten nabbed at two different border crossings. Had to imagine Liv and his daughter taken from him and each other as a result of the life he was dabbling at. Maybe he *was* nothing more than a boy playing international rogue, a lazy amoralist unwilling to give up his dreams of adventure for a life of the endless castration of taxes, paid holidays, and putting a little something away every week. But he'd come too far. Had already broken too many promises to himself and those he loved. And this was just too much money.

I think not, he said. *I'll deliver the car.*

He'd just gone from as far as you can go to as far as you can go on the Continent in thirty-something hours and was too tired to argue when Ödd replied, *Then it looks like you have a partner. Let's go meet the spics.*

Gibraltar was rotten with sunstroked tourists, a densely packed, indigenous polyglot stew of Maltese, Jews, Arabs, and Britons— a two-and-a-third-square-mile British territory where Spanish-speaking bobbies directed traffic on the left. The rock itself was, if you believed that kind of thing, one of the Pillars of Hercules, and home of late to screeching Barbary macaques, military installations, and villas for the wealthy. Most of Gibraltar's citizens lived on the west side of the coast, in Catalan Bay. The marina looked out onto the straits, an eight-mile cobalt puddle between the mainland and Morocco. On a clear night, the lights from Tangier were visible, and the scent of cinnamon and laurel wafted on the water.

Stefan and Ödd walked into a chop shop in the industrial park at the southern end of the Queensway Marina. Volkswagens/Mercedes/Porsches/Audis/Peugeots were raised on hydraulic lifts, doors spread like wings, parts getting stripped and swapped. The entirely illegal operation was right out in the open. While they waited for the buyer, Ödd made it clear to Stefan that he would not get a cut of the money from the car. That was fine with Stefan—he wasn't a car thief.

A Spanish mechanic showed the men into the manager's office, and after Ödd got his price for the car, Stefan said, *There's some other business. Who do I talk to?*

You can talk to me, the manager said.

I'm talking to you, if you're the last person I'll need to talk to.

You want me to get the boss for this?

Stefan just looked at the dark, fat man with a hairline that started just behind his ears.

José Luis Martín López was the head of the Gibraltarian mafia. Fifty-something, darkly Semitic—a natty dresser. Sevilla via Savile Row. José Luis spoke perfect English, with a heavy Catalan lisp. He owned the chop shop, half the Zodiac boats moored to the quay, and the restaurant he was having lunch in.

He was pissed off. Some kid had asked to meet him, but that was forty minutes ago. He didn't like to be kept waiting.

Where is this guy? He glared at Ödd. *You got me the car, what else do I need from you? Why am I waiting here?*

Ödd fidgeted. He didn't know where the fuck Stefan had run off to. Maybe the American had gotten cold feet and beat it out of town.

Stefan jogged over a few minutes later, misted with sweat.

This your partner? José Luis asked as he picked through the shell of his spiny lobster. Ödd shrugged. José Luis looked Stefan up and down. *So where were you? Seeing the sights?*

My apologies. I had to get some things.

What kind of things, that couldn't wait? José Luis asked, ducking his fingertips into the finger bowl. Half of the restaurant was indoors—the other half sat baking on a terrace facing the marina, ten or twelve tables with plastic cloths fastened to their undersides by metal clips, grains of rice in the salt shakers. José Luis motioned for Stefan to sit. Stefan put his rucksack on an empty chair.

First off, who am I talking to? Who's in charge? José Luis asked, wagging his finger between Stefan and Ödd. *Am I talking to you, or you?*

Two minutes later, Ödd was inside the restaurant, at a table with the garage manager, while Stefan and José Luis leaned on elbows at right angles to each other at the patio table.

Stefan took the stones from the plastic bag and laid them on the table.

José Luis grinned. *You just walk around here, carrying these with you? Not too smart.*

Nah, Stefan deadpanned him. *I found a good hiding place for them.*

This is my town . . . you've been here five minutes and you found a good place for them? You can tell me where the good hiding places are in my town. I should know things like this.

Stefan smiled.

José Luis gave up. No cracking this nut. *In any event . . . I'm not in the stones business, I'm in the making-money business.* He turned some of the gems between his fingertips. *I like this one . . . la, la, this one would look good on my wife.* José Luis put the stone back in the pile.

What are you doing in Norway? You don't look Norwegian, José Luis said. *You look Spanish. But your Spanish is lousy.*

Stefan liked this guy: he was no bullshit and he looked you straight in the eye when he spoke. For some reason, he opened up to him. Maybe to prove that he deserved to be sitting there. Maybe because he hadn't slept in two days. He told him about growing up in Ibiza for the first few years of his life. About how he'd trained to become a diver but couldn't get a work visa.

José Luis edged forward in his seat. *I understand it gets pretty rough in the North Sea . . . you must have been good.*

Stefan shrugged.

José Luis deliberated for a beat. Then, *I understand these stones have a certain value . . . so maybe you can help me out with another matter . . . and then we can do business.* He leaned back in his chair and pointed out over the marina. *See that line of black Zodiacs?*

Stefan cupped his hand over his eyes and clocked the handful of rigid inflatable boats bobbing against the quay at the southern end of the marina.

They belong to me, José Luis continued, *and now—I want you to watch.* He checked his Omega Speedmaster with a jerk of his wrist, barely taking his eyes off the water. A forty-one-foot utility boat flying Spanish coast guard colors cruised past the fortified cement gateway to the strait.

A Zodiac—with two guys prone, commando-style, along its sides to keep it weighted down—roared across the bay. Its pilot cranked the outboard, balls-out for a small patch of undeveloped beachfront. The Spanish coast guard ship clocked the Zodiac, turned, and gave chase. On the beach in front of the marina, a Daewoo pickup truck reversed into the sand until it was at the water's edge. The Zodiac light, impossibly fast. The coast guard ship gaining. The Zodiac fifty yards away from shore. The coast guard double that. The Zodiac slammed into the beach. An assembly line of men slung cases of cigarettes into the bed of the pickup truck. The Zodiac pushed back into the water and the pickup spun its wheels into the sand, fishtailing foam and beach in a muddy arc as the vehicles sped away from each other. The coast guard couldn't follow onto land, and by the time their ship had turned around, the Zodiac was too far away to catch.

Three minutes from start to finish. In broad daylight. Business as usual in Gibraltar.

Marlboros, Gauloises, Marquise . . . the bestsellers, José Luis said. *So . . . Mr. Diver,* José Luis started, *two days ago, my men were making just such a run, but . . .*

He looked at his men in the café. Rolled his lips between his teeth. *The coast guard got too close, and they were forced to dump a half-ton cargo of placas—hashish—in the strait.*

José Luis explained that while it wasn't exactly Plan A to dump a shipment, it wasn't unheard of. In fact, the more valuable cargoes—like hashish—were wrapped onto waterproof pallets ringed with buoys and weighted with Dunlop bags of salt just in case. If dumped, the location would be marked by the smugglers, the pallet would sink, the salt would melt, and the package would float back to the surface a few days later. All José Luis's men had to do was keep an eye on the location of the drop, and pluck the package up when it arose from the deep.

The problem is, he said, *I have X amount of money out there in the bay, but because MY FUCKING DUNCES FORGOT TO MARK THE LOCATION, I HAVE NO WAY TO GET IT.*

His men kept their heads tucked into their papers. Knew better than to look up.

So, José Luis continued, *the Moroccans always put a . . . naff . . . five-quid light on the placas, a . . . a . . . ?*

Transponder? Stefan volunteered.

That's right . . . but it's already been two days . . . and the salt will melt. . . . A wave of his hand toward the bay. *If someone could help me resecure my investment, I'd be grateful.*

José Luis looked at Stefan, chin in the palm of his hand. Stefan stared out over the water, then back at José Luis. He looked like shit in the reflection in the older man's Police brand sunglasses. All he'd done was answer a page four days ago. Since then he'd home-invaded an innocent couple, stolen hundreds of thousands of dollars' worth of gems, beaten the shit out of his upstairs neighbor, and driven across a continent on no sleep. All he wanted to do was unload the stones and go home.

Stefan stood a lot better chance of walking away with something—anything—with José Luis on his side than without. This Spaniard was a fucking *don.* Wouldn't hurt to have someone like José Luis indebted to him. And as José Luis had said—*he was in the making-money business.*

Seven hours' sleep between the cool, starched sheets in one of José Luis's hotel rooms and the massive lunch of swordfish au poivre and strong beer gave him back some of what the road had taken. That night, he felt good. And the equipment was all top-notch—Aqua Lung aluminum tanks, Bali wetsuit, Mares face mask—everything he'd asked for.

It was midnight in the Straits of Gibraltar.

Two hours of bounce dives and there was still no sign of the transponder. All this for some hashish. If he thought about it too much, the drug angle of the job bothered him. So he didn't think about it too much. Told himself that hash wasn't really drugs. Little more than pot, really. Bob Marley smoked pot, along with the oppressed, righteous brothers of Judah, and if it was good enough for those *right Rastafari,* it was good enough for *I and I.*

He climbed back into the Zodiac and ripped into an orange. The wake from a passing ship lifted the Zodiac and slapped it back down. The busiest shipping port in the world, José Luis had warned him. *Don't get smooshed.* Even at this late hour freighters, cruise ships, and coast guard patrols clogged the strait. Running lights were out of the question given the nature of their mission, so they had to hunt in the dark. The pilot—one of the men who'd ditched the *placas* a day earlier—white-knuckled the outboard throttle in case they had to pull out from under a looming ship.

Stefan felt safer in the water. He synched the dial on his Tissot to the amount of air left in his tanks and flipped back over the side. His AIDP training paid off in the depthless black with just the glowing needles on his wrist to mark the way. He'd cursed the instructors who'd dumped him into the ocean and left him to find his way back, but he thanked them now. Without them, he might have gotten disoriented in the black, with just the sucking sound of the regulator and the occasional bump from the tiger sharks that kept nosing him. It wasn't so bad at the bottom of the dive, but as he ascended he looked like prey and they came at him mouths closed and nosed him. A flashlight would have ruined his night vision, so they were all in the dark together.

Above him, the ten-foot blades of cruise ships and freighters threatened to pull him into their vacuum and slice him to ribbons. This kind of mission required a team of divers with high beams and a line man, not one man dropped from the sides of a Zodiac with two tanks and a half-witted pilot. He'd give it one more descent and then call it a night. Not worth dying for. José Luis had plenty of money.

Then, twenty-two meters down: a glowing amber circle, winking from the ocean floor.

The transponder.

At dawn, José Luis's men went to the location Stefan had buoyed and towed back the *placas* with a recreational fishing boat. A couple of his guys sat in the fighting chairs and pretended to haul in swordfish, while a chain lugged the *placas* back. The coast guard had paid them no mind.

He told José Luis he'd meet him at the car park, and called Liv from the phone in José Luis's restaurant.

Gotta stay a little longer than I thought, baby. How's my other baby? Liv said their daughter was fine. They missed him, though. He missed them, too. But José Luis's man was waving him over to the Mercedes and he had to go.

Thirty minutes later, at a café in downtown Gibraltar, he became a member of a Gibraltarian smuggling consortium.

Chico—bueno. José Luis smiled at him as he piled into the car. *Hurry up, we have a meeting about our placas.*

Our? Stefan asked.

Finder's fee, Chico. José Luis had started calling him Chico instead of Alex. *You don't look like an Alex.* Stefan didn't argue.

At the meeting, in the small business center of José Luis's hotel, the men spread around a Formica table while a fax machine blipped in the corner. There was an Englishman—a ginger, doughy, middle-aged shipper—whose job was to arrange for the trucking and transport paperwork for the goods they would be smuggling. There was Ödd, already part of José Luis's car ring, promoted into the group thanks to his "partnership" with Stefan; there was José Luis; and there was a Spaniard—mid-thirties with the underbite of a bichon frise—exceedingly polite—who owned a bonded warehouse.

Stefan quickly realized that the real money in Gibraltar was being made from the shipping of black-market goods like alcohol and tobacco. Even the hashish money was to be poured into the acquisition of more booze and cigarettes. The consortium laid it out for him: he could either keep his share of the hashish and sell it on his own steam, or he could parlay the value of the hash into a stake in the consortium. The choice was easy. Dope dealing had never appealed to him. His minority share of the hash wasn't worth all that much, and the consortium needed a good-faith deposit from all members that would cover the value of their next shipment of four eighteen-wheelers filled with booze and cigarettes bound for northern Europe. Ödd and Stefan agreed to put up the stones as the rest of their collateral. Stefan figured that once the money from the first run had been collected, he'd get the gems back and find a buyer. Profit upon profit. Based on the kinds of people he'd met after a day and a half in Gibraltar, finding a buyer shouldn't be all that tough.

And to a young man deeply conflicted about engaging in anything illegal, the enterprise was a far lesser evil than blowing up safes. José Luis's consortium had the veneer of a legitimate operation. His personal attorney was a former solicitor general. José Luis's counsel had easily set up a dummy offshore trading company called High Seas Traders. Since Stefan had experience in brokering, José Luis's attorney gave him space in his office by the Queensway Marina. Stefan—using the name Alex Burgess—was listed as the beneficial owner of the shipping company, whose registered shareholders were members of the consortium. It was a shell corporation—a place for the money to land—with Stefan ostensibly an agent in the company he himself owned.

Reputable and crusty Barclays of London handled the account into which the monies would be funneled.

The first stage of the operation revolved around the VAT—the value-added tax. In order for any goods to leave Gibraltar and travel through Europe, the cargo had to be bonded—insured for its full value—as determined by the VAT. The VAT was 15 percent of the total worth of the shipment. This percentage would have to be paid in order for any goods to travel through European borders, no matter the destination. Legally, if the final destination was a non-EU country, where the VAT did not apply, the 15 percent VAT fee that had been paid up front would be refunded by the customs office of that government.

Now, since the goods—the booze and tobacco—had been purchased on the black market, and were on their *way* to the black market, there was no official bill of lading, or proof of purchase by which any actual VAT could be determined. Or any way to collect the VAT refund that had to be outlaid to secure the bond.

José Luis's attorney simply forged the bills of lading. There was, however, no way around paying the 15 percent VAT fee necessary to secure the bond. The fee—which came to roughly $10,000—was paid up front by the consortium. Even with this expense, the low prices they paid on the black market for the alcohol and cigarettes made the enterprise profitable. The consortium had paid $4.50 per liter of alcohol, which then was sold to the Scandinavian black market at $10, and turned around on the street for $20, which was still a third of the state price: neutral grain spirits in Norway were strictly controlled, sold at government stations, which was why the black market was so robust. Each truck carried 35,000 liters of palletized alcohol and fifty ten-pack cartons of cigarettes: Johnnie Walker Red, Stolichnaya, Marquises, and Marlboro Reds were the primary loads. The entire investment consisted of about $200,000. They stood to make between $500,000 and $600,000.

The rest of the operation worked like this:

The Englishman was in charge of the transport; Ödd was in charge of the black-market distribution in the north; José Luis provided most of the capital and oversaw the acquisition of the alcohol and cigarettes coming into Gibraltar. Stefan wasn't responsible for all that much—the scam was practically on autopilot by the time he showed up. He was mainly an investor, by dint of the stones and the hashish he'd recovered for José Luis. Mostly he lounged around the office at the marina.

Stefan's end, after splitting it with Ödd, would likely be around $45,000 per shipment. He committed to four shipments, with José Luis personally holding the stones as collateral. If he managed to sell the stones after that, then great. If not, he'd still clear almost two hundred grand for his trouble.

He lived in a studio condo José Luis rented to tourists off George's Lane, on a villa-lined street set back from the marina. José Luis floated him a grand while the paperwork for the shipping was being processed, and he sent eight hundred back home to Liv and Mai-Sunniva. He ping-ponged between giddy optimism and guilt. He went along with the score, but his body betrayed his guilt. It was difficult for him to eat without wanting to vomit. He felt seasick on land. His conscience would be heard, whether he tamped it down or not. His hands started to shake again. He clenched them into fists so nobody would notice.

For all of this, he felt somewhat at ease among these crooks. This was a business where men wore seersucker suits and Bally loafers, and life was lived in the daylight. There were no ski masks, no guns, no *real* victims.

A problem he hadn't counted on was the separation anxiety he'd felt over leaving his family. This was not the kind of father and mate he'd set out to be. Liv was living with her mother, and Stefan wrestled with whether the money he was trying to scrounge was worth his absence. In the end, he determined it was. Togetherness wouldn't buy baby food, medicine, diapers.

But before a dime could be made from the smuggling operation, they needed to turn the hashish around to help fund the shipments. José Luis had a plan.

Ödd says he can get a good price up north, Chico.

Whoa . . . I'm not running drugs, José Luis.

No, Chico, we'll get a mula.

A mule. A *drug* mule.

The Admiral was a retired British sea captain, a lean, runny-eyed alcoholic in his sixties who'd made a couple of drug runs for José Luis over the years to supplement his pension. He was the *mula*. José Luis had donated one of the cars from the chop shop—a white Vauxhall with its doors hollowed out and stuffed with Saranwrapped hashish. Stefan would follow the Admiral in a SEAT Málaga four-door, from Gibraltar to Norway, where Ödd's network would take the hash and distribute it. Each man had a two-way radio to maintain communication if they lost track of each other on the road.

The four-day trip to northern Europe was meditative. Owing to their cargo, caution was the order of the day. Stefan and the Admiral stayed in hotels, ate regular meals, and stayed below the speed limit. Nice and easy. Over dinner, at the end of each day's drive, six or seven glasses of claret lubed the Admiral into a charming raconteur. He told Stefan that this *mula affair* was a recent avocation. Originally, he'd made some side money as an extra in Spaghetti Westerns. A dozen years prior, the director Sergio Corbucci had seen the ruddy, thin-lipped ex-seaman in the desert town of Almería, Spain—and thought he looked a helluva lot more like a cowboy than any of the swarthy locals. The Admiral had done two or three films, until the genre died out. Then he'd moved to Gibraltar, where his one or two runs for José Luis a year—at £5,000 a pop— made for a comfy twilight.

On the second of March, they reached the Swedish-Norwegian border at Holtet. The plan was for Ödd to join the caravan on the Swedish side, which was not as heavily guarded as the Oslo checkpoint.

On the Swedish side of the border, Ödd flashed his lights at the caravan and exited the highway onto a dirt road surrounded by trees. That wasn't part of the plan.

Alex . . . what's all this? Stefan's radio crackled. The Admiral didn't like improvisation.

Ödd probably wants to catch up before we head across. . . . No worries, Admiral.

Stefan followed Ödd's car. The Admiral followed him.

The Admiral was old. Jittery. No one had told him that someone else would be meeting them at the border. That someone was Mike.

By the time he came upon Stefan, Ödd, and a strange blond man in a Moncler ski jacket and velour track suit, the Admiral was so convinced they were setting him up for an ambush that he sat in the car screaming *Don't kill me, don't kill me, don't kill me* while Stefan tried to calm him down—*Easy, Admiral . . . take it easy.*

The Admiral took it no such way, and when Stefan made a grab for the keys in the ignition, the geezer got so spooked that he peeled off with Stefan dangling from the driver's side window for fifty feet until a tree branch clubbed him from the car. The Admiral ground the gears into reverse and spun a 180 back onto Highway 22 toward Norway, while Mike, Ödd, and Stefan scrambled into their respective vehicles in pursuit of the rummy with a ton of hashish in his car.

Twenty minutes later, the three of them were outside the Siste Reis Pub, a dank local hangout in the sleepy border town of Halden, just over the Svinesund Bridge in Norway, staring at the white Vauxhall parked at the curb. Next to the Vauxhall was a Norwegian customs police sedan. There was even a fucking cage in the back for a drug-sniffing mutt. *Brilliant.* Not only was the Vauxhall stuffed to the mufflers with dope, it had Gibraltarian plates. It wouldn't take much more than a Norwegian Barney Fife to start asking the tough questions like: Why would anyone who lived in sun-kissed Gibraltar, the smuggling hub of Europe, drive into the glacial moonscape of Norway?

You freaked him out, and now he's in there getting pissed with the customs police! Stefan yelled. *Who told you to come, anyway, Mike?*

Who told me to come? He's—pointing at Ödd—*my contact! We sent you down to sell the stones and you go on holiday? I'm in on whatever you're in on, man . . . fair's fair.*

Ödd looked away. Of course he'd told Mike about the run. Probably felt like he needed some ballast against Stefan.

Somebody's gotta go in there and get the keys to the car, Mike said.

Stefan waved toward the door of the pub: *Be my guest.*

Ödd and Mike hemmed and hawed . . . *Do you know how many warrants I've got?* and . . . *The old geezer doesn't know me, he'll splatter his diapers and go embolic, I walk in there.*

Let me get this straight, Stefan interrupted. *You want the only brown guy—the guy with the Gibraltarian license plates—to walk into that bar and take the keys to the car filled with hashish, from a drunken mule who may or may not have already slobbered out a confession to customs police?*

Mike and Ödd nodded. The plan sounded excellent.

The Admiral looked up from his drink thirty seconds later as tears zigged down his face.

Alex . . . something bad happened to me once . . . in the war. They tortured me, and . . .

Stefan sat down. *It's okay, Admiral. Just give me the keys.*

The airless room was mostly empty. A fat trucker played an electronic quiz game at the end of the bar, and the barmaid leaned over his shoulder and waved a bag of chips between them. The customs officer stood in the doorway of the kitchen, holding the swinging door open while he talked to someone just out of sight. The Admiral sniffled, and the barmaid gave a lazy glance their way. In a minute, she'd come over and ask if Stefan wanted anything. Then she'd see the old man crying into his claret, a young black man across from him, and maybe head back to the trucker, or the customs cop, and remark how odd the whole scene was. Maybe they'd look over and wonder what the fuck the black guy had done to Gramps and maybe feel like asking questions.

Pull it together, Admiral, Stefan murmured.

The Admiral nodded. Palmed the keys to him under the table. Still a bit of the soldier left in him. *I'm sorry, Alex,* he whispered.

Ödd drove the Vauxhall to a garage outside Oslo and off-loaded the hash. While they waited for the car to come back, Stefan took the Admiral to the Svinedusparken Motell, a cheap and cheerful three-story off the 22, and sat with him while he napped. So drunk by that point that Stefan had had to help him off with his pants. The Admiral protested that he didn't deserve his cut—that Stefan should keep it for himself.

You earned it, cowboy, Stefan said.

I was a cowboy, Alex—did I ever tell you . . . ? the Admiral started, the memory curling his lips as he blacked out.

He hadn't seen Mai-Sunniva in almost a month. She'd had a growth spurt—looked like she'd eaten whatever baby he'd left behind. Liv was overjoyed to see him, if understandably frayed at the edges from whatever had swept him from home and kept him from home. If he'd bothered to think about it, he'd have been struck by the similarities to his parents around the same time in their lives: Roye's long absence, Ebba's life defined by motherhood and waiting for his return. But there had been no such reflection, only the forward momentum the life he'd chosen demanded.

He'd left behind more than just the baby to look after: the neighbor he'd beaten before his departure had decided to pursue legal action.

There was a bill from the hospital for three broken ribs waiting for him at the apartment on Hjelmsgata, and a Post-it note from a detective who'd stopped by to follow up on the incident. He thought of José Luis and the mechanisms the man had in place to keep himself at a safe remove from the dirt he did. He'd need some of that, if only for his family's sake.

The day after his return, he packed Liv and Mai-Sunniva into the Vanden Plas and took them on a day trip to Copenhagen. He didn't explain to Liv why he wanted her to apply for her and Mai-Sunniva's Danish citizenship, but he didn't back down outside the Danish passport office, either. Scandinavia had fairly lax citizenship requirements for members of its bordering countries. Danish citizenship would give Liv and the baby a legal avenue of escape if they had to get out of Norway in a hurry. Liv cried and demanded to know why. He slunk in the driver's seat. He didn't know if there were security cameras stationed near the entrance, and he couldn't risk being seen.

Everything I'm doing is for you, he said, and Liv bundled up the baby and pushed open the car door.

Thank you. For six hundred years my family has wanted only to be Danish.

When the detective returned to pursue the rowdy neighbor's charge, Stefan invited him into the living room to talk. Kept Liv and the baby front and center, in the man's line of sight. *What would you have done?* Stefan shrugged. The detective was in his early thirties, fluent in English he was dying to try out, the heavy muscle around his shoulders and chest melting into fat at his waistband.

I would hope there would be another accommodation, the detective said.

But in the moment . . . ?

Yes, things must have been very intense, the detective said. *If you choose not to be accountable for the monies . . . for his injuries . . . then that is for your counsel to advise. I don't think there is any evidence of criminal intentions on your part.*

As he was leaving, the detective turned to him. *I don't see it . . . but I know it is here.*

Stefan cocked his head.

The detective flared his nostrils. *Marzipan?*

Stefan smiled. *Yes . . . would you like some?*

Ecch. The detective frowned. *I am severely allergic, so I have to know the scent well.*

Too bad . . . I love it, Stefan said and wished the other man good day. When he shut the door he looked at Liv and bit his knuckle to stifle the sigh. Relieved, mostly, that the man had been allergic to marzipan: if he'd taken Stefan up on the offer for a piece of almond candy, he would have been disappointed, for there was no such candy in the home. Only the wafting scent of almonds from the bars of gelignite sweating in the footlocker beneath the bed.

Things were quiet for the next three weeks. He'd forgotten what the creak of the floorboards and the crying of the baby sounded like. When José Luis finally called, his voice seemed to come from another time, a rerun of a caper movie on the Late Show.

José Luis informed Stefan that his share from the hashish came to just under $7,000. Stefan asked if he could use his take to provide for his family, instead of putting it back into the shipment. José Luis agreed. He remembered what it was like to be a family man, just starting out. The stones alone could be Stefan's stake. There were only four shipments and then Stefan could take his money and the stones and walk away from the life.

The first two shipments of booze and cigarettes came through in mid-March.

Stefan's share was £20,000 on each shipment. He took great pride that the money was routed through Barclays. Wherever the money had originally come from, it lay in his bank account as sanitized as hospital linen. Technically, he was just a broker. His involvement in the operation began and ended in Gibraltar— *how* the booze and cigarettes were distributed up north was Ödd's affair.

Ödd was a greedy motherfucker.

Ödd had gotten it into his head that despite the long-established presence of a Scandinavian smuggling ring run by Swedish Yugoslavians—Yugos for short—he'd undercut them and take over the lion's share of the trade. Ödd had failed to understand that the competition wasn't in it just for the money.

Arkan—real name Zeljko Raznatovic—was the leader of the Tigers—a Serbian volunteer guard responsible for much of the ethnic cleansing during the Yugoslavian wars of the 1980s and early 1990s. A charming ex–bank robber cum revolutionary, Arkan was one of The Hague's most wanted, trafficking black-market goods all over northern Europe to buy guns and munitions.

One of Arkan's lieutenants was a man named Gunther. Gunther had been in the game a lot longer than Ödd, and didn't appreciate his smuggling business being undercut by some upstarts in Oslo. Gunther had historically tipped the police to small runs, with the understanding that they'd let the bigger shipments go through. The cops could show their superiors that they were diligently cracking down on smuggling, and Gunther made sure they got a taste of the more lucrative shipments. Everybody won. The drivers who got nabbed did their time without complaint: Scandinavian prisons were like Ikeas with cells; the sentences were rarely more than six months to a year; and they were feted as heroes to the cause upon their release.

Ödd understood none of this. He'd assumed that there would be a pissed-off pool of labor willing to work for bosses that wouldn't toss them to the cops. He courted some of these drivers, none of whom were willing to jump the fence. They were, however, willing to share the Norwegian's advances with their boss, Gunther. He started keeping a close eye on the lanes, and paid his Yugo drivers extra to sniff around Ödd's operation.

The last two truckloads Stefan was committed to were nabbed by the police at the Göteborg-Norway border.

Both the shipments and the drivers belonged to José Luis and

the Gibraltarian mob. The trucks belonged to the ginger Englishman. Since Stefan had guaranteed the shipments with the stones,
José Luis was now the owner of the stones. Stefan was now the
owner of sweet fuck-all.

But shit got deeper.

Down south, Ödd and the Englishman had decided that it
would be a good idea to—without telling José Luis *or* his drivers—
add a couple of kilos of Moroccan hash and some methamphet-
amine to the trucks on the second shipment, right in the back of the
eighteen-wheelers, to boost their cut.

José Luis and his syndicate were profligate dopers—no doubt—
but they had mules and the chop shop and *procedures* for that. The
shipping/VAT scam relied on the appearance of legality. The drugs
and the attention they'd elicited changed all that. José Luis's drivers were being charged on an order of magnitude beyond simple
smuggling—they were now being charged with trafficking in nar-
cotics as well.

José Luis and the consortium didn't like losing shipments and
they didn't like surprises. Stefan and Ödd were the newest members of the consortium, and the suspicions for having larded the
shipments with dope fell on both of them.

Things unraveled quickly. José Luis stopped taking his calls,
and Stefan was unsure of what the older man might do by way of
reprisal. Stefan decided to find Ödd and compel him to level with
José Luis about his role in the shipment.

Mike called to tell him he'd found Ödd, but the Yugos had gotten to him first. When Stefan arrived at Mike's place, he found Ödd
holding a bag of frozen peas to his mottled and swollen face, one of
his canines missing and a burst blood vessel around his eye. One
of the drivers Ödd had attempted to recruit had passed along Ödd's

contact information to Gunther and his men, and they'd grabbed him outside a kiosk in downtown Oslo. They'd tortured him into giving them—in addition to the names of his partners—the details for the shipments en route, which was how the police had known which trucks to search. The only reason they'd let him go was so that he could inform the rest of his gang that there was a contract out on all of their lives: Mike's, Stefan's, and Ödd's. A contract the Yugos would eagerly fulfill, at a time of their choosing.

Stefan flashed back to the marina, when Ödd had blurted, *Hello, Stefan.* Which name had Ödd given Gunther? Gunther, who smuggled booze and cigarettes as a sideline to his day job of killing Muslims by the thousands. Gunther, who had a working relationship with the police. How much had Mike confided in Ödd? Mike had been to Stefan's house—a house with his woman and child inside its walls.

Ödd had gone to recruit Yugo drivers at the BNS Trucking container/depot, a fenced-in cul-de-sac thirty minutes on the E6 northeast of Oslo, in a dilapidated industrial park. Thirty-odd eighteen-wheelers were lined up lengthwise against the chain link, the business's office a double-wide trailer near the entrance to the yard.

Stefan and Mike—pretending to be in the market for drivers who could help them ship coffee from Oslo to Madrid—probed three or four of the men on-site about their experience. Stefan's plan had been to select a Yugo from the group, follow him when he left, and then force the man to convey a message to his boss to back off.

Thom was a snowy mountain of a man, an Aryan supremacist who hated Gunther more than he hated Stefan's brown skin. He watched Mike angling the Yugos and sneered, *Those guys are scum. . . . You should work with Norwegians only, if you want your shipment to get where it's going.*

Stefan nodded at Mike: that was the man. Thom was happy to talk. He'd unknowingly taken a job as a driver on a run that Gunther had hipped to the police, and served eight months in Oslo prison. Thom hadn't signed on to be a martyr for the Yugos or anybody else. He and Mike reminisced about the joint and Mike asked Thom if he wanted to make some money and even some scores.

Yes, Thom said, smiling. *I know where the Yugos keep their trucks.*

Stefan and Mike drove Mike's car around to the garage Thom mentioned. There were six or seven eighteen-wheelers lined up against a corrugated metal fence, workers shooting the shit and filling out manifests at the entrance. It was broad daylight.

You sure about this? Mike asked.

Stefan thought he was going to puke. His hands shook like Muhammad Ali on an espresso bender. He wasn't sure about anything anymore. But something had to be done and this was the best he could come up with.

Stefan pulled his ski mask over his face, *Fuck it, then, let's go, man,* and Mike got out of the car and swung the Heckler & Koch 50mm fully automatic machine gun over his shoulder. Stefan crossed ahead of him, a Steyr AUG .45 submachine gun held low. The men working at Gunther's depot saw them, but nobody moved: *It's broad daylight and these are Gunther's trucks and nobody's that crazy and this must be a joke, a trick of the light.*

Stefan jerked back the selector and he and Mike sprayed two of the trucks. Stefan's truck was empty, Mike's sieved booze from the side in eighty-proof streams. Stefan backed away and hit another truck with a burst until he heard glass shatter inside the hold. This was the best they could do: send a message.

Gunther had taken two of Stefan's trucks—now *he* was out two trucks. Stefan and Mike raced back to the car, tossed their subs into the back seat, where the barrels sizzled grooves into the vinyl upholstery, and took off before the Yugos got back to their feet.

Mike knew that George had connections in the Oslo police department, so he told George he was marked for death, along with everyone else. This was a lie, as Ödd hadn't known enough about George to give him up—but Mike's gambit worked. In a panic, George begged one of his former police colleagues, a female detective he'd fucked once after a drunken party, for a last known address for Gunther.

Two days later, at two in the morning, Mike and Stefan arrived at Gunther's small, lovingly detailed house in the suburb of Butterudveien, an hour outside downtown Oslo. Mike had suggested they take George along for extra muscle, but Stefan wasn't having it. *We don't need muscle, we need brains,* he told Mike. Adding, a beat later, *But I'm taking you anyway.*

The alarm was point-of-entry—not motion-sensitive. That was good. They'd have thirty to sixty seconds before it went off. More than enough time. Stefan wasn't scared. Shooting up the depot had emboldened him. It was hot behind the ski mask and he realized how familiar the view from the scratchy, almond-shaped slits had become.

Mike had to use two bump keys before he found the right one. Stefan had already cocked his .45 auto and was moving toward the stairwell when Mike snapped his fingers and pointed at the alarm. It was unarmed; the green stand-by light blipped benignly on the wall pad. They could take their time. Both men exhaled and took a beat to let their eyes adjust to the dark. They'd made it to the base of the stairwell when they heard the click of something against the wood. Another set of eyes caught some light and glinted beneath them, the German shepherd growling low bass.

Shoot . . . it, Mike hissed. Stefan slowly dropped to his haunches.

Back home in Baltimore, a lot of poor people had guard dogs—pit bulls, German shepherds, Dobermans—that they kept locked up outside, in summer heat and winter snow, in order to keep them hard. These dogs were not pets—they were there to keep whatever meager belongings the owners had safe from the have-nots a little lower on the food chain. When Stefan was a kid, snaking through the alleys where these dogs would froth and clamber and snarl against the chain link fences, he had always stopped and sat a few inches away, until the dogs lifted their ears and stuck their rosy tongues through the links, licking his fingers and lolling about in appreciation of warmth and human contact. The kids in the neighborhood used to exclaim, *Damn! I ain't never seen nobody pet Mr. Evans's dog.* His own dog, Quasimodo, had given him years of experience in how to move around an animal bent on establishing dominance.

He curled his fingers and let the black and tan bitch lick his lips through the opening of his mask.

Let her smell your hand, he whispered to Mike, who stuck out a shaky fist. Stefan lay on the floor for another ten minutes stroking the underside of the dog's chin until he figured it was safe to move onto the stairwell.

Gunther was in bed with a woman. They were both naked, the covers twisted around them. Gunther was tight, compact. Maybe forty. A Caesar haircut and the tattoo of a pouncing tiger on his right calf. The woman slept with a pillow over her head, a squat, boyish figure with the exception of a perfectly round ass that looked like the heart from a Valentine's Day greeting card. Gunther farted and the woman half turned at the sound. Mike snatched the woman from the bed by her forearm and Stefan jammed his gun into Gunther's temple just as he lunged for the nightstand.

Stefan put his boot into the back of Gunther's neck and cocked the .45—*You hear that?* He pulled a Taurus 9mm auto from Gunther's nightstand with his free hand and handed it butt-first across the bed to Mike, the woman's forearm going blue in his grip.

Mike yanked the covers off the bed. Stefan took his boot from Gunther's neck and motioned toward a chair next to a teak ward-robe across the room. Gunther rose slowly. Made no move to cover himself. He was proud, defiant—even naked at the wrong end of a gun. Maybe Stefan had been right to take the threat from this man seriously.

He shoved Gunther, a rough kick into the small of his back that wobbled him toward the chair. He would sit when Stefan said sit. Fuck the preening macho bullshit. Stefan pulled out his flex cuffs and looked over to make sure Mike was doing the same to the woman. Too late—Mike had already fucked up. He'd set the Tau-rus on the bed while getting his cuffs out and the woman grabbed it and tossed it. Gunther leaned forward in his chair and caught the butt of it, as Stefan wedged his .45 auto into his waist and choked the Yugo out with his own arm, while the woman screamed and the shepherd yapped between the two men, unsure if this was a game or cause for alarm. Gunther was losing consciousness from lack of oxygen, his fingers loosening around the Taurus. Stefan grabbed it, spun Gunther, and smashed him across the bridge of his nose with the butt. As Gunther tottered back onto the chair, Stefan unloaded a canister of CS gas—Mace—into his face, then hooked him with a rabbit punch to the solar plexus that billowed the air from him and forced the Yugo to suck the pepper spray deep into his lungs. Stefan held Gunther's face between his thumb and forefinger and stuck the canister's nozzle into the bloody pulp of his nose and emptied the rest of the canister until nothing else came out. Gunther puked blood and streamed pink snot while Mike zipped the cuffs taut into the woman's wrists and whispered, *See what you've done? See that?*

Put something on her and get her out of here, Stefan told Mike. Mike wrapped the sheet around her and pushed her into the hallway by the nape of her neck.

Gunther was hunched over in the chair, trying to lift his head from his chest. He snorted deeply and hawked up a pink blob of phlegm.

Stefan stood back and waited for Gunther to regain his composure. There was a psychological point to all of this, and he needed to make sure Gunther took in its full meaning: he had been violated. Stefan had come into *his* home, beaten him in front of *his* woman, both of them naked, and would, depending on how things played out, put a hollow point into the back of Gunther's head. When Gunther finally opened his eyes, the first thing he saw was a big man in a ski mask standing in front of him. Petting his dog.

Even within this bloody chaos, Stefan had been careful, had colored inside the lines. He'd made sure Gunther's woman was clothed, had let his dog live. If any of those personal boundaries had been crossed, Stefan would have had to have killed Gunther as a matter of protocol. Gunther's honor would have required that he seek revenge. It was a tricky psychological gambit. He needed to make Gunther suffer, while leaving him enough dignity that he wouldn't see the sense in escalating things. But Stefan had to make sure.

Open your mouth, he said.

Gunther just stared at him. Stefan cracked him in the temple with the .45. *Open your fucking mouth.* Scandinavians didn't speak to each other that way. It got the man's attention almost as much as the violence had. Gunther opened his mouth and Stefan stuck the barrel of the .45 just past his teeth and cocked it.

I hear you've put out a contract on me . . . is that true?

Gunther shook his head.

So we can talk, then?

Gunther nodded.

Stefan uncocked the .45 and sat on the edge of the bed. *You know who I am?*

Gunther nodded. Off Stefan's shrug: *Alex.*

Good. This meant that Ödd hadn't given up his real name. Killing Gunther was one of a couple of options now.

And what did I do to you? Stefan asked, in Danish-inflected Norwegian. If he let Gunther live, he wanted to leave him with as confusing a portrait as possible, no face, and an unplaceable accent.

You tried to take over my business, Gunther wheezed.

Is there no room for two?

No, Gunther answered evenly.

But we're even now, Stefan said. *You lost your shipments, and I've lost mine.* Gunther was wheezing pretty bad. *Can you breathe okay?*

Gunther nodded. Naked and beaten and being looked after by the man who'd shamed him. Stefan whistled for Mike. Mike appeared with the woman in the doorway.

Cut her loose. Mike flicked open a pocketknife and split the cuffs from her wrists. Stefan picked up Gunther's Taurus, ejected both the clip and the round in the chamber, and pocketed them. He put the gun back in the nightstand.

You know what it means if you ever see me again, yes?

Gunther nodded.

The woman could cut him loose. By that time, Mike and Stefan would be just turning on their headlights as they slid onto the E6 toward Oslo.

Oslo was finished for him. He cleaned out the apartment. One of the last phone calls he received there was from Ödd: the ginger Englishman had gone missing down in Gibraltar. His wife had been calling the cops and the British consulate looking for him. Ödd freaked. Rightfully so. It had been his idea—along with the Englishman's—to run dope. They were the reason Stefan had had to visit Gunther in the middle of the night. They were the reason he'd lost the stones. Stones he'd never even wanted. All he'd done was answer a page. And Gibraltar was burnt for him now, too. José Luis likely assumed that he'd been in on the dope angle with Ödd: they were partners after all.

Stefan rented a farmhouse in northern Denmark. He had the bulk of the money from the first two shipments, which was enough to bring the whole family together. Ebba had developed carpal tunnel syndrome from years kneading patients' muscles, and found it harder to practice therapy. The Boyesen Institute was losing money every year. Gerda was in poor health, and Ebba's brother had mismanaged the company's finances so badly that the institute's future was dubious. The castle was in receivership and she and Rene had split up. Their preteen daughters, Veronique and Emmanuelle, came to live with Ebba and Liv and Stefan and Mai-Sunniva at the farmhouse. Everyone was looking to Stefan for support. The money he'd made wouldn't last forever.

To try to save the Boyesen Institute, he spent thousands in legal fees in an attempt to block Ebba's brother from access to institute funds. He spent another few grand on his baby sisters. Rene was getting married. After he and Ebba split, he'd taken up with an American TV actress—the star of a 1980s weekly mystery/comedy series—and their wedding was set for Kenya. Rene had called the girls and told them that while he'd love to have them at the ceremony, he just couldn't afford their airfare. So Stefan bought the girls' dresses for the wedding, along with two plane tickets from Heathrow to Kenya. He didn't mind spending the blood money on family. He did mind when he was in the supermarket buying diapers for his daughter a few weeks later and the two-page spread in *Hello!* magazine read:

Stars' Glittering Wedding in Kenya!

There were pictures of Queen Noor, Whitney Houston, and a bunch of stars in attendance, along with the 15-carat diamond wedding ring Veronique and Emmanuelle's "too broke to fly them to his wedding" father had bought his new bride. By the end of the summer, the strain of caring for all the women in his life was becoming unbearable. But no way was he going back into the life. He needed something that would give him a financial cushion, and he thought he knew what that thing was.

Stefan had risked life and limb for those fucking stones. He'd kept his end of the bargain, and those trucks that had gotten nabbed? Well, those were on Ödd and the ginger Englishman. Maybe José Luis had taken out the Englishman, like everybody said. Maybe he'd taken out Ödd, too. But Stefan couldn't just let them go. He'd traveled across a continent and dived below her; been a jewel thief and a home invader, a black-market smuggler and an absent father. There was a quarter of a million dollars back in Gibraltar and he'd *earned* every penny of it. He could have just let it go. Or moved back to the States with his family and gotten his degree and done what honest hardworking men from good families have always done. But by the time he thought about those things, the turbines were blowing the 727 Lufthansa Airways flight out of Oslo, southward.

———

I want my stones. I kept my part of the bargain. The Englishman was your guy. Ödd was one of yours, too, when it comes right down to it. I never met those guys until I met you.

José Luis is silent. The macaques on the Rock of Gibraltar howl and scuttle as the car makes its way up the rise. The southwest side home to an English military base, the rest of the slope inhabited by apes and the rich.

José Luis's villa is a two-level Georgian/Spanish colonial hybrid set back from a small driveway with four or five men laying an intricate stone wall around the gravel.

José Luis yells *Comida!—Lunch!*—to the workers from the car window, and they scatter to the rear of the house. Stefan isn't sure if the signal is a code. For all he knows, they've gone around back to get clubs or knives or shovels to dig a grave. He shakes it off. José Luis rolls up his sleeve, picks up a slab of slate, and slathers a film of mortar onto one side in a brisk, expert stroke.

I used to be a stonemason, he says, laying stone upon stone in perfect order. *Got tired of fucking working.* He scrapes the trowel clean. *You are real,* he says, *like me, a man—you get in there, do things that need to be done.* He rolls down his sleeve and buttons the cuff.

Stefan takes in the tiles, the tools, the dirt. What was that story he'd read in second grade—"The Cask of Amontillado"?—about the guy who'd gotten buried alive, brick by brick? Poe had written that . . . he was from Baltimore, too. The world follows you wherever you go. He wonders where the hell the workers have gone.

You'll smoke with me? José Luis asks. In the kitchen, a large room fronted with bay windows and covered in burnt orange terra-cotta tiles, he pulls a Bustelo coffee tin from the shelf. He fills a pipe with hashish—Zero-Zero, the best—from Morocco, and lights it. Zero-Zero is the first scraping of the pollen from the Moroccan marijuana plant, a powdery, sticky resin that produces a trippy high more akin to LSD than cannabis. José Luis puffs and passes the pipe and makes a salad—oranges and almonds and sherry vinegar—and opens a bottle of wine.

I'm very disappointed with the way things turned out, he says. He pours them both a glass. The wine is bitter and grips the tongue and dulls the rough edges of the high. By the time Stefan notices José Luis isn't drinking, he can't stand up. José Luis smiles. Excuses himself. Stefan hears him on the phone in the other room, but can't make out the Cádiz-tinged conversation. He's gotta get straight. Breathes out, long and slow, emptying his lungs. An old diver's trick—helps to oxygenate the blood. But nothing's working against this high. It's like swimming through honey. Where are those fucking workmen? José Luis comes back after a minute, Stefan trying to rise again, wobbling back into his chair.

Whoa, Chico Bueno. José Luis smiles. *You better stay put.*

José Luis just watches him, his back to the sink. A monkey shrieks outside the open kitchen window, and when Stefan turns from the sound there are two men beside him. One of the men reaches inside his pocket, and Stefan slides the chair back a few inches—maybe he can take the guy's knee from under him without standing up—*Easy,* José Luis says gently, as the man pulls a drawstring pouch from his jacket. José Luis jerks his chin at the man and the man puts the pouch on the table next to Stefan. *When you came here, I asked you to do something, and you did it, without knowing anything about me. Those other men, the men I work with, would never jump into the ocean for me. If you tell me you didn't know, I will believe you.*

I didn't know, Stefan says.

José Luis shrugs. *Okay.* He points to the pouch. Stefan takes it and spreads the stones out on the hammered copper table. They are all there. A glowing mound of green and purple and translucent pressed carbon soaking gold tint from the table.

Which one did you say your wife would like? Stefan asks.

José Luis takes a draught of the wine and edges forward in his chair.

Yeah? he asks.

Stefan nods. The room has slowed down and the floor feels solid again. José Luis points out two simple brilliant-cut diamonds, and Stefan places them in the other man's palm and closes both his hands around it. Outside, he can hear the clang of tools as the men return to building the wall.

On their way down the mountain, an hour later, Stefan tells him, *Thanks for being honorable. You could have kept the stones, left me with nothing. . . .*

José Luis shrugs it off. *I was just holding them for you. Right in my desk, most of the time.*

Stefan laughs. A quarter of a million dollars' worth of gems in the guy's desk. Probably hadn't even locked it.

Chico Bueno . . . that day, when you came to me . . . and you said you had a good place to hide the stones? Where did you hide them?

As they get to the base of the Rock of Gibraltar, Stefan points a lazy finger out the window and says, *I hid the little stones in the big one, jefe,* and both men plus the driver howl to beat the monkeys in the trees.

X

THE COOL-OUT

After the Gib, he'd returned to the rented farmhouse in Hals, and Ebba; Liv; his sisters, Emmanuelle and Veronique; and Mai-Sunniva all lived there for the summer. He'd kept the stones in a strongbox and resolved not to sell them. They would be a reminder to him of the life he'd lived. And they were an insurance policy he could cash in if things got desperate. He still had some leftover money—dwindling fast—from the shipping score, but he was angling for something long-term, and *legal*, to secure his family's future. The more he thought about it, the more he became convinced that his family held the key. They'd already created something worthwhile. It just needed a bit of aggressive administration.

Ebba and Gerda had never been any good at business. Like all people who'd been raised with wealth, they trusted in the beneficent money gods to provide. But Stefan knew that getting and hanging on to money was a 24/7 hustle. All the hippie therapeutic shit Gerda had pioneered in the 1960s and 1970s was becoming big business in the New Age era. It wasn't just shamanic Germans who were interested in past lives and misaligned chakras: everybody wanted to get into the act. By the mid-1990s, Kundalini yoga, reflexology, and shiatsu could be had in any gym or day spa, without all the psychic distress and primal screaming that went along with Biodynamic Therapy.

This change in the landscape, coupled with the shoddy management of the institute, led to a financial crisis. The castle at Lugny—the main breadwinner—was too expensive to maintain. They still had Acacia House in London, and a small center in Cap d'Ail, Monaco, but the institute was withering. Stefan was determined to save it.

For all his occasional skepticism of Biodynamic Therapy, he was proud of how the women in his family had practically defined a field. And some of that stuff *did* work. As a kid, he'd seen people relieved of cysts, arthritis, mental anguish. If he hadn't witnessed the power of that therapy, he wouldn't have studied emergency medicine. A break in a different direction—less of an adrenaline jones and more intellectual discipline—and he might even have tried medical school.

He knew that if Gerda and Ebba wanted to hang on to the remainder of their foundation, they'd have to modernize. Computers. The patenting of their techniques and the licensing of practitioners in their methodology. "Brand" the treatment. And Ebba's brother had to be replaced. There was a daunting list of measures that needed to be taken. He was sure he could do it.

Gerda lived at and managed Acacia House in London. He didn't want to step on her toes at the flagship location of her institute. Ebba lived mostly in London with the girls, but gave frequent seminars at the mostly dormant Monaco branch. Monaco—*that* sounded promising. Stefan had come to Hals to decompress, but there's unwinding in the snow and four hours of daylight, and there's unwinding on the French Riviera. He'd turn the Monaco clinic around, secure his family's legacy, and soak up some rays. The Norwegian climate was hell on Mai-Sunniva's asthma anyway, and Liv, well, she could use some sun and lavender and beautiful people.

In the fall of 1993, he took over a two-bedroom balcony apartment belonging to the Boyesen Institute, on Chemin des Mimosas, in Cap d'Ail, southeast France. Tina Turner lived right across the street, in a circular stone villa, and Monaco was a seven-minute zip down the Riviera.

He and Liv made friends quickly, spending days at Plage Mala, a pebbly idyll lapped by the Mediterranean, and evenings on their tiled veranda, or, rarely, in Monaco, playing boulevardiers with millionaires and movie stars.

He set about trying to patent Gerda's methodology, something she'd never thought to do, but the process was akin to patenting yoga, and he had little luck. It was impossible to prove that his grandmother's theories were the bedrock of many of the current holistic trends. His whole exercise was distinctly *American*. Europeans didn't tend to toss around lawsuits and slap a brand name on everything. He was in over his head, lacking the money or legal expertise to solidify Gerda's business.

He and Liv had little to do. She took up cooking. He picked up the guitar again, started making jewelry—simple beaded necklaces and woven bracelets—and tried a little sculpting. He was rested. Well out of the life. And bored out of his fucking mind. He was a young father living in a vacation paradise for the rich, the old, and the celebrity. He was none of those things. He did not take vacations. His daily life had already been one long escape. For Stefan, the paperwork and legal grind of navigating obscure patent laws and sitting on the beach became deadly dull.

Liv went to London twice a month to get her license in Biodynamic Therapy. She was still in her teens when they had met, a parent soon after. He had been the locus of her life. Her classes were the first step in forging an adult identity besides girlfriend or mother. And because she was the—de facto—daughter-in-law of one of the founders, the institute's classes were free.

While Liv was in London taking classes, he loafed around Monaco. Hung out at the Sportsman's Lounge, a cabaret/casino, and nursed twenty-dollar *pressions*. That's how he'd met Dana, a Southern California bombshell who'd gone to Cal State Long Beach in dance, and toured Europe with a famous black American choreographer's dance troupe.

When he met her, she was on a date with Prince Albert. He'd gone for a piss and left her alone long enough for Stefan and Dana to exchange numbers. Dana didn't care that Stefan had a live-in girlfriend or a kid. An artist living on her looks, she figured she might as well live it up with someone who looked as good as she did.

But Dana evolved into more than just a way to occupy time. In some ways, they were more suited for each other than he and Liv. Dana had interests outside of Stefan, and she wasn't looking for Stefan to rescue, support, or dazzle her. She found his history entertaining and appealing—but she had her own stories. She'd been dancing in America—New York, Los Angeles, Europe—since her late teens. Made her own way. Her art, while important to her, enabled her to do the thing she really loved: travel. She'd never met anyone who'd seen as much of the planet as she had. Long hours were spent regretting the places they'd been without the other. New, slate-cleaning trips were planned, at the beach at Plage Mala, or over citric bottles of rosé at the old port overlooking the harbor at Monaco-Ville. They'd point out the boats they thought most capable of seeing them around the world. Nothing too showy. In Monte Carlo, a simple boat was anything under fifty feet, without a Jacuzzi on deck. They dreamed big, breathless dreams of a life of adventure together. The rush Stefan had chased found no outlet in sleepy—if ritzy—Monaco, and with Liv and his child gone, romance was the stimulant that stepped in to fill the void.

They had sweaty, postcoital professions of love. He started to feel alive again. There was an electric *illegality* to the whole thing. The excitement of the affair was almost as intense as the high from a heist or a dive.

Eventually, he got sloppy. Monaco being a small town like any other, Liv found out. Stefan was never home when she called. Could only talk for a few hushed minutes when she did. When she came home from her studies, his "five-minute" trips to the market often lasted hours, his return punctuated by the scent of sweet perfumes and salt and musk that were foreign to her, but known, in the way death smells only like death.

She was devastated. She'd never assumed he was the faithful sort, but *this* infidelity, piled on top of the long absences and financial instability he'd subjected them to, was too much. In the winter of 1995, she moved to London with Mai-Sunniva. Shortly after, Dana left for Paris, after receiving an offer to pose for French *Playboy*. Stefan was alone, doggedly determined to dig the Boyesen Institute out from under, but it was too late. The institute was bankrupt.

While he was packing up the Cap d'Ail apartment, Dana called.

She'd chickened out of the *Playboy* shoot. *What if my father sees it?* She'd decided to go to Tokyo instead, and dance with the Jay Fox cabaret, where a white woman of her charms could make a few grand a week. He'd never been to the East.

Originally, she'd gotten him a job as an extra in the show. He couldn't dance for shit, but all they'd wanted him for was to stand around onstage in a sailor suit and toss the girls in the air when they ran in for a jump. He hated it. Had no aptitude for performance of any kind. In his own skin, he was comfortable—occasionally haughty. But he did not understand showmanship. As outsized as his persona was, it was his—the idea of pretending, for *entertainment's* sake, to be someone or something else was asinine. He didn't even like to read fiction. He bailed on the show after a few weeks and retreated into the Myouzenji Temple dojo in Roppongi, near the studio apartment Dana had rented. The dojo was where the truth lived, among the blood- and sweat-stained floors and the discipline. He trusted that once he got back in the dojo, work would find him.

The Australian, Grove, spotted him on the heavy bag that first day at the Myouzenji Temple dojo, happy to work out with somebody over five-seven and 170 pounds. At nearly six feet, and his largest ever weight of 190, Stefan was a monster, a Godzilla in Tokyo. Grove worked at a neon pit called Giant Robot! He told Stefan to come in and see about working the door.

The money was good. He salved his conscience by sending most of it back to Liv and Mai-Sunniva, but he enjoyed his newfound freedom. It seemed to him that everything he'd gone through the last few years had been due to his obligations as a provider. Fuck it. It was *his* turn. There were rumblings in the dojo about a new annual martial arts competition called K-1, held in Tokyo's Dai-Ichi Stadium. K-1 promised to determine the baddest fighter on earth in one night's fighting. Stefan thought he had a pretty good shot at the '96 title if he trained hard enough. He worked the door of the club nights, trained days, and stayed out of trouble.

Except for going to jail.

One night, a group of drunken Iranian guys, maybe six of them, stumbled up to the door and demanded entry. Stefan turned them away. One of them stepped up. Got a broken nose for his trouble. The cops came. The Iranian had blood everywhere. Could barely stand. Assault was a mandatory twenty-one-day bid in jail. Giant Robot!'s manager tried to talk the cops out of it, but the Iranian was so utterly fucked up that even Stefan had to admit it looked a tough case to prove self-defense.

The sergeant processed Stefan at the Roppongi station and checked out for the night. The intake sergeant told Stefan to take his ring—a thick silver band—off. It was dangerous, he said. The arresting officer was long gone and all this new officer saw was a big black American covered in blood, refusing to take his ring off, not because he was a troublemaker or a hard-case, but because despite all he'd done, Liv, his first true love, had given him that ring, and in that moment he decided that taking it off was breaking every connection to home and family, and that she and Mai-Sunniva would be lost to him forever in that simple action. Too bad if the sergeant couldn't see it that way, or the line of miniaturized cops tapping their batons into their palms in the processing room didn't see it that way, as long as they understood that *nobody better put their hands on him.* A line of four of them came at him, and he shoved them off with clenched fists, careful not to strike them, just enough to back them off. Sometimes he'd just let them charge, tiring them out, deflecting their momentum with jujitsu as they tried to grab a wrist or a limb and pin him.

Ten days' solitary confinement and bread and water was his punishment for resisting arrest. He kept his ring.

At the end of the ten days, they put him in the violent offenders ward, in a twenty-by-twenty-foot cell in the central island of the jail. There were five guys to a cell—all Yakuza. Cots hung from the walls and there was a Plexiglas closet for a toilet. Most of the Yaks had full sleeves—tats of dragons, tigers—and black circles marking each crime they'd committed. They thought Stefan was a nutcase.

He got up every morning at six and did a hundred push-ups on his knuckles and sat in a corner doing splits until breakfast. Still had it in his mind to try for the K-1. Couldn't risk twenty-one days without training.

The U.S. embassy rep came in the first week out of solitary, asked him if he wanted them to notify his family. He hadn't spoken to Roye—except for a few phone calls—in almost a decade. There hadn't been a reason, outside of distance. Roye had remarried, had three more children—two boys and a girl—and had sold the house on McCulloh and moved to rural northern Baltimore County, just shy of the Pennsylvania border. He was busy raising a new family, and Stefan was an adult, living his life an ocean away. Neither Stefan nor Roye was a sentimentalist. On one of Stefan's rare phone calls, informing his dad of Mai-Sunniva's birth, Roye had good-naturedly congratulated him and said, *Hope she doesn't drive you crazy like you did me.*

Both men had laughed. Stefan promised to send pictures. It was another year before they spoke again.

But a call from Tokyo, informing his dad that he was in jail? This was not how he wanted to reconnect with his father. And no way did he want them to notify Liv about how far he'd fallen. She'd probably think he'd gotten what he deserved for running off to the Orient with some American dancer. He told the rep there was no one.

For the rest of his bid, he hung with the Yaks and asked them to teach him bits of Japanese, and he tried to teach them some English. The Yaks were so well connected they had bento boxes brought in for lunch, and after a few days they made sure he got one, too. None of the other prisoners—mostly overly aggressive touts or wife beaters or drunks—got those perks.

On the last day, the owner of Giant Robot! met him at the jail with an envelope of money—all of his salary from the time he'd missed—and asked him to come back to work immediately, as head of security. Stefan had gone to jail for protecting his business. A guy willing to take a bullet like that was worth keeping.

Barely two weeks later, he went in on his night off to get his paycheck and they told him that some Yaks were getting out of hand and he'd gone over to talk to them and that's when the Yak winked to his buddies and grabbed him by the belt and tossed him over the railing. The Yak was dead, for all he knew. The Yakuza would avenge their member. Just out of jail for a previous violent offense, Stefan knew the Japanese legal system would be no refuge.

———

The Lanna Muay Thai training camp is a twelve-hour bus ride into the hills of northern Thailand from the Mo Chit station in east Bangkok. He leans across two sagging vinyl seats and tries to doze, rucksack pillow against the window absorbing bumps from the road. Flocks of motorbikes and tuk-tuks swarm the bus on the four-lane highway until death-race congestion gives way to single-track road and jungle and oxen as the bus climbs into the mountains of Chiang Mai.

Outside, it is a hundred degrees. Inside the half-filled bus, it is frigid. Thais like it cold. They stop at Phitsanulok, and a lithe, flat-faced girl in her twenties gets on. She moves through the aisle selling salted peanuts from a woven basket. He buys three bags. A handful of monks stream on behind her and cluster at the back of the bus. He smiles to himself: back in Baltimore, only the toughest kids dared sit in the back of the bus—it was the lawless zone, out of range of the driver's mirrors. In an otherwise empty bus, the hard-cases would still take the last row, and if you sat back there, you were at their mercy. In high school, he'd always taken a seat in their midst, legs spread wide into the aisle, looking bored, just *waiting* for some thugged-out motherfucker to tell him to move, or deliberately knock into him. Here, in this other place, a group of ascetic men took the back of the bus so as not to bother anyone. He is glad he has seen the rear of both buses and wishes more brothers from back home could.

He tears open the bag and upends a stream of peanuts into his mouth. He should have bought just one. Have to be careful with money. Fifty dollars left. That's a lot in Thailand, but still.

He hasn't seen Liv or Mai-Sunniva in almost six months. Not since Monaco. Not since he moved to Tokyo to be with Dana.

He crumples the empty bag, jams it into the ashtray on the seat arm. He's on the run. *To* something as much as *from* something. In twenty-nine years, he'd only ever heeded his own need for adventure, no matter what it had done to the people around him. He hadn't done so out of cruelty. No, he recognizes it now for what it has always been: hubris. A sense that he lived outside of the conventions that made others so passive, so meek, so *dead*. But there was spiritually dead and there was *real* dead, and no amount of philosophizing could change what had happened in Tokyo.

It was his fault. He'd organized his life so that tragedy was inevitable:

He would not have been in Tokyo if he hadn't taken up with Dana.

He wouldn't have met Dana if he hadn't been in Monaco.

He wouldn't have been in Monaco if he hadn't had to flee Norway.

He wouldn't have had to flee Norway if he hadn't gotten involved with Mike and slid into the criminal world.

He wouldn't have slid into the criminal world if he'd had enough discipline to knuckle down and finish his education.

He'd lived in the moment, convinced that life had grander plans for him, that he was destined for a life of wealth and adventure. A woman and child weren't going to get in his way. He'd provide for them *and* satisfy his jones. What if it had been him in the street outside Giant Robot!? Mai-Sunniva would grow up without a father. And whatever memory she'd have of him would be clouded by the circumstances of his death: *My daddy died in a bar brawl.* There were niggas back in Baltimore who'd never left their neighborhood, never had half the breaks he'd gotten, who managed to be there for their children.

He has dragged his life and the happiness of the people he loves here with him—to jungles and dark places—and no one is the better for it. He looks back at the group of monks. That might not be a bad idea. Devote himself to something greater. Better luck next lifetime. *No.* No more running. He is going to make amends. He looks out the window, nothing but dark and his reflection in the glass. Thirteen hours later, the bus pulls into Chiang Mai. From there, he takes a tuk-tuk to the Lanna Muay Thai camp.

Even in the dawn, with the outline of the boxing rings shrouded in grey and the jungle just starting to warm from the sun, he knows that he will find something in this place. And that it will hurt.

This is his morning:

0600—Warm Up/Stretch
0610—10-Km Run
0710—Drills (Knees, Kicks, Punches on the bag)
0730—Shadowbox (5 to 6 rounds)
0800—Bag Work (4 to 5 rounds)
0825—Pad Work (2 to 5 rounds)
0850—Clinching/Sparring (5 rounds)
0915—Drills (as before)
0935—Exercises (sit-ups, push-ups, chin-ups)
0950—Shadowbox (2 to 3 rounds)
1005—Cool-Down Stretch

This is his afternoon:

1600—Warm Up/Stretch
1610—3- to 5-Km Run
1635—Skip (4 rounds)
1655—Shadowbox (5 to 6 rounds)
1725—Bag Work (6 to 8 rounds)

1805—Pad Work (5 to 6 rounds)

1835—Clinching/Sparring (5 to 6 rounds)

1905—Drills (as morning)

1925—Shadowbox (3 to 4 rounds)

1940—Cool-Down Stretch

In the evening, he adds another five-kilometer run. If he can shut down his body maybe his mind will follow. Every day hurt comes for him with elbows and knees. His nose is broken. Every day they kick his ass. He deserves whatever they give him.

Chiang Mai is an odd mixture of growing metropolis and traditional hill village. Elephants and oxen lumber along the shoulder of the bustling Huay Kaew road, right past the 7-Eleven and the university. Lanna Thai is a new Muay Thai fight gym at the foot of the Doi Suthep mountain in northern Thailand. Heavy bags swing from the open-air hangars; a ring anchors the far side.

A Scot owns Lanna Thai, but it's run by veteran Thai fighters. There are no Westerners, save Stefan and a French ex-army guy. Everyone else is Thai. Most of the students are grown men, but there's a thriving pool of boy fighters as well. Muay Thai training starts early. It takes years to build up enough scar tissue on shins and elbows and fists to withstand the blows. If a boy shows promise, sometimes the trainer will razor slits from his shins to his kneecaps to kill the nerves. Sometimes they break the cartilage in the kids' noses so there's no risk of caving in a fight. Fights are big business in the villages. Once a week, locals cheer their fighters, the frenzied mob slurping Singha lager, munching griddled coconut balls—*kanom krok*—and waving money. There are few tourists this far north. Tourists do not come to fight. In 1996 there is no such thing as adventure/immersion tourism or paying a hundred dollars a month for the privilege of puking jungle curry and splintering a forearm.

No, this is Thailand near the Burmese border. Burma's military junta, SLORC—the State Law and Order Restoration Council—is shelling the Muang Thais and the Karen rebels up the road at Mae Sai. Gems and drugs and civil war flood the Golden Triangle. You come here to *not* be somewhere else.

Every day he gets better. But that's not the point. He is here because the dojo has provided him with the only refuge he's ever known. Muay Thai is rumored to be the most challenging— physically and spiritually—martial art there is. He needs to be subsumed again by the thing that's always saved him.

He realizes after only a few days here that he has never known how to fight.

Muay Thai is the distillation of the most effective methods for human animals to hurt each other aside from love or guns. There are no *katas,* no forms. Only what works. Shins, knees, elbows. Bone on bone. He is on his ass or spitting out blood or wondering where that kick just came from for the first month.

During the break, in the hottest part of the day, he goes to the wat, the small Buddhist temple at the monastery a kilometer outside camp. The wat is a thirty-foot cone, covered with hundreds of thousands of shards of broken glass, maintained by a school of monks.

For the first few days, he'd sat at the edge of the clearing and watched the monks, shaved heads and orange robes, sweeping the dirt from around the temple, chanting, meditating. Amazed at how isolated their existence was. They went into Chiang Mai's villages each day collecting alms but were not allowed to ask for money. Villagers who had nothing came up to them and pressed food or money into their hands. Paying off the next life in this one.

One of the monks sits on the steps of the wat, and stares directly into the midday sun. Tears stream down his flat, round face from the effort, but he barely blinks. He doesn't even squint. After an hour, he comes over to Stefan and hands him a bristled brush. Wordlessly leads him by the elbow to the wat.

Every day, in between training, Stefan limps up the stick ladder and scrubs the bits of glass on the wat. The sun one-two punches him, searing his back, bouncing hard off the glass into his face. He doesn't remember where he leaves off every day. There's no way he could ever finish the task, not in a thousand lifetimes. Each glass tile on the wat must be scrubbed. Look at it as a whole and you'll never finish. Start with one. Keep going. Mosquitoes, stuck in the film of sweat and blistered skin on his back, drink deep. Some days he can't close his right fist, the last two knuckles in his hand mashed into the cartilage. He ties the brush to his hand with a rag and scrapes the fragments of cola bottles and colored glass. When he thinks it's too much he looks down.

Below him, the monk stares into the sun.

———

A few days later. In a bar. A hollowed-out storefront with low wooden benches at angles next to tables, people and noise and the Sai River flowing past the open frontage. There is no training today, and he wants to cross "Friendship Bridge," the hundred-foot cement slab separating Thailand from Burma, at Mae Sai. From his seat at the open window, he can see robed villagers straggling across the bridge in both directions, on bicycles, Enduros, two legs, with the brown rush of the Sai gurgling below. A blue, hand-painted *You Are Now Entering the Republic of Myanmar* sign crowns the brick archway where Burmese border guards smoke and check passports and hawk spit into the river.

Don't waste your time, dude.

A man with a dirty blond ponytail creaks up a bench. Maybe forty, dingy khaki shorts and an Obie T-shirt.

Jinx—he holds out his hand and Stefan shakes it. *Where you from?*

Just now, Lanna Thai.

That ain't no Thai accent, dude.

Stefan laughs. *How about Baltimore?*

I'll buy that.

Jinx is a gemstone dealer out of Santa Monica, California, just now doing some work with the Gemological Institute of America.

Nothing to see across that border, man, except what they want you to see.

Stefan looks out onto the dreary high street. A collection of flimsy gem-trading outposts and cut-rate jewelry stores. Bars, like this one, every hundred yards or so. Most without names or signage. A few crates of beer and some nuts and a few bottles of Mekong cane liqueur. He might as well pop over into Burma—Myanmar, whatever the fuck they're calling it—seeing as how he is so close.

Tourist trap. Jinx wags his head. *Used to call this road—here all the way to Sub-Soi, a few clicks east—"the trail of tears." When war broke out, it was all the hill people got fucked the worst.*

They sit in silence for a bit, just watching the market circus outside the bar. The inevitable question, *What the hell are you doing here?* Jinx digging the edited version of Stefan's history, remarking, *You gotta meet this guy, hang on, you're gonna love this guy,* getting up from the table and disappearing for a good ten minutes before coming back with another guy, late forties, hair buzzed past his bald spots, *Stefan, meet my buddy Barry—Barry, you gotta talk to this guy, he's a trip.*

Barry Heffernan is the U.S. consul for northern Thailand. He runs a gemstone business. He'd been a pilot during the secret bombing campaigns over Laos, had stayed after the U.S. pulled out, married a Thai, had a son, assimilated into Thai life. Didn't even speak English in his own home. They order another round of Singhas. Stefan sees a Karen tribeswoman, long white gown stitched with ocher trim, pushing a bicycle laden with silver-beaded jewelry. Transfixed, he goes silent in the midst of all the bullshit small talk.

Whoa, where'd you go? Barry says, snapping his fingers.

Stefan racks focus back to the other men. *I saw people like that— like that woman, that one, with the bike—when I was in South America.*

When was that? Barry asks. *I was there in the early eighties, fucking hairy. People getting disappeared all the time.*

I was there after. But up in the hills, there were still all these people caught in the middle of that shit, just cut off, or used as pawns.

He tells them about the Arhuaco Indians, and his time in the Sierra Nevada. Brown, indigenous people living high in the mountains, left behind by the forces of politics and modernization. He doesn't drink much, and the beer bubbles some of his past to the surface. He recounts the first time he saw a man die, on the banana boat on the Amazon, at the hands of the Brazilian police, and Barry and Jinx sit slack-jawed.

Jesus, what were you doing there, you were just a fucking kid, alone on the Amazon? I know spooks—goddamned CIA—who wouldn't ride that river alone.

Stefan leans in, spurred on, goddamn it's been a while since he's spoken English to anyone, even longer since he's been able to unload. *It wasn't Plan A.* He laughs. *It started out as a lark, but then we got to do some other stuff.*

Like? Barry asks.

Help out a bit. Really basic shit, like treating kids for infections. A lot of times these village populations get encroached upon, people wind up living so close to animals that infections exist where none did before. They used to shit two hundred meters downstream, but now downstream's controlled by the government, or guerrillas, so they're jammed into a smaller environment. . . . They shit right at the source, where their animals bathe, or where they get drinking water. Kids always get sickest, they break your heart. Kid doesn't know why he's sick, or what a doctor is—outside of some village quacks who dance, and chant, or rub beetle shells on him and hope his dysentery goes away. He upends the rest of his beer. *Free elections, clean water, and antibiotics could save half the Third World. Shit, two thirds. Easy.*

Jinx nods solemnly. *Kudos, my man. Good for you.*

Stefan shrugs off the compliment. Stares into the dregs at the bottom of his bottle. The men press him for more stories but just now he can't muster the spirit to talk about himself. He can't even meet their eyes. Barry and Jinx stare awkwardly at each other.

Finally, Jinx leans in, asks, *Hey, man—you know anything about gems?*

Stefan deflects. *Used to be kind of an amateur collector . . . just the cheap stuff . . . for fun.*

Barry yells for three more beers in Thai. *Listen,* he says, *I used to buy rubies from the mujahideen, back in the eighties, they'd use the money to fight the Russians, you know? Now that bridge they have there, I can cross there, buy rubies, okay ones, too, come back, sell them, no problem.*

But, Jinx leans in, Barry interrupting him—

—that money goes to the Burmese.

And? Stefan shifts in his seat.

And, Barry says, *there's people who could use the money more.*

You know how to ride a bike? Jinx asks.

———

Eight days after that.

The Yamaha DT250R Enduro's forks bottom out as he sinks into a hole in the riverbed. He stands on the pegs and gives it throttle, the bike lurching forward in a spray of mud, fishtailing a bit but staying rubber side down. This part of the Mae Sai River, about a half click below the Takileich crossing, is rough and fast but not very deep. He roars up the embankment on the Burmese side and disappears into the tree line. After the initial thicket of trees lining the edge of the river, the forest gives way to slashed and burned fields. The Karen hill people deforest the jungle: they need the open space for their pigs, water buffalo, chickens, the animals lumbering and basking in the mud, their owners above them in stilted bamboo shacks. People shouldn't live this close to livestock. Maybe that's why he has dengue fever. He kills the engine and lets the bike fall over onto the mud, too weak to put the kickstand down. A wiry Karen woman, neck extended by a stack of gold hoops, calls out to her husband, brown and tattooed, wearing floppy army fatigues and a tidy Hitler mustache.

Stefan unhooks the bungee cord holding the rucksack on the rear of the bike and leans back against one of the stilts holding the house aloft. The world swims. A group of women in a dirt plot between the houses, hunched over hand looms or grinding spices in wooden mortars, shimmy out of focus. He can barely keep from gagging. The smell of pig shit is overwhelming and his fever makes him shake. The man with the Hitler mustache squats next to him and unfolds a cloth square filled with rubies. Rose and light purple—the size of pinky toenails—the stones are high-quality.

He opens his rucksack and hands Hitler a bulging plastic sandwich bag of bhat. Thai currency worth more than Burmese, even in Burma. Hitler shakes his hand and walks off, counting the money. Stefan waves some of the kids darting in and out of the animal pens over to him. He fishes another bag from the sack and huddles over it so they can't see what it is. They hide behind stilts and stare blankly at him or giggle. A few of the older ones come over first, and he bug-eyes them, Bill Cosby–style, until they creep closer. Soon, he's swarmed by brown children, moon-faced and muddy, dying for a peek into the bag.

He pulls out a Jamaica Sac lollipop or a sugared tamarind nugget and holds it up, and if the kids look healthy, he gives it to them. If the kids look sick—plenty of them do, runny eyes rimmed red from dehydration—he makes them down a Cipro he's got mixed in with the candies, making sure they wash it down with the Pepsi or Fanta he's packed in the rucksack, and then, when they've wiggled their tongues for him, he gives them the candy. This is how he spends his days now.

Since his knee started acting up again, he's had to ease up on the training. He'd started traveling with the school to different villages and fighting the locals, but some fifteen-year-old kid had cracked him on the side of his patella with a rocket of a kick in the middle of a fight. He'd just started winning a few bouts, too. Lanna Thai's owner let him stay and train for free if he took local bouts. He was a good draw—big black American—never went down easy.

But his knee has been whingeing these last few days, so he'd taken up Barry and Jinx's offer. He knows they think he's just some hard-case who needs a few bucks, but he's not doing it for the money. He spends everything they give him on antibiotic blister packs and candy he buys from the pharmacy on Huay Kaew road.

He'd appreciated the symbolism of cleaning the wat every day, but he wanted his amends to be *active*. His first instinct had been to say no. The mention of gems and smuggling caused his hands to shake—but what Barry and Jinx were doing wasn't immoral.

And the stones from the Gib had given him an advanced education in gemology—he knew now how to spot flaws, figure carats. Even though he'd resolved never to sell the stones, he'd studied them often. Once he'd even taken a few of them to the luxe Fred Boutique in Monaco, under the pretense of comparing different setting options. He'd taken a friend of his along, an international pop star—who happened to be a black American from Maryland, as well—he'd met on the beach. The jeweler had just assumed Stefan was another wealthy playboy. The woman behind the counter bent over the gems with Stefan and showed him how to use a loupe, and he'd scoured the nascent Internet to round out his knowledge. He couldn't get a job at Chopard, but he knew more than the average Kay Jewelers employee.

He'd never studied the geology behind it, though. The villagers took him into the mountains and showed him the veins that run parallel to the waterfalls and the Sai, showed him how they dug and sifted and mined. He'd learned that precious elements are often found together: where there is gold, there is often silver. Where there are diamonds—rubies and sapphires are usually close at hand.

Burmese rubies were better quality than Thai rubies. SLORC now had the villagers on their side of the border—who'd mined and farmed on a subsistence level over the last eight or nine hundred years—under their brutal, repressive control. And SLORC wanted its cut.

Barry and Jinx were gonna get their gems anyway, so Stefan figured he might as well rig the game in favor of the Karen. He's on the right side in this fight. A hill tribe against a nation's military? Not a difficult choice for him.

The last of the kids gets dosed and Stefan looks over, where one of them is squatting under the house, loosing a stream of diarrhea. He'll never have a bag of meds big enough to make a difference. His heart sinks. Maybe his spotty antibiotic runs are as symbolic as his scrubbing the glass of the wat.

It's getting dark. He can't stay here. First Lady of the United States Hillary Clinton is visiting the region in three days and security along the border is ramping up. He's not supposed to be in Burma, and he's damn sure not supposed to be buying gems from the Karen without SLORC knowing about it.

He can barely lift his bike, and some of the men rush over as it slides in the mud. He thanks them and kick-starts it and feathers the clutch until he's down the hill. It's hard keeping the front tire between the trees he's got the shakes so bad.

But. He's on a motorcycle in the middle of the jungle, running medicine to an endangered population. In the middle of a civil war. A junkie is a junkie is a junkie. The best he can do is manage his addiction. He thinks of the diarrheic kid and the bag of meds that would never be enough. He knows what he has to do.

XI

STRANGE FRUIT

I n the spring of 1997, he'd come back to the U.S. after twelve years away. He'd returned from Thailand determined to follow a nobler path, but it wasn't easy. The time away from Dana had clotted over the rawness of his love for her. Their love had been wild, free. But reckless abandon—in his mind—had been the cause of every bad choice he'd ever made. Penance was about deprivation: ignoring the basest, basic impulses he'd always indulged. He had begun a family with Liv, and the honorable, responsible thing to do was to see that through. He ended things with Dana. It had not been messy. She was at a different place in her life than he was. Stefan came with the baggage of a family. And the spectre of violence and unpredictability seemed to cling to him and his life. A lot for a twenty-three-year-old girl to sign on for. She was unfettered, and had lots of the world left to explore. With or without him.

He and Liv decided to work things out. By then, the Boyesen

Institute had foundered, and there were no employment prospects for him on the Continent. He also wanted to make sure Mai-Sunniva got dual citizenship. Lack of work visas had hampered him his whole adult life and he wanted her to have a geographic mobility he'd never enjoyed. Liv was ambivalent about the move. She was a small-town girl who'd spent her youth traipsing across Europe at Stefan's whim. After his extended and frank betrayal, it was a difficult decision. But the promise of more opportunity for herself and her daughter tipped the scales in favor of America.

Stefan stayed on a friend's couch in D.C. for a month while he looked for a job. Initially, the only job he could find was as a telemarketer, but it was enough to secure a $500-per-month apartment at 3000 Connecticut Avenue, right across from the National Zoo. Liv and Mai-Sunniva followed.

At first, the couple was busy navigating their new environs, and it took a while for the rifts to show. Mai-Sunniva acted out, her anger at Stefan's long absence manifested in temper tantrums and asthma attacks. Liv traveled back and forth to London and continued her Biodynamic Therapy studies that first year—which consisted of, by then, assisting Ebba and Gerda—while Stefan chafed at his new job. He'd never sat behind a desk, and the smallness of fluorescent lights and Quiznos lunches made him want to put a bullet through the back of his skull.

America, he quickly discovered, was every bit as boring as he'd remembered. The national news was full of people screeching about the president having gotten a blow job. For fuck's sake—in Europe, mistresses were practically cabinet positions. And everybody was so *fat*. He'd been in the best shape of his life in Southeast Asia, but barely a year later, excess layers clung to him.

Always an early adopter of technology, he thought he saw a

niche market in the burgeoning world of the Internet. He collaborated on an online start-up with some new friends in the Adams Morgan neighborhood down the street. They would develop a kind of Web-based resource for people searching for experts within a given field. Businesses would pay to have a listing—best doily knitter, or geologist, etc.—on their site. It was a typical dot-com era hustle, a pan-for-gold on the Information Superhighway. But with no college degree, résumé, or work experience that didn't make him sound like the Man from U.N.C.L.E., he had to make his own way.

The Web site was called Yearbook. When it launched, in the winter of 1998, the site had so little content he'd listed himself as one of the clients—as an "Adventure Travel Expert." He'd traveled. He'd had adventures. Fuck it.

Life was hand-to-mouth. Once or twice there was an eviction notice posted to their door. He'd go down to the rental office and charm Eunice, the thirty-something black lady, into giving him a few more days. Somehow, he always made rent.

But poverty and his new, sluggish routine were a lethal combination. He was miserable.

Then the phone rang.

Is this Randall Templeton, the adventure travel expert? Stefan said yes, and the voice continued, *I got a plane, loaded with medical equipment, about to fly out of Key West into Honduras—I guess you know what's going on down there?*

Stefan knew. The whole world knew. By October 29, Hurricane Mitch had crashed into Honduras with winds exceeding 150 miles per hour. Honduras, Nicaragua, and huge swaths of South and Central America were flooded. Thousands were dead.

I looked at your thing here on the net and I need a partner to fly out with me, distribute medical equipment, and I don't know, what the hell, I thought I'd give you a call, see if you'd be interested in partnering up, the voice drawled.

Rodger Harrison was the avuncular founder of a nonprofit organization called Paramedics for Children. Rodger and PFC worked on a shoestring budget, providing medical care for villagers in Central America, and as soon as Mitch hit, he'd set about getting supplies out to the disaster zone. He'd been trolling the Internet for hours looking for qualified volunteers when he'd seen Stefan's listing.

Stefan was happy to be held to the promise he'd made to himself back in Thailand. There were 10,000 people already dead in Honduras and 100,000 displaced. He immediately agreed to meet Rodger in Charlotte, North Carolina. He packed his compass, his Merck manual from his days among the Arhuacos, and his old boots from AIDP and spent money he didn't have on a Greyhound bus ticket.

When he got off the bus six hours later in Charlotte, Rodger was in the terminal waiting for him, a big smile under his floppy hat and grey hair.

You came, he said, grinning, pumping his fist. *I can't believe it.*

I said I'd come, Stefan said.

They drove a rickety old ambulance from Charlotte to Key West, and talked the whole way. Stefan was in awe of Rodger, a guy with a heart that seemed too big for this world, a man who'd retired after a career as a medic and devoted his middle age to villagers in Central America. This was that *thing* he'd hoped to accomplish back in Thailand. Adventure, plus helping people on a large scale. He hadn't been this nervous or amped about anything since the jobs back in Scandinavia. But this was different. Rodger was no Mike or José Luis, and the mission wasn't about gems or booze or hashish. Stakes were real.

Rodger told him that they'd be on a beat-to-shit DC-9 transport. He screwed up his lips as he told him that he had to level with him, one just like it had already crashed the day before en route to the disaster zone.

The DC-9 flew into San Pedro Sula, northern Honduras, an old Cuban pilot at the wheel and pallets of medicine rattling in the cargo hold. The landing strip was so battered by the storm that the nose dipped into the mud, the tail shimmied and spun, and for a couple of seconds they looked like they were breaking up, but the leathery Cuban righted the ship at the edge of the landing strip.

San Pedro Sula, like most of the coastline, had been flattened into a muddy pitch. The landing area was a military airstrip, teeming with U.S. Army Corps of Engineers, Humvees, and the Honduran military.

Their flight was low priority among all the military machinery. Rodger and Stefan needed to get their supplies off-loaded and into the field—an impossibility without a forklift. After a futile attempt trying to rally the Honduran military guys into getting some machinery to the plane, Stefan walked over to the Corps of Engineers and asked to talk to the commanding officer. A big black guy in his fifties—a master sergeant—came over.

The sergeant told him he'd seen him trying to get the Hondurans' shit together and that it was *Good to see a brother out here taking charge.*

When the sergeant asked where he was from, and Stefan answered Baltimore, the sergeant beamed and said he was from Cherry Hill. Stefan told him how he'd been a lifeguard at the Cherry Hill community pool for a few weeks back in '85. Small goddamn world. The sergeant recognized the name Templeton from the Baltimore City school named after his grandfather Furman, and whistled for the forklift operators to *Get on over here and help this young brother out*.

Rodger and Stefan managed to wangle an old Russian UAZ-469 jeep from the Hondurans, a real beast, and they slogged through the mud into villages handing out food and electrolytes and medicine to the displaced locals. There were a lot of kids, stranded and homeless, and bodies half buried in the mud along the La Ceiba riverbed.

They walked through them and over them and sometimes they saw kids straining to flip the corpses stuck in the mud, looking for parents or brothers and sisters and they knew that in the heat and this far out that the kids would be next, some of them would be dead soon, too, there was no way to save them. Sometimes Stefan would look over and see Rodger crying.

He was getting an education in the realities of large-scale disaster management. He'd assumed that there were finely tuned international response mechanisms that sprang into action in times of crisis, but that wasn't the case. Instead, there were huge, lumbering enterprises that had a hard time getting supplies to the people who needed it, bullshit red tape, situational unawareness, and a crippling lack of communication. It was dispiriting *and* energizing: he figured that if *he* could see the inefficiency—with little formal training—then solutions couldn't be that hard to come by.

After two weeks in the field, he finally knew what he wanted to be when he grew up. He knuckled down and began doing interpreting work as a way to pay the bills, while taking disaster management courses at the American University, Johns Hopkins, and Switzerland's University of Neuchâtel. Whatever happened, he would be *ready,* not just jonesing.

In the summer of '99, Liv went to Norway, and left Stefan and Mai-Sunniva to their own devices, in the two-bedroom condo they were now renting in Adams Morgan. No one—least of all Liv— was surprised by what happened next.

Around the corner, on Adams Morgan's Eighteenth Street, was a semibohemian café-lounge—aptly named Tryst—where Stefan saw a gorgeous young Russian girl working the floor. She noticed Stefan, too, the big American always hunched over his laptop. Sometimes a little girl, with sandy hair and butterscotch cheeks, fidgeted by his side, or mad-dashed between the low-slung vintage couches and kitsch on a scone- and soda-pop-fueled bender. The waitress noticed, too, that Stefan and the manager—a Japanese woman named Keiko—were chums, quipping back and forth in Japanese. But still, the waitress and Stefan never spoke. The timing was invariably off, but no matter what else he had going on, he made a point of smiling at her a few seconds past appropriate.

Elena Sotnikova was from a picturesque town in southern Russia—Pyatigorsk—at the foot of the Caucasus, lodged between the Caspian and Black seas. Her mother had been a professor of linguistics at Pyatigorsk State Linguistics University, so she'd been fluent in English from an early age. After two years at PSLU, Elena got a student visa to travel to the States, where she hoped to finish her college education. She'd been to the U.S. once before, when she was fifteen, and had made some friends in Virginia. These friends had helped her secure a job as a nanny, to a family outside Houston, which in turn would help her get a student visa. She'd been in D.C. all summer, saving money and dating and getting ready for her new life, when Stefan came up to her one sweltering August afternoon and asked her if she felt okay. She was rubbing her temples and leaning back on the couch. Monster headache. Stefan knelt across from her in a reclaimed armchair and told her to give him her arm. He told her he'd learned some shiatsu while living in Tokyo and he pressed a spot on her forearm he said was a pressure point for headaches and told stories about the Yakuza and the neon craziness of Roppongi. After a few minutes of his burrowing his thumb into her arm, he said, *It's working, yes?* And she nodded yes, even though now all she had was a sore arm to go along with her headache. But the stories were fascinating. She wanted to hear everything.

Told you it would work, he said, and asked her to come to his house for dinner the following night. He would cook. His daughter would chaperone.

You can't cook, she said.

You're Russian—you'll never know, he said with a laugh.

She came for dinner the next night. Three days before she was supposed to leave for Conroe, Texas. She stayed each of those days with Stefan and Mai-Sunniva. After she left, they spoke every day. Separation was unbearable.

You have to come back here. I miss you. Mai misses you.

But I can't stay if I'm not in school.

So we'll get you in school.

In October, after seven weeks apart, Stefan arranged for her to meet with the admissions people at Montgomery County College, in the D.C. exurbs, and she was accepted for the spring semester, her student visa intact.

He and Liv were cold ashes in the fire—had been for a while—but nobody'd broached it. Liv was only in the States because *he* was. Because *he'd* moved the family. Liv returned in December, and she and Stefan were forced to confront the end of their relationship. Liv was furious, mostly at what she deemed the loss of her youth, nights and days and months spent waiting, raising their child, while Stefan traveled far, wide, loose.

But Stefan would not be moved from Elena. Anguished from the hurt he was causing Liv and Mai-Sunniva, he pulled Elena aside and told her, *Find someone younger, without all this bullshit, someone you can start fresh with.*

When she ignored his request, he wept, far from her sight. He'd never been happier.

Elena's immigration status—a J-1 student visa—was only good for one year. In December of 2000, she had to leave the country. She returned to Pyatigorsk, to finish the last year of her linguistics degree. Stefan visited a few times over the next six months, but they needed a base somewhere closer to him. Ebba had friends in Buenos Aires, in the upscale San Ysidro neighborhood, and they had space. At the end of the spring semester, Elena packed up and moved for the summer.

It was cheaper and easier to get to than Russia. Stefan visited Elena three times during an intense eight-month period. On December 1, he came for a six-week visit. On January 2, they were married. Unknown to her, she was three weeks pregnant.

That month, she moved back to Russia, determined to get her degree, and waddled through her final semester alone. One month shy of her due date, Stefan returned to Russia and brought Elena to Paris, where, once again, Ebba had friends who agreed to let the couple crash in a spare room while they waited for their baby. If he couldn't bring his bride to America, then his baby would be born in Europe. No way did he trust the Russian hospital system.

On August 31, 2002, Stormy-Ilios Templeton was born in Paris's Pitié-Salpêtrière hospital. The boy's name came from the *Iliad*— Ilios is the male form of Iliad—and Stefan's tenuous thematic connect-the-dots of Paris's rescue of Helen from a storm, which Stefan had extrapolated to mean that Elena (Helen) had been sent to Paris (the city) as a rescue from the "Storm" of their lives. But he really just thought the name sounded cool and exotic, and his boy would no doubt fulfill the promise of a name so awesomely imperious, kind of like how girls named Jasmine usually wound up being hot.

Elena became just as enamored of Europe as she had been of the States. And Stefan hadn't seen much of his mother since the mid-1990s, when he'd left Monaco. So he and Elena decided to stay. No reason not to. The translating work was a treadmill to nowhere. He had completed several disaster management courses, and had even volunteered for some NGOs, but found the system relatively closed. They favored young, untethered idealists with ink-wet degrees. He had plenty of time in the field, and lots of theory and official accreditation to back it up, but taking off for months at a time with a wife and two kids to support was a luxury he couldn't afford. Mai-Sunniva was content in school, Liv had married a D.C. boy Stefan had introduced her to, and there was nothing keeping him from showing Elena and Stormy the Continent. Ebba set them up at her place, in Elmshorn, Germany, from the fall of 2002 until the summer of 2004. The usual problems of visas and employment abroad hounded him, and, totally broke, they decided the best bet for their new family was back in D.C. At least he could get some work translating, and as his wife, Elena, was now an American citizen, free to make her own way, too.

Upon his return, his primary income was doing translation work for D.C. law firms, notably for Chile's prosecution case against Augusto Pinochet. But his passion still lay firmly in the world of disaster management. Hurricane Mitch and Honduras were never far from his mind. The classes and certifications he'd gotten in D.C.—in water sanitation for large populations, hydrology, and disease containment—provided a larger context, an insight into the bureaucracy of the aid world. He hadn't had cause or opportunity to put any of it to use, though. It was back to the grind.

But the earth was as restless and discontented with stability as he was.

When the tsunami slammed into Southeast Asia, on December 26, 2004, he was visiting Ebba, in Elmshorn, for Christmas, after dropping Mai-Sunniva off at Liv's parents' house in Norway. The day the storm broke, Ebba was in the kitchen, breaking boiled potatoes into fish soup, the windows steamed, a loaf of black bread laid out on the counter. The TV in the living room interrupted its programming. Mother and son sat glued to the screen for hours. It was the second biggest tsunami ever recorded. Hundreds of thousands were dead.

Two days later, the aunt of one of Stormy's playmates from D.C. called. Soren, her nephew, had been on holiday with his parents on the island of Koh Phangan, Thailand. Soren's parents were fine. They'd been running to higher ground when the wave hit, Soren between their hands, and the wave came and they looked down and he'd been washed away.

The Thai government had posted digital pictures of the dead on a Web site, but neither the parents nor the aunt had the stomach to scroll through the ever expanding roster of corpses. Stefan knew Soren by sight. And he had experience with natural disasters. They'd called him first.

The digital images were obscenely resolute. Swollen muddy faces. Corpses grouped by age. Stefan had clicked numbly past the faces of hundreds of dead children. Next to the computer screen was a picture of Stormy that Ebba had taken when he was a few months old, on his back wiggling his fingers and toes up at the camera. Stefan turned for a minute, had wanted to linger on the picture of his boy before going back to the pictures, but the bodies on the screen burned into his eyes, and the images fused into one. His baby, all gums and smiles, millimeters away from lost children staring through milky eyes up at him. Too close. Too much.

He hadn't found Soren in that first batch of photos.

He couldn't stomach more than a few hours of the chore and had taken a walk to clear his head when a name popped into his head. He returned to Ebba's house and punched the name Ihab Ishtawi into Lycos. Ihab was rich. Ihab was a friend of a friend, working at the London School of Economics—the son of an Arabian oil baron—a pretty nice guy from what Stefan could remember. It had been a one-in-a-million shot, but he'd racked his brain for anybody with money *and* heart.

Hey man, you know for the price of that DB7 you roll in, you could send some paramedics down to help some of your Muslim brothers out.

Inshallah, done my man. Where do I wire the money?

The second person he'd thought of had been Rodger, and Paramedics for Children. He'd been so impressed with PFC during Hurricane Mitch, and Rodger had since expanded his organization into a coalition of two dozen EMTs from the United States and Canada. They usually focused on Central America, but Stefan knew they'd be able to hit the ground running if he could manage to get them into the South Asia theater.

Unfortunately, Stefan was an action guy, with no talent or patience for the logistics required to undertake a movement of people and supplies.

After that first phone call, when his buddy Ihab had pledged some money, Stefan had called around and gotten lots of *Sure, anything I can do to help.* An acquaintance had gotten him a hotel room at Indonesia's Medan Metro hotel. Another friend's father was Richard Ness: the president of Indonesia's largest mining concern, Newmont Mining. Ness pledged Stefan—and PFC—free accommodations. Connections and promises of aid snowballed with each phone call. Stefan vaguely remembered an Egyptian ambassador he'd met in D.C. The ambassador guaranteed flights for the PFC crew on Egypt Air. It was all coming together. Stefan called Rodger and told him, *Get the team together. I've got money for travel and accommodations for everyone. I'll fly in and scout the area, you guys join me as soon as you can.*

He packed a bag with combat boots he'd purchased at an Elmshorn army surplus store, bought a *Let's Go Southeast Asia,* and talked his way into a free ticket at the Lufthansa desk at Hamburg International Airport.

Eight days after the tsunami, Polonia International Airport in Medan, Indonesia, was overrun with aid workers, press, and military, the small terminal a sweat lodge filled to bursting. Stefan pushed his way into the registration line. The Indonesians had waived visas for humanitarian workers, but they were ball-busting the few Americans registering along the queue. Really going over their credentials and affiliations. The Iraq war had the Muslim country spooked.

Some Indonesian Armed Forces soldiers pulled a handful of men in short-sleeved Arrow shirts and North Face backpacks out of line and Stefan heard the word "FEMA" barked in a Texas twang, *Doesn't anybody speak English around here, we're trying to help you people for chrissakes.* Fucking hell . . . if they were rousting FEMA, there was no way they'd let him enter. He hadn't thought this through. He'd assumed that he could use PFC as a calling card, but the last he'd heard, there had been a problem with their travel arrangements and they were still stuck in the States.

The Indonesian army scrutinized the line of people in front of him for their accreditation. Then they started shouting at the group of aid workers. The men—maybe a dozen of them—shrugged and mugged back at the Indonesians in French.

Stefan edged in and started translating for the Frenchmen. Let them know which forms the Indonesians were asking them for, where to sign, and which line to stand in. The Indonesian soldiers grunted and moved down the line, assuming that Stefan was with the Frenchmen.

ELISA—Equipe Légère d'Intervention de Secours Aéroportée—was a light medical airborne tactical unit, a spinoff of France's GIGN—Groupe d'Intervention de la Gendarmerie Nationale—an antiterrorism unit. The ELISA crew of a dozen medics and surgeons had adapted their rapid deployment training for natural disasters, lending themselves to other nations' military units. They'd never been to Indonesia, and spoke only French. Stefan asked them if he could act as a security lookout. He told them of his training at AIDP, his disaster management and medic background, alluded to some military prowess, and they'd agreed to let him become a member of the team for the mission. It didn't hurt that he was bilingual. Right there at the airport, they gave him an ELISA laminate filled in with a Sharpie and he piggybacked their security clearances.

That night, Stefan checked into the Medan Metro hotel—a hovel for transients, decorated with an army cot, spiders bigger than the TV, chipped lead paint—and went through his makeshift kit. He Sharpie'd his vitals onto the inside of the collar of the orange jumper ELISA had given him. *NKAB+: No Known Allergies—Blood type B positive.* Just in case.

The only other stuff he'd managed to pack besides the *Let's Go Southeast Asia* and his boots was a massive bag of candy. He'd started taking candy with him ever since his medicine runs into Burma. As a stranger, a good way to get kids to feel at ease was by bearing candy. What was creepy in the First World was endearing in the Third.

He looked over some of the phrases in the back of the *Let's Go,* and tried to get some sleep. ELISA was deploying at dawn. He arose early to take the last hot shower he'd get for what might be weeks. Four minutes and a few gallons of tepid, rusted water later, he twisted the spigot and it came off in his hand. A jet of water shot from the wall into the closet-sized bathroom, soaking everything, flooding the room. He looked around for something to stop the flow, but there was only a squeegee the maids used to wipe the scum from the mirror. *Shit.* His friend had been nice enough to vouch for the room. Management would try to stick him with the damages, and all the guy had done was try to help Stefan out.

He raced to the other room, ripped open the bag of candy, and crammed half a dozen gumballs into his mouth, chewing like a camel until the wad was pliable. He jammed the rubbery clump into the geyser shooting from the wall, capped the plug with the ashtray on top of the toilet, wedged one end of the squeegee against the ashtray, the other against the door to the bathroom, and backed out of the room. The thing would hold five . . . maybe six minutes. Tops. He was into his clothes and in a cab to the Humanitarian Information Center at the Medan Novotel hotel, where ELISA was deploying, four minutes later.

ELISA only dropped into places most in need. That was a hundred kilometers west of the epicenter of the tsunami. Banda Aceh.

––––––––

Meulaboh, the western Sumatran capital of Aceh province, used to be a city. Now there is nothing left but a muddy pitch. The ocean, having done its worst, has receded offshore. The sheared foundations of houses are the only sign that anything has ever stood here.

Five hundred feet above what was once a beach, Stefan stares out at a mud field. The Black Hawk's blades ripple the mud, and the slop is dotted with the neon orange of a sarong, the reflective silver of a Diadora running shoe, the bright blue of a Hilfiger T-shirt. The bodies have started to swell, extruding the clothes to the surface. There are thousands of them.

The smell.

As soon as the rotors slow to a bass thump, the decay punches through. Sweet and gassy and intimately unfamiliar.

They extract their gear from the chopper. A hundred yards off he sees a cluster of U.S. Marines. Small recon units from the USS *Bonhomme Richard* and the USS *Abraham Lincoln,* both anchored a mile out to sea. The marines can't come more than a mile inland, and they can't carry any weaponry. The Indonesians hate the U.S., global disaster or no.

Stefan edges up. Waits for a chance to introduce himself. Colonel Tom Greenwood from the 15th Marine Expeditionary Unit beats him to it, asks who he is. Stefan shows him his flight clearances from the Singaporean military, then asks if the 15th can get him and his crew farther into the disaster zone.

Where's the most damage? he asks, and Colonel Greenwood

thinks for a minute. The question is relative in a land where nothing is left standing.

Well son, we've seen Calang . . . doubt if anyone's left alive there, but if you want, we can move your unit in.

The marine Black Hawk swoops in from the *Bonhomme Richard* and drops the ELISA crew into Calang Aceh, the hardest-hit area in Southeast Asia, forty-five minutes after the crew has landed in Meulaboh.

The earth has been churned for miles inland. There are almost no geographic reference points. A mosque, ornate and defiant and incongruous in the muck, unscathed. A snaking line of survivors dots the beach up to the water's edge, where the Indonesians hand out food and water from World War II–era amphibious units. Indonesian soldiers patrol the beach, M-16s slanted in front of their chests.

The force of the wave has bent palm trees parallel into the mud. An arm juts from the soup, hand curled into a static wave. Thousands and thousands and thousands of bodies. Swollen, purple and brown, to bursting. It is over ninety degrees. In the wake of the tsunami, weather has stood still. The ocean mocking them now, waveless and calm. A child napping peacefully after a tantrum.

A Land Rover—"Sporty Motor Sports" decal affixed to its door—fishtails up to them. It's packed with Indonesian military. They tell the ELISA group that they must present themselves to the command post before they will be allowed to provide any aid. An ELISA doctor, a middle-aged surgeon named Stephane Grandame, asks Stefan if it's a trap. The Indonesians distrust Westerners. Stefan doesn't know. Either way, they have to go. It's forty-eight hours before the marines are coming back for them, and the marines don't have guns. These soldiers do.

They drive to the command post, two hundred meters west on the beach, where a military tent city has been hastily assembled. At the gate entry, a young soldier mans a tripod mounted with a .50 caliber machine gun.

Since 1976, Banda Aceh has been embroiled in a civil war, as separatist guerrillas have attempted to claim the area as part of Sumatra, rather than Indonesia. There has been sporadic fighting, even after the wave hit. Next to the guard is a stake, with a human head on it. War doesn't stop for natural disasters, and the Indonesians want any locals with dreams of independence to know they're still running things.

Stefan and the ELISA crew file past the sentry. Planks of wood stretch over a drainage ditch of water. As he crosses the ditch, he makes a mistake. Looks down. Dozens of bodies suspended there, men and women and kids staring up at him through fixed dead eyes.

Inside the command tent, a tiny Indonesian general sniffs over their credentials. *What is an American doing with so many Frenchmen?* he asks.

I'm not here as an American, just here to help.

The general squints. Look on his face suggests he can't decide if Stefan is full of shit. Advises the team that they'll berth in the tent next to his, along with the Indonesian army's 505th Amphibious Unit. It's too late for rescue operations so they'll have to start in the morning.

As the other members trail out of the command tent, the general pulls him aside. Winks and asks him to ask the Americans if they've heard anything about GAM—the Free Aceh Movement—forces in the area. Stefan says there's no way he'd have access to that kind of information and the general winks again and says, *That's what you CIA fellows always say.*

The ninth day after the tsunami, he walks the perimeter of the beach at Banda Aceh and crests a hill and there's a tall man with copper hair and a beard and hiking boots and a blue T-shirt that reads "German Emergency Medical Doctors." The man looks up, but doesn't seem to notice him. He's sitting on an overturned piece of driftwood, eyes red, drifts of mucus streaming from his nose. Stefan squats next to him, the man focusing now. *You're too late. We're all too late. Go home.* The man rises unsteadily, sits back down. Rises again. *Go home, go home. It's too late.*

The only people who'd survived the tsunami were the ones who knew what it meant when the sea retracted. They'd run for higher ground. But unless you knew that the sea's departure meant that it was going to return with a vengeance, you stayed and marveled at the ebb and the calm and died.

The villagers out in their fishing boats had been safe. The energy of a tsunami is compressed: out at sea it's harmless. The energy increases proportionate to the shoreline, forward and upward. He has been here three days. He understands the doctor's sense of futility, but resists the temptation. There's too much to do here to leave. Just pick a place and start and don't think too much about it. Like scrubbing the wat, his penance years earlier in Chiang Mai: each glass tile on the wat must be scrubbed. Look at it as a whole and you'll never finish. Start with one. Keep going.

Since the Indonesian general is convinced that he's CIA, he exploits the man's insecurities. Asks him to let him use the satellite phone to reach the *Bonhomme Richard.* The general is happy to oblige. While the Indonesians hate the U.S. military and government, they fear the CIA. Stefan tells Colonel Greenwood to forget about the extraction. No need to send that Black Hawk today at the end of their forty-eight-hour mission. They're staying awhile. It is January 5, 2005. He has been a member of the ELISA team for less than a week.

———

Two weeks after the wave. There are already scores of children with dysentery. Three kids—two five-year-old girls and an eleven-year-old boy—have lockjaw. The children's parents are dead: the kids were that much faster clawing up the hill away from shore, their parents sucked behind them in the maw.

The children need to be airlifted out before they slip into comas. The girls are worse off than the boy. Their throats have begun to close, and they haven't been able to speak enough to give their names. He calls one of them Honey, and the other Pie. Honey has already started convulsing, twisting into a rictus and gasping for air between panicked breaths, the air whistling between the space where she's lost her front baby tooth. He sticks his forefinger in her mouth to keep an airflow going until she passes out. Pie has a blistering fever, 102 and rising, and before long her spasms will start. Without help, Honey will die first, Pie next, some others soon after.

He doesn't speak Indonesian, but he fumbles through some phrases in the back of the *Let's Go*. Tells the IAF he needs a medevac helo. They seem to understand. They point and gesture and mime that a battleship a half mile out to sea is going to Meulaboh, where the marines are stationed. The ship can take him, and he can arrange for the Americans to fly him back with a helicopter to medevac the children. They tell him the trip to get the chopper will take *three hours*. It's longer than he'd like but better than nothing.

On the battleship, two nautical kilometers out to sea, he thanks the captain for letting him hitch a ride. The captain speaks English a bit better than the soldiers on the beach. Enough to correct Stefan's misunderstanding regarding the three hours the trip would take: three *days* was what the soldiers had meant to convey. The landing vessel is a dot heading back to the beach now. The captain has no way to contact them to get them back. Three days from now the kids will be dead. Stefan cinches his backpack around his waist. Climbs the bow. Dives into the ocean. He closes the distance from the ship to the shore in an hour, wangles the sat-phone from the general for "official CIA business," and calls in a medevac. Honey and Pie are helo'd to Meulaboh dawn of the next day. They get to live.

The days bleed into each other. A family four kilometers inland, house still standing, drowned in their beds—on the *second* floor. Endless burial parties. Tens of thousands of body bags arrive and do not go to waste.

The earth isn't done: an aftershock hits and Dr. Grandame, his tent mate, is tossed from his cot onto the floor, so bone tired he doesn't even get up, just lies there in the mud until Stefan carries him back to bed.

Each day it begins again. The back three pages of his *Let's Go* are the only blank paper he has to plan the day's operations:

17/01/05: 0730: call in Medevac. 2 mos old girl. Abscess on right side near carotid—stable but dehydrated, lose if not transported.

0830: Burial party. Disinfect party after.

0900: get WFP the 30 ton ferry; get jet fuel; see Coxswain.

0930: tetanus vaccination for kids. Make sure to dab kids already vaccinated with red nail polish to confirm.

1100: deploy to IDP camp across bay to vaccinate/tetanus. Need Zodiac/fuel/charts/gear.

1200: helo to Banda Aceh, French Military Consul.

1200 (if no helo): Brief US consul Paul Berry via Satphone.

He is getting frustrated. Few of the relief workers seem to know what the others are doing. The marines thought nobody had survived in Calang, but as soon as they'd gotten there, survivors had trickled in from the hills looking for food, water, and their dead. Even now, the U.N. has no consensus on how many IDPs—internally displaced people—there are. A shipment of rice has been sitting on a barge a mile offshore for two days. The World Food Program people don't know whom to clear a landing with.

Earlier, an ABC News Australia camera crew had asked him how the relief effort was going and he'd gotten so pissed at the bureaucracy of the aid machinery that he'd sneered, *If you ask me, the response has been inefficient . . . mind-bogglingly slow.*

Almost three weeks after the tsunami, the ELISA team has treated over three thousand survivors and helped bury almost that many. There's no electricity, no fuel, and aftershocks rattle the island every few hours. Forecasters say it's even money that there'll be another tsunami in the next week. The team's primary goal is to contain the spread of disease and gather the survivors before the fatalities multiply. They haven't spent much time away from the shoreline, where most of the victims were concentrated. On day eighteen after the tsunami, they load up on water and hike into Banda Aceh's interior. Not much relief has made its way inland.

The heat is nuclear. For the first part of the hike, there are no trees. They've been ripped from the earth, leaving a desert of mud.

The sweat pours off him. One foot in front of the other. He's been here before. The discipline. Muscles told to swim, push, punch, kick, against anything in their way. The training. From the crib. The sum of his parts that made no sense together. The warrior father and the healer mother and the beatings he'd caught until he'd been able to return the favor and the bad guy gone good because he'd never really been that good at being bad. All the things he could do—skills gone after or accidentally on purpose laid in his path—things other men couldn't do, or wouldn't do, and not a single thing in his life being possible without the thing that came before. A lot of those things he's tried to forget, washed away in a flood of guilt and some kind of penance. And these last few years. He'd studied. Waited to be needed. Cursed his life behind a desk back in D.C. Chomped at the bit to be part of something like this. But would give anything right now to be back there, behind that desk, for the villagers swelling the vinyl bags doused with lye to be back home, too. Thankful that he's able to do anything at all; miserable at the necessity.

Higher ground. Skin cooled now, the sun finally broken by trees the sea couldn't take away. He looks up, grateful for the shade, suddenly aware, as he's never been, that life's gifts are cursed with conditions. Gratitude for the relief from the heat turning to something else now: the leaves are not cooling him. There are no leaves. There is no shade here, no, it's the people he has come to help who block the sun, their bodies draped across the tops of the fronds, a human canopy deposited by the sea, the relief not sweet except for the smell. Maybe the German doctor was right: *Go home. We're all too late.*

Who does he think he is, some savior come to fight against nature? His whole life has been a fight against nature. He has lost as often as he has won. Maybe none of them, the living or the dead, able, in the end, to escape their fate, some washed away and some carried along.

A few more feet and he will signal for the crew to turn back. No point to this. For these last few feet, he won't look up. He can't. Not if he expects to make another step. A tune now, from somewhere deep and unbidden, the lyrics puckering his lips. Billie Holiday's "Strange Fruit" on his tongue, in his head, drowning out the slosh of their boots. At that tree up ahead, they will stop looking for survivors. There are none.

He stops at the tree and catches his breath. The others will catch up in a moment and he will shake his head and start the slog back to the beach at Banda Aceh. The song louder still—

. . . Here is a strange and bitter crop

—Lady Day and him and their blues.

Then. A few hundred yards past the tree line. Children. Six or seven of them, lips cracked, caked with mud, scrambling toward him. *Anda memiliki air?—You have water?* He waves the ELISA crew over. Races toward the kids, big dumb smile. Doesn't look up. Doesn't need to. Everything right in front of him now.

Yes, he says, in the half dozen words of Indonesian he knows, *I have water.*

EPILOGUE

Bullshit.

————————

I mean, c'mon. After he told me the whole story, I remembered why I'd never paid much attention to his adventures when we were kids. They were so outsized—so improbable—that my snarky defenses, my marrow-deep cynicism, had rebelled. People didn't do such things.

At the same time, on that winter night in 2007 when we'd reconnected after so many years apart, I was struck by the *way* he'd recounted his past. It was classic Stefan—served irony-free and with a heaping tablespoon of deadpan seriousness. He'd communicated the same way for the thirty years I'd known him. He ordered an espresso the same way he described blowing a safe. The man was incapable of flourish. I *knew* there was no way his tales were true, but he'd never been much of a talker, and even less of a story-teller. The guy didn't read fiction and couldn't tell a joke. I couldn't reconcile the—what had to be—overblown whoppers I'd just heard, with the reticence he'd always shown in personal dealings.

Fifth grade, Baltimore School 66. Show-and-tell in Mrs. Jones's English class. Stefan had neglected to prepare anything. Mrs. Jones said to him, *I understand you do karate, Stefan . . . why don't you show us something?*

Stefan rose, said, *But there's no need,* and sat down.

The guy was not interested in impressing anybody—he already thought he was a bad motherfucker and the opinion of his small-town peers didn't mean shit to him.

Still, I was left, after hearing these stories, with the gut assumption that Stefan had probably fluffed up marginal adventures into something larger. I'd never known him to lie, but we'd been apart a long time. Maybe his life hadn't turned out as he'd hoped. Maybe the opinion of his boyhood chum meant more to him than the truth.

I determined to find out what had really happened to him during those years. I recognized that my relationship with him made me a suspect purveyor of information. So I erred on the side of skepticism. I'm not proud to admit, I half viewed the undertaking as a potentially heartbreaking unmasking. Of him. Our friendship. The long shadow his presence had cast upon my youth.

He was reluctant to let me write any of this. This was a guy who'd spent half his life staying off the radar. *Not* leaving a trail. I didn't want to undo any of the recent foundation he'd laid as a di-saster management expert and humanitarian. But I felt that the story of a guy who'd gone from as low as he'd been, to a place in the world where he could make a difference, was an important one. The story was, in theme and literal scope, universal.

Yet strangely American. Americans love second chances. The trip from there to here, bad to good and back again. Here, a street hustler named Malcolm Little could go from petty hood to fiery moral icon, *Little* no more, past obliterated and redeemed and crossed out by the letter X. Here, a family fortune could be made bootlegging booze, and parlayed into public service and the Kennedys' Camelot. Stefan's story, though smaller and less grand in its reach, had some of that. I had to go where the story took me, knowing where it wound up.

There *was* the chance that I was heading into waters deeper than I'd anticipated. The stuff in those Pelican cases couldn't be bought at the corner store. Whatever I found out, I found out. But there were stakes beyond my desire to sniff out a good tale. He had responsibilities: a wife, two kids. People depended on him.

So I promised him that no matter what I discovered:

1) I would not get him arrested,
2) or divorced.

Researching the childhood stuff was easy. *I* was a primary source for much of it, and his recollections, along with his parents' and our former classmates', gave a pretty thorough accounting of his first eighteen years. The years he'd spent at the castle, and in France, I hadn't been privy to, so I journeyed there with him in the fall of 2007.

The fucking thing *was* a castle. Had everything but a moat. Suffice it to say that all those years I'd heard about the place—he'd undersold it. He'd left out the griffins, the oceans of marble, the postcard beauty. When we pulled into the grounds, the castle at Lugny was deserted and overrun with weeds. The building was still majestic, but gone to seed from years of neglect. The manager of the property—Philippe Deschamps—came out of the servants' house and asked us what we were doing. He remembered Stefan, and Ebba and Rene, and he allowed Stefan to take me on a tour.

Stefan nearly cried. The place was so dilapidated that it rusted over memories he'd held dear. He knew how lucky he was to have had teenage years spent in such a romantic location. Other kids of our generation had escaped via Dungeons and Dragons, but he'd had the real thing. Philippe and Stefan and I roamed the grounds for hours, until the light faded, recounting long-ago as well as recent Mâcon histories.

After Philippe had left, Stefan snuck us into Rene and Ebba's old living quarters across the road from the castle. Stefan hadn't been back there since 1981, when Rene kicked him out for spilling chocolate milk on one of the rugs. In what used to be Ebba and Rene's room, we found an old copy of *Lolita* in French, Ebba's name written on the inside flap. He pocketed it to give to his mother as a Christmas present.

Over the next few days, he took me to all the local haunts he'd frequented as a teenager: vineyards and caves and mountains. One midnight, he'd even made me stand in the midst of the Burgundian forest where he'd learned to conquer his fear of dark and solitude. I lasted five minutes.

I believed his stories about the castle. He knew too much about the place, and too much had been added and confirmed by Philippe and his mother and sisters for it to have been either the concoction of an imaginative young boy or the gilded memories of a middle-aged man. My own memory stepped in to validate this past as well:

his stories had not changed substantively since he'd relayed them—in a deadly dull monotone—to me nearly thirty years prior. But as I listened again, I heard something I'd missed on the tales' first tellings. The even pitch of his voice, and the uninflected passages hid something. *Pain.* The coolness tamped down the hurt, forced him to recount his past not as he'd wished it had been, but how it was. Part of that pain was tied up in our history, though I'd been too self-absorbed to notice it as a kid. His years away had been lonely. He had missed me.

In 1980, on his mother's last visit to him in America, he and Ebba had asked my father if I could spend the summer, and perhaps even attend school for a semester alongside him, in Burgundy. I was desperately afraid that the adventure would not come to pass, matched only by my fear that it would. My father was too poor to afford even the airfare, so I had stayed behind. Spared the adventure and the growth.

When I visited the castle on that day, decades later, and saw the vast expanse of the woods and the downright lonesome exile of the clock tower, where he'd roamed by himself as a boy, I was ashamed at having doubted his story, because I hadn't known how much my absence had affected him. And I had missed him, too. The *almost-ness* of our youth spent together in the French countryside, riding motorcycles across lush forests, playing Robin Hood, or French Resistance, torturous romances—salty, aching, and heartbreaking first kisses and maybe more—with Burgundian nymphs . . .

I had hidden my pain away, too, under a shell of cynicism, doubt, indifference. Easier to admit that the life every boy dreamt of never existed than to wallow in the small, bloodless life I lived.

Those years in Burgundy were easy to verify, though surprisingly hard to take. For both of us.

The period during Oxford and St. Selby's had plenty of documentation. Peter Reichhardt, Ricardo Alvarez, Juan Camilo, Wilfred Chilangwa, and Mathilde Tessier were all still alive. The story of the yobs on Banbury Road and the fight, still apocryphal. The Brazilian girl, Esme, even had a cool remembrance I couldn't fit into the story: when one of the yobs sucker-punched him from behind, Stefan had the imprint of the guy's sovereign ring branded in the back of his skull all semester. I also had his grade book—middling—and St. Selby's class pictures. The *Miami Vice* jacket really was hideous.

For the South American chapter, Peter and Juan and Ricardo were present, although Ricardo, as of this writing, is in jail in Colombia, for having ties to a paramilitary group. So take from that what you will.

And the Gib. For me, the Gib hinges on two things: the stones and Stefan's dive training. I'd just *seen* the stones back in his D.C. apartment. They were raw, and uncut, and as described. In and of itself, that proves nothing.

But, as it turned out, I'd seen the jewels once before.

In 1995, I'd been traveling through Europe, and had stopped for three days in Cap d'Ail, to visit Stefan. I hadn't seen him in a decade. When I asked him how he was making a living, he said he'd made some money shipping. Then he'd showed me a necklace he said his grandmother had given him. The necklace was a huge emerald surrounded by diamonds. Again, that proves nothing. Maybe it was a mass-produced bauble and not a stolen gemstone. You never know. I can't help but think he was trying to tell me what he'd become, even then. But he couldn't.

Then there's Stefan's training as a deep-sea diver. I went with him to Marseille, to AIDP. Stefan showed me the whole place. He knew where every piece of equipment was stored, where the bunks were, everything. We watched some of the divers come back from an exercise, and gabbed with some of them at the quay. I would not describe them as friendly. We went into the administration building to look over the offices. While we were there some instructors happened to be exiting the building and Stefan stopped them and asked a few questions.

I don't speak much French. I understood enough to hear him ask if Commander Menard was still running the place. Then I saw one of the instructors look at his watch and point over his shoulder and say Menard *was on his way down, right behind them.* Then I saw Stefan do something I'd never seen him do before.

He ran.

I ran with him. He didn't stop looking over his shoulder until we were in the rental car speeding down the Boulevard des Neiges.

I might still owe those motherfuckers money.

Later, back home in D.C., I saw his AIDP-embossed dive logbook. Tucked inside the cover flap were photographs of him—just out of his teens—in full dive gear on the quay at AIDP. The logbook listed the dates, locations, and specifics of each dive. Each entry had been made by an instructor and stamped with an AIDP seal. When I called AIDP six months later, to ask about the special training Stefan said he'd received, my limited French got me to a receptionist who said, *Why would we have anything to say about something like that? Where do you hear this?* It's not like I expected them to come out and confirm the spy shit—but it was a detail I couldn't nail down with any certainty. It's not like I'd seen him handle a bunch of tactical weapons or advise a military.

Yet.

But I gave him the benefit of the doubt that he'd received the type of dive training necessary to at least pull off the hashish dive of the Gib. José Luis and the consortium led me into territory where there was no such thing as too much caution. These guys *are real*. Some of them are still living. Others—like the ginger Englishman and Ödd—are dead. I spoke to some of the participants in the operation independently of Stefan, and they not only confirmed his version of events, but fleshed out details he'd either forgotten or considered unimportant. Stefan petting the dog in the hallway of Gunther's is one example. Mike and the details of the armored car robbery are another.

I met one of his cronies from that time period, on the same research trip to Europe. When Stefan introduced me as a writer, the Scandinavian grabbed him by the elbow and whispered, *How much does he know?* Later, the crony gave me a tense, terse recounting of Stefan's criminal years in Scandinavia, and made me promise not to name or portray him (I haven't). I had three people who'd vouched for the goings on in Gibraltar, independently of each other, all of them terrified of being caught, nearly fifteen years after the fact. Again, perhaps a hoax. A big, Grassy Knoll–style cover-up. I should note, however, that I was forwarded—by one of the participants in the Gib—several articles about the Gibraltarian black market confirming that stuff like the Gib was more the rule than the exception. These articles and further research revealed that some of the participants were still either active, or currently under investigation. Ultimately, I believed the story of the Gib. Too many people confirmed it, added to it, or were panicked by it.

The same meeting at which I'd met one of Stefan's former partners was, incidentally, at a dinner for a South American businessman living in Scandinavia. The businessman was a Cuban exile who'd started a construction business in Stockholm. He had security guards stationed around the restaurant, and he'd made a point to sit next to Stefan. On the way into the room, Stefan had advised me, *Keep your mouth shut and your eyes open and for fuck's sake don't tell anyone you're a writer.*

What happened at that dinner is another story for another time, but the end result was that the man—nicknamed the Lion—was using his construction company as a front. He was sending hundreds of thousands of dollars to anti-Castro forces in Cuba. He wanted Stefan's help. At one point during the meal, I observed Stefan slide the man a business card. The card had the imprint of a well-known military contractor written on it. I am *not suggesting for a second* that Stefan is affiliated with any such organization—he *hates* those guys. I am just saying that he had one of their cards and passed it along. He lives in Washington, D.C., and that city, like the world we now share, is a small place.

I had gone to the restroom halfway through the meal, and found the Lion at the sink washing his hands. I decided to test out a wan, shabby pet theory—that maybe Stefan was just a really good bullshit artist—on someone who'd just met him and had no allegiance to him. I looked over and smiled at him in the vanity mirror. *Some character, huh?* I smirked in the direction of the dining room. The Lion's face changed. He dried his hands and looked at me and said, *Your friend is a great man.*

I was taken aback. I knew that the Lion had an agenda—as did Stefan, who wanted him to invest in ruggedized computers they could distribute in the developing world—but the guy was ostensibly a crime boss, and did not seem gullible. At the end of that dinner, the Lion clasped Stefan's hand and hugged him goodbye. After the man had piled into his Mercedes E-320 and sped off, Stefan opened his palm. Inside was a hefty silver ring, with the head of a lion carved onto its face. Engraved on the band's interior was the Lion's name—which I won't repeat—and the date *1972*. After knowing him for two hours, the Lion had given Stefan a ring he'd worn on his finger for thirty-five years.

For the Monaco, Tokyo, and South Asian stints, there were a variety of sources, some more fecund than others. As I've mentioned, I had personally visited the family in Cap d'Ail. Liv—Stefan's longtime girlfriend—confirmed most of the details of that period, as did Ebba. Dana refused to talk to me, but gave no reason. She has a career and a husband and kids now. Maybe she'd like as much of that era in her rearview mirror as possible. Grove from Giant Robot! spoke to me at length. He'd met Dana, and had worked side by side with Stefan at Giant Robot! for several months. He filled in much about that time that Stefan hadn't remembered, or had tried to forget. Most important, he was an eyewitness to a crucial turning point in Stefan's life, and story: the balcony incident with the Yakuza.

Still too deeply troubled to remember some of the details, Stefan had relayed to me only the basics of the story. Grove filled in specifics, and in the end provided some long-awaited closure: the Yakuza hadn't died. He'd spent some time in the hospital with a broken face, and was released after a few weeks. When I told Stefan over the phone, in 2010—fifteen years later—he cheered, *No shit? That's fucking great, man.*

Even through the phone line, you could hear him swim free of the iron-guilt anchor he'd nearly let drag him to the bottom.

No one was with him on those gem-smuggling runs along the Burmese border, and all Stefan had for Jinx was a nickname. Barry Heffernan, owing to his position as U.S. consul for the area, would not go on the record. Turns out gem trading, though not illegal in the strictest sense, is not an endorsed form of moonlighting in U.S. government circles. I did have photographic evidence, however: pictures of Stefan fighting at Lanna Thai camp; the monk staring into the sun; crossing into Burma on the Enduro; his cleaning the wat. He was either in possession of the most extreme vacation pictures ever, or had actually done the things he'd said.

For Hurricane Mitch and the tsunami episodes, there was plenty of documentation. Some members of Paramedics for Children contacted me—none with very favorable things to say about Stefan (they praised his performance during Hurricane Mitch, but his promises of travel arrangements for their deployment into Indonesia had fallen through, and the organization was nearly bankrupted when Rodger decided—heroically—that PFC would make good on its promise and complete its mission in Indonesia without his help).

For the tsunami, several of the ELISA surgeons provided me with a thorough accounting of their mission, and Stefan's involvement. There was also an ABC News Australia video interview with Stefan in theater, where he railed—somewhat high-handedly—about the lack of response and coordination the international relief effort had exhibited. It's easy to see, even in that short clip, his inability to deal with inaction, real or perceived. He was like a humanitarian microwave: he wanted results, *now.*

Successes and failures aside, he had really gone to those wrecked places. Boots on the ground. I was almost satisfied. My grain of salt had dissolved . . . *somewhat.*

I wanted to make whatever I wrote about Stefan as honest as I could. Hagiographies bore me, and illuminate no truths about the human heart. I kept researching, sure that something would crack the veneer of what Stefan had told me.

Turns out, there was a plan that could definitively sort truth from fiction: in November of 2007, he would be leaving on his third mission to Sudan, on another well-building expedition.

I would go with him.

In the autumn of 2007, Stefan was hired by the NGO KUSH to plot water coordinates in the Abyei province of Sudan. Abyei was the epicenter of the genocide in Darfur. Stefan had become a water sanitation expert by then and had already been to the region twice. Seeing him in action would provide a flavor of his temperament and character during stressful times. I could see if he really could walk the walk. He'd also hinted that this Sudan water mission would lead us into "deep waters." He was not making a pun. Stefan does not make puns.

First off—I thought he was ridiculous for making us fly into Addis Ababa, then into Lokichokio, Kenya, then into southern Sudan, instead of having us fly directly into Khartoum, the capital of Sudan. He said he didn't want us to be *on Khartoum's radar*. We would head into the disputed southern territory so that the Islamic dictatorship of the north would have no paper trail of our movements. Nobody would. If anything happened, we would have ceased to exist. *I* was not an adventure junkie. I wanted *some* government, somewhere, to know where I was.

Nope. Stefan said he'd rather risk us traveling off the ruling government's grid. (His advice turned out to be prescient: while we were in Sudan, a British teacher was imprisoned by the Khartoum government for naming a teddy bear Mohammed.)

When we were getting onto the Ethiopian Airlines flight to Addis Ababa, on our way out of D.C., the stewardesses swarmed around him. They acted like he was Haile Selassie back from the grave. They promptly scooted the first two middle rows of passengers in coach class toward the rear of the craft, lifted the armrests, and loaded us up with extra pillows and free champagne. We had it better than first class. When I asked Stefan why they were making such a fuss, he just shrugged. *I helped them out on a flight once.*

I took my champagne and went over to a cluster of stewardesses—Ethiopian women, *not* ugly, by the way—and asked them why Stefan was getting the star treatment.

One of them looked at me and said, *He saved two people on a flight.*

I scratched my head. *Two people got sick and he helped them?*

The stewardess shook her head. *No—on a flight out last year, a man had a heart attack, and he gave him CPR and saved him. On a different flight, a Somali girl had a panic attack and started throwing up, and choking on her vomit, and he cleared her mouth, you know, so she could breathe.*

He wouldn't have even mentioned that story. Just another day on the commute. I would have found it unbelievable if I'd heard it from *him. Two* lifesaving emergencies on two separate flights? But these women told me—their regular route was D.C. to Addis—he didn't. They had been there. I had the champagne and extra fluffy pillows and a row to myself to prove it.

So. The mission. The primary cause of death in the (second) Sudanese Civil War (1982–2005) had been lack of access to water, as villagers fled into the bush. With renewed tensions in the area, Stefan's assignment was to plot coordinates of freshwater locations into a GPS: an escape route villagers could use in the event of war along a water-lined corridor. That was the plan. There's an old military saying: *Everybody's got a plan until they get hit.*

In *way* too condensed form, the village of Abyei was—and is, at the time of this writing—the flashpoint of what could be the next civil war in Sudan. (What we think of as the "crisis in Darfur" largely has its roots in the Abyei conflict.) All the way over, Stefan had fretted about how he felt the West had failed Sudan. How the bullshit "neutrality" ethos most NGOs swore allegiance to enabled genocide. By his side on that flight was the dog-eared— and excellent—polemic against the business of humanitarian aid Graham Hancock's *Lords of Poverty*. Stefan chafed against the notion that once trouble—the man-made kind—started in Sudan, all the aid workers would be rushed out, leaving the region to fend for itself.

Like they did in Rwanda, or for the last twenty-five years in Sudan, he fumed. *The CIA used to go in and fuck with dictatorships like Bashir's* [Sudan's repressive Islamist leader]. *Now we send microfinance advisers. These people need support, or else we'll all be sitting around saying "How did this happen?"* He was profoundly angry. Impotence was a cheap, confining, scratchy suit to him. *Somebody should do something to help them,* he said with a sigh, and wondered how I had no idea about what had happened in East Africa aside from reading Eggers's *What Is the What.*

When we reached the NGO compound in Agok village, just outside Abyei, four days later, Stefan set about visiting potential water sources and well sites. He also made sure to question the villagers about the likelihood of a return to war in the region. He wanted to know how real the threat was, among the people who would have to deal with it. He made it plain to the majority population of Dinka tribespeople—the primary victims of the Sudanese genocide—that he was with them in spirit, that someone from the West stood by them. Many of the villagers had lost family members in the decades-old war, and scores of boys and men were members of the resistance: the SPLA—the Sudanese People's Liberation Army.

One nuclear dawn, 115 degrees as the sun crested the acacia trees, Stefan ducked his head into our tent and said, *Get your ass up, we've got shit to do.*

A small SPLA contingent, slung heavy with AK-47s, drove us deep into the bush. There, by a fetid swamp, vultures sprouting from tree branches, the local SPLA commander asked Stefan to inspect his troops.

Can you help us? Tell us how to be ready?

I'm just one man, Stefan deflected. The long, lean, blue-black commander frowned at the ragged assortment of men and boys. Some had no uniforms. Some had no shoes. Some stood at attention with sticks shouldered where weapons should have been. You didn't have to be Patton to tell: they weren't ready.

Is there anything we can do? the commander asked.

I nearly chimed in, *Yeah, isn't there anything? We're fucking Americans. Don't we help people like this?*

Stefan chewed the inside of his cheek. Won or lost some internal argument, until finally:

Let me see your weapons, he said. The commander unearthed a cache of arms: rocket-propelled grenade launchers, bazookas, .50 caliber machine guns. Most of the weaponry was Vietnam era or older. A sorry, dilapidated arsenal.

I'm not a soldier, Stefan told the commander. *But if I were, I'd advise you to build a berm along the track road outside Abyei . . . that's where Bashir's men will come. It's the only road big enough for motorized vehicles.*

After a few hours with the commander and the men, the older man asked Stefan to address the troops. *A man such as yourself, from our big brother America, would be inspirational,* he said smiling. Stefan is not a public speaker. He kept it short. Told the men that America had not forgotten them—a well-intentioned lie—and that we all shared a common enemy.

Please remember that the Janjaweed and Bashir are your enemies, but that Islam is not. Islamist militants are not Islam. . . . . It's political Islam that must be defeated.

Maybe not the Gettysburg Address, but the men seemed to take comfort in it. Comfort is as good a form of humanitarian aid as any, as far as I'm concerned.

We traveled close to the north's front line. Stefan showed me the oil fields that were at the heart of the recent conflict: huge reserves were in the south, where Christian/Dinka tribes had lived for centuries, and was coveted by the Islamic north. The north had tanks and planes and Janjaweed militias on horseback. The south had grit and rusted weapons.

We went so far afield of where NGOs were allowed to go that the head of the United Nations mission in Sudan (UNMIS) told me that it was impossible we'd gotten that close to the front lines. *I've been here two years and I've never been out there,* he said. Stefan—one man, with no political or military affiliation—had gotten out there. And because I was with him, so had I. I had witnessed for myself a story I would otherwise have declared—if not impossible—highly improbable. We really were in "deep waters."

The next day, when I expressed concern to Stefan that our sorties may have broken some kind of impartiality code of the humanitarian world, he looked genuinely pained. *Man, all these aid groups pack up and leave when shit goes down . . . that's what they all do in Africa. These people have a right to protect themselves.*

Soldiers who'd been fighting in the bush for a quarter of a century, hard Africans with rubber tires for shoes and eyes rimmed red from the parasites burrowing into their bloodstream, pulled me aside and told me the same thing the Lion had told me, back in Stockholm, almost verbatim: *This man, he is great.*

On our sixth or seventh day at our camp in dusty, desertified Agok town, a U.N. plane crashed into the bush right outside the fence. The Antonov twin turboprop's front landing gear caved into the dried clay runway and skidded to a halt on its belly. There was a plume of crimson dust and then dead quiet. Within minutes, some of the Western aid workers from UNMIS and Médecins sans Frontières rushed into the compound. They all said the same thing: *Where's Stefan?* These were workers who'd been in country for months, even years. Stefan had been in Agok for a week.

At the moment of the crash, he was instructing some of the tribal chiefs in an evacuation plan for all the villages around Abyei. He went out to the crippled plane, where it was determined that all the passengers were okay. All except one. One of the women on the plane—a south Sudanese who'd come to take a seminar in microfinance—was nine months pregnant. The crash sent her into labor.

I was less than useful in any emergency that didn't involve getting wine stains out of carpet, so I didn't see Stefan until three hours later. The woman still hadn't given birth, but she had refused to let anyone but Stefan deliver her baby. He'd sat in her hut for hours, his arm inside her, feeling for contractions. Finally, a village chief found a midwife, and brought her to the woman's side. She'd agreed to let the woman stay with her and Stefan left. He found me outside our tent, loafing on the hammock. I asked him how it went.

I would have done it—but I gotta say, I'm better at making 'em than delivering 'em. He laughed.

I told him he was lucky he'd gotten out of it. Something close to horror, or more generously, pity, flickered across his face. For a full moment, he just stared at me. Like I was a bug. Or some animal wandered off a frozen plain, mesmerized by the warmth of humans and their fires.

And then it hit me.

The world as I thought I knew it was small, and safe, and adventures were for other people. My experiences and the experiences of everyone around me were proscribed by ethnic, cultural, moral, physical, geographical boundaries. The notion that these boundaries could not only be crossed, but *exploded,* by a life like his, strained credulity. It was easier to suggest that it was the stuff of fiction, the stock-in-trade of thrillers and James Bond movies. His life was all of those things. And it was the truth. As ugly or beautiful as anything can be when exposed to hard light.

It must be acknowledged that much of what made Stefan's life possible was circumstance and privilege. As much as I'd wanted to flit off to Burgundy for junior high, or beat up anybody who'd ever shoved me off the cafeteria lunch line, life had other plans for me. For most of us. Countless books and movies and therapy sessions are spent on all of us who didn't slay the dragon, score the touchdown for the big game, marry the homecoming queen, or create a computer operating platform at twenty. But there was more to the making and the worth of Stefan Templeton's life than just access and privilege.

Stefan *consciously created himself.* Most of us make do with what we've got. He refused to be a passive participant in his own life. Many of the fantastic situations he found himself in were the result of his perpetual motion, his preparation, paired with receptivity to chance. Sometimes what needed to happen was good. Often, he chose poorly, and what happened was toxic. But *something always happened.* And that thing, good or bad, laid a foundation, which almost always led to growth. Moral, professional, spiritual. The kind of growth that comes not from being alive, but from living.

Stefan Templeton is no saint, and only lately a kind of hero. He can be, and often is, a bit of a prick. He's lived so hard and wild that interacting with him on a personal level can be exhausting. He is not the guy you want to help plan your bachelor party, or the shoulder you need after a bad breakup. He's on a whole other trip.

Truthfully, he's as confounded by my existence, and the existence of most of his peers, as I am by his. He cannot believe how little we've seen and done. The rarity and sameness of our sex, our appetites, our curiosity. His experiences are not mine. (Probably not yours, either, unless your last name is Bourne or Bond.) His incredulity bristles at the idea that we are fat, happy, and static.

I had posed thousands of questions to Stefan Templeton and those who knew him, loved and/or hated him, had been touched, bruised, healed, by his presence. But the most important questions posed by my examination of my childhood friend had to do not with him, but with the nature of life and living. In each detail of his adventures, I found myself first dubious, then accepting, and then, occasionally, awed. By my own complacency. By whatever contract I had unknowingly signed with life that confined morality, or race, or culture, or experience, to neat and tended plots where no weeds went wild or animals rutted or flowers bloomed hidden from view.

All of those questions I had asked and answered of Stefan Templeton left me with a memory of one he had posed to me, over a quarter century ago.

We were fifteen, maybe sixteen. I'm thinking 1983. Walking down Baltimore's North Charles Street, late at night. Springtime, finally. Out looking for girls. We were coming up on rough-and-tumble North Avenue, an alive and ghettofied intersection sprinkled with liquor stores, black dance clubs, and fried chicken joints. Stefan turned around—eyes always in the back of the head at that time, in that place, where gunshots and beat-downs seemed always just around a corner or lounging in a doorway—and saw him.

Muhammad Ali. The Champ. The Greatest. Right behind us on the sidewalk, surrounded by six hulking Fruit of Islam bodyguards. I saw him, too. But in an instant, Stefan did something I did not, would not, could not do. He spun, put up his dukes, and danced and threw feather jabs back and forth at the Champ—motherfucking Muhammad Ali—the Champ not the man he once was, the shake already there and the shuffle the worse for wear, but that grin with some of the devil in it still strong, jab still true, some butterfly left in him. Even the bodyguards, who'd edged in when Stefan spun, backing off and letting these two glance whisper-fists at each other. After thirty or so seconds, Stefan beamed, panted, *Thanks, Champ!* And turned and put his arm around me as we kept walking.

Man! I just boxed with Ali!

I shrugged.

Do you know how big that is? he said.

I shrugged again.

In many ways, this book is the answer to his question, more than twenty-five years later. Now I get it. And I care. Life doesn't just happen. It is lived.

Turn and put up your dukes and dance and fight the Greatest.

ACKNOWLEDGMENTS

The author would like to thank the following:

First and foremost: Stefan Templeton, Roye Templeton, Ebba Boyesen, Liv Thulin, Elena Sotnikova, Mai Templeton. They were all patient, kind, and supportive, in the midst of endless questioning and profane intrusions into their privacy. Thanks as well to the various good and bad guys, both on the record and off, who helped point me in the right direction and away from harm.

Last, these people, who, known to them or not, make everything I do possible: Ralph Matthews, Kate Lee, Lauren Sandler, Stuart Adamson, Vanessa Mobley, Steven and Laura, all at WME, and the Enoch Pratt Free Library, where all this shit got started, in the time before time.